Theology and Philosophy

Signposts in Theology

Theology, Death and Dying
Ray S. Anderson

Theology and Religious Pluralism
Gavin D'Costa

Theology and Philosophy
Ingolf U. Dalferth

Theology and Politics
Duncan B. Forrester

Theology and the Problem of Evil
Kenneth Surin

Theology and Literature
T. R. Wright

In preparation

Theology and Feminism
Daphne Hampson

Theology and Philosophy

INGOLF U. DALFERTH

Basil Blackwell

Copyright © Ingolf U. Dalferth 1988

First published 1988

Basil Blackwell Ltd
108 Cowley Road, Oxford, OX4 1JF, UK

Basil Blackwell Inc.
432 Park Avenue South, Suite 1503
New York, NY 10016, USA

British Library Cataloguing in Publication Data
Dalferth, Ingolf U. (Ingolf Ulrich)
    Theology and philosophy
    1. Theology — Philosophical perspectives
    I. Title
    200′.1
ISBN 0-631-15354-3

Library of Congress Cataloging in Publication Data
Dalferth, Ingolf U.
    Theology and philosophy.
    (Signposts in theology)
    Bibliography: p.
    Includes index.
    1. Christianity—Philosophy. I. Title. II. Series.
BR100.D25 1988   230′.01   88-5028
ISBN 0-631-15354-3

Typeset in 10/11½ pt Century Light
by Colset Private Limited, Singapore
Printed in Great Britain

Contents

Introduction   vii

Part I   Background and Beginnings   1

1 The Rationality of Theology   3
2 The Origins of Theology   18
3 Christian Theology   35

Part II   Faith and Reason   61

4 Perspectives and the Quest for Harmony   63
5 The Two-Books Model   67
6 The Nature-Grace Model   71
7 The Law-Gospel Model   76
8 The Reason-Revelation Model   89
9 The Difference-in-Unity Model   99
10 The Unity-in-Difference Model   112
11 Harmony without Identity   127

Part III   Revelation and Reflection   149

12 Reflection and the Quest for Clarity   151
13 The Content of Revelation and the Knowledge of God   158

vi *Contents*

14 Types of Reflective Knowledge about God   164

15 Metaphysical Theology in the Paradigm of Reflection   169

16 Metaphysical Theology in the Paradigm of Self-Reflection   174

17 Revelational Theology   188

18 Revelation and Orientation   204

Bibliography   224

Index   232

Introduction

This is a book about the relationship between theology and philosophy in the Christian tradition. It explores some of the most important ways in which theologians and philosophers past and present have conceived of the place and role of philosophy within Christian thought; and it discusses some of the main problems posed by the various uses of philosophy in Christian theology. It does not aim at an exhaustive account of Christian thought on these controversial matters. That would be quite impossible within the limits of a short book like this. All I propose to do is to introduce the reader to some central aspects of one of the perennial problems of Christian theology: How to define its own nature and status *vis-à-vis* philosophy without obscuring the differences or ignoring the dependencies.

Theology is not philosophy, and philosophy is not a substitute for religious convictions. But whereas religion can exist without philosophy, and philosophy without religion, theology cannot exist without recourse to each of the other two. It rationally reflects on questions arising in pre-theological religious experience and the discourse of faith; and it is the rationality of its reflective labour in the process of faith seeking understanding which inseparably links it with philosophy. For philosophy is essentially concerned with argument and the attempt to solve conceptual problems; and conceptual problems face theology in all areas of its reflective labours.

From the beginning the fate of these two intellectual disciplines has been closely linked. Throughout their long and distinguished career in Western thought they have faced similar problems. And although in our century they have at times been further apart than ever, the theologian and the philosopher are in fact related more closely than is sometimes admitted. The philosophical task of sifting straight from twisted thinking does not stop short of theology and religious matters, for here perhaps more than elsewhere it is true, as Bishop Berkeley caustically observed, that all men have opinions, but few men think. And although clarity is not enough, it is not lightly to be dismissed in theological or any other sort of thinking. Christian theology, in any case, cannot consistently pursue its task and dodge philosophical questions for at least two reasons. Methodologically it cannot convincingly expound the Christian faith and critically reflect the beliefs of the Christian community without a close logical scrutiny of its own concepts and arguments. Materially it has to expound a faith which, although it is a stumbling-block to the Jews and foolishness to the Greeks, is not meant to be blindly accepted by the faithful few but claims universal significance for all men and women. If the wisdom of the world fails to understand it, then it should be because of its own blindness, not because the Christian faith is unintelligible or inaccessible to rational elucidation.

The thesis which I shall develop and defend in this book is that the rationality of Christian theology and the intelligibility of the Christian faith both ties theology to philosophy and divorces it from it; and that the difference between the intelligibility of faith and the rationality of our reflection on faith has been the driving force behind theology's various ways of relating to philosophy. Unlike faith theology is a rational enterprise - not because it unfailingly pronounces the truth but because it proceeds by argument. It presents reasoned beliefs, not non-debatable dogmas for the faithful to believe and the godless to ignore; and although it aims at truth, its reasoning (as all human reasoning) is not invariably valid or sound. Few theological opinions have stood the test of time, fewer still may turn out to be true. For all that, theology is rational, if and when it argues, for it is the idea of reasons, not of true reasons, which is central to rationality.

Reasons are things which favour or disfavour other things, and without a clear grasp of the difference between a claim and a reason for or against a claim we are merely on the way to rationality. There are many rudimentary forms of rationality, but it can flourish only in an atmosphere of argument. Arguments, however, are mostly controversial and rarely conclusive. So a part of being rational is learning how to cope with the unpleasant truth that in almost all areas of life and thought conflict is not only possible but to be expected, and that we have to live with conflicting views about virtually everything that matters. This is difficult at times, but it has advantages which are not to be lightly dismissed: in theology as much as in all other disciplines we can learn most from those who disagree with us.

I have learned much (though no doubt not as much as I should have) from Hugh Mellor's and Christoph Schwöbel's acute criticisms of parts of this material and from Lyle Dabney's helpful comments which have saved me from many linguistic blunders. I am much indebted to all of them for the improvements which they have suggested at many points in this book. Whatever remains of an unsatisfactory nature about it is entirely my own fault.

The plan of the book is as follows. The first part traces the background and beginnings of the relationship between theology and philosophy from the Presocratics to the rise of Christian theology. After an introductory chapter on the rationality of theology I discuss the origins of theology in Greek philosophy (Plato, Aristotle and the Stoics) and the quite different kind of theology emerging in Christian thought. Two basic and perennial problems are shown to underly its multifaceted relationship with philosophy: the 'problem of perspectives' (the difference between external and internal views on faith and theology) and the 'problem of reflection' (the difference between faith and theology, or revelation and reflection).

The second and main part discusses the problem of perspectives. It shows that the theological quest for harmonizing the perspectives of Faith (internal perspective) and Reason (external perspective) has led to different types of solutions in the Two-Books Model (Augustine), the Nature-Grace Model (Thomas Aquinas), the Law-Gospel Model (Luther), the Reason-Revelation Model (Enlightenment), the Difference-in-Unity Model (Schleiermacher) and the Unity-in-Difference Model (Barth). Each model has its particular strengths and weaknesses, but none offers a final solution to the problem. Indeed, the problem of perspectives is fundamental precisely in that it allows of no definitive solution: it cannot be overcome without re-emerging in a different way. All we can (and must) do, therefore, is to secure harmony between the perspectives of Faith and Reason by designing rational means of translating between them.

A similar case is the problem of reflection, the topic of the third and final part. Theology's quest for clarity about faith requires the figurative expressions of faith to be conceptually reconstructed - a permanent task not to be solved once and for all, and the source of perennial problems in theology's relationships both to faith and to philosophy. In particular, these reconstructions are easily mistaken for philosophical constructions prompted by quite different problems and considerations. Whereas philosophical theologies are based on problems of reflective (cosmological, ideological and rational metaphysics) or self-reflective knowledge (transcendental, absolutist and interpretative metaphysics), revelational theology is based on the paradigm of demonstrative knowledge and faith's claim to respond to God's self-identification in Jesus Christ as saving and creative love. Its fundamental reflective task is thus twofold: it must explicate the orientational knowledge derived from revelation in a system of doctrines, and elucidate the whole of reality in the light of it. In neither respect is theology infallible. Neither task can be completed once and for all or in only one way. But it is the tasks, not their solutions, which constitute the identity of Christian theology. And while its problems are markedly different from those of philosophical theology, their methods and solutions need neither be incompatible nor mutually exclusive.

In the course of the book I have reused, with permission where necessary, material contained in the following: '*Esse est Operari*. The Anti-Scholastic Theologies of Farrer and Luther', *Modern Theology* 1, 1985, pp. 183-210; 'Theologischer Realismus und realistische Theologie bei Karl Barth', *Evangelische Theologie* 46, 1986, pp. 402-22; 'Karl Barth's Eschatological Realism' (In S.W. Sykes (ed.), *Karl Barth: Centenary Essays*, forthcoming at Cambridge University Press).

Ingolf U. Dalferth

PART I
BACKGROUND AND BEGINNINGS

Chapter 1

The Rationality of Theology

I

Theology, as a distinctive intellectual discipline, is a Greek discovery. Its beginnings are intimately bound up with the rise of reason in ancient Greece; and although its relationship to philosophy has had a chequered career, it has remained a rational enterprise ever since.

The rationality of theology is sometimes misunderstood or mistakenly denied. There are those to whom theology ceases to be of religious import if it attempts to be rational. They follow Kierkegaard in celebrating the irrationality of the leap of faith and the suprarationality of the divine mystery which theology professes to explore. They claim Christian theology in particular to go beyond the confines of human reason in that it seeks to expound a faith which is a stumbling-block to the Jews, foolishness to the Greeks, and if not against, then at least above reason. Others arrive at similar conclusions for quite different reasons. For them, theology belongs to a pre-rational past; it is an atavism in the scientific culture of our time; it lacks nothing except a basis in reality; and it fails to meet the contemporary standards of science and reason by which we sort out the sound from the unsound, the legitimate from the illegitimate.

Neither objection stands up to examination. That which is rational is not necessarily the product of reason or of reason alone, and that which is religious does not necessarily rule out rational elucidation nor is it obviously unsound. Even if it were true that 'religion is basically irrational' because 'at its worst it is below reason, at its best for above it', it would still be true that 'it can be studied rationally, and should be and must be, "for reason is God's scale on earth" ' (Zaehner, 1962, p. 12). Theology need not be irrational in order to be religiously adequate and true to the mystery of faith, nor does it cease to be rational by refusing to be rationalistic or by rejecting the natural sciences as the sole standard of rationality. The dispute, quite obviously, turns on the question of what can rationally be asserted to be rational. This will require some brief elucidation.

II

First, what is rational is not limited to what we can prove. We may not be able to prove that there is life after death but still have reasons to believe it to be true; on the other hand, even if we have good reasons for believing it to be so, it may be false. A rational belief is not necessarily true, and a false belief not necessarily irrational (Dalferth, 1981, pp. 507-16).

Second, what is rational need not be a self-discovery. We do not have to think up everything for ourselves in order to be rational. Borrowed beliefs are not necessarily irrational; and egocentric reason is not the sole or even main source of rational beliefs. Knowledge is a social product, and rationality is not tied to a foundationalist epistemology which begins by dispensing with vicarious information and ends up with cognitive solipsism (cf. Rescher, 1973, ch. 13).

Third, rationality is not the prerogative of (natural) science. Even if we were nothing but reasoners (which we are not) our rationality would not be exhausted by science. Reason 'is omnivorous; it does not pasture exclusively in scientific fields'; and we have no reason to confine our 'reasoning powers to a monotonously scientific diet' (J. Barnes, 1982a, p. 4). Scientific rationality with its canons of generalizable experience and mathematical construction and its procedures of conjecture and refutation are an important but by no means the sole form of rationality.

Fourth, rationality pertains primarily to method and not to content. Our beliefs, including our scientific beliefs, are rational not because of what they hold but because of the way they are held: they are, ideally, beliefs which in the light of critical discussion appear to be the most warranted thus far (cf. Popper, 1972, p. 22). Of course, what it is for a belief to be warranted, and which methods are appropriate for warranting it, may themselves be matters of dispute; and as our beliefs are not homogeneous, the answer will vary with the area and type of belief under discussion. What is appropriate in physics is not necessarily so in theology. However, it is as inappropriate in theology as it is in physics to hold at the same time a belief and its contradictory or to ignore evidence against that belief while knowing it to be relevant. Beliefs, in whatever area and of whatever type, may be held dogmatically or rationally. They are rational if they are supported by argument, buttressed by reasons and established upon evidence (J. Barnes,

1982a, p. 5); and they fail to be rational if they are held contrary to the rules of logic, the canons of argument and the criteria of evidence relevant to the area under discussion.

Fifth, it follows that the notion of a 'rational belief' is ambiguous. It can mean that the content of the belief is rational, i.e. that the belief is *justified* or *justifiable*; but it can also mean that the way the belief is held is rational, i.e. that the belief is *reasonable*. The two senses are not to be confused, for the justifiability of *p* and the reasonableness of believing *p* are two very different things (cf. Dalferth, 1981, pp. 495ff). In the first or logical sense a belief is rational if what is believed can be supported by argument and justified by reason (Green, 1978, pp. 14ff); and our concept of rationality will be narrow or broad depending on whether we expect those arguments to conform to the requirements of proof (cf. Mavrodes, 1970a, pp. 22ff; Penelhum, 1971, pp. 21ff; Dalferth, 1981, pp. 520ff), of strict probability (Swinburne, 1979; Mackie, 1982) or of the nature of a cumulative case in the sense argued by Basil Mitchell (1973). In the second or practical sense it is not the belief, but the believer's believing which is rational because she or he has good grounds for holding this belief (Mavrodes, 1970a, pp. 11ff; 1970b, pp. 2ff; 1979, pp. 40ff). But (practical) grounds for believing are not necessarily (theoretical) reasons for a belief. A person may not be able to show that God exists, yet be reasonable in believing it. We can share this belief and yet differ widely or even irreconcilably in our grounds for believing it, as is the case with Christians, Jews and Moslems. But although we do not have to deny the reasonableness of each other's believing, we cannot accept something as a cogent and convincing argument for this belief without expecting it to be in principle acceptable to all persons of ordinary intelligence and intellectual capacity. In either sense, however, rationality is not primarily a quality of the belief in question but of the believer's relationship to his or her belief or believing (Kellenberger, 1985, pp. 21ff). For a belief is rational if it is held rationally; it is held rationally if we have reasons to believe it; and one, though by no means the sole, kind of reason to believe it is the justification of the belief.

Sixth, rationality is not uniform, but comes in different sorts. If the rationality of a belief depends on the reasonableness of our believing it, it will vary according to the kinds of reason we have for believing it; and if, as is often claimed, we can believe something on internal and/or external grounds, we have to distinguish between internal and external rationality. This distinction is as easy to state as it is difficult to explain; so it needs to be elucidated.

The distinction between external and internal rationality has played a major role in philosophical discussions in the wake of Wittgenstein. It is grounded in the awareness of the diversity of scientific, moral, religious, political and other kinds of beliefs and the corresponding diversity of criteria for rationality. Scientific beliefs, for example, are held rationally if they are held tentatively and in proportion to the evidence available. Religious beliefs, on the contrary, are not tentative, but unconditional. Believers - as Wittgenstein has pointed out (1970, pp. 55ff) - do not hold their beliefs with a conviction proportionate to evidence as is the case with scientific beliefs. Their beliefs are neither probable nor well founded in a scientific sense; and the apologetic attempt to make them look scientifically respectable is completely misconceived. For not even their indubitability would be 'enough in this case. Even if there is as much evidence as for Napoleon. Because the indubitability wouldn't be enough to make me change my whole life' (p. 57). Wittgenstein concluded from this that religious beliefs are neither reasonable nor unreasonable; they are not the sort of belief to which reasonability would apply.

The conclusion, obviously, is too strong. All he can reasonably claim to have shown is that *scientific* reasonability does not apply; but it is not clear that this is the only sort of reasonability. Followers of Wittgenstein like Peter Winch (1958; 1967) and D. Z. Phillips (1970; 1976) have therefore modified Wittgenstein's view. For them, religious and other kinds of beliefs can indeed be rational or irrational; but the criteria of rationality by which we draw this distinction are embedded in the way of life to which the belief in question belongs. Thus Phillips writes (1967, p. 63):

> Religious believers, when asked why they believe in God, may reply in a variety of ways. They may say, 'I have had an experience of the living God', 'I believe in the Lord Jesus Christ', 'God saved me while I was a sinner', or, 'I just can't help believing'. Philosophers have not given such reasons very much attention. The so-called trouble is not so much with the content of the replies, as with the fact that the replies are made by believers. The answers come from within religion, they presuppose the framework of Faith, and therefore cannot be treated as evidence for religious belief.

That is to say, religious beliefs are rational or irrational in a sense *internal* to religion and not according to some objective norm taken from, e.g., science; and in order to find out how this distinction operates in a given case we have to pay heed to actual religious practice.

The upshot of this line of argument is that the question of rationality takes on two different forms. On the one hand there is the question of the rationality or irrationality of a given belief which has to be decided according to the criteria internal to the way of life to which it belongs. On the other hand there is the more fundamental question of the rationality or irrationality of this whole way of life. For Phillips (and here he echoes Wittgenstein) questions of this sort are illegitimate because all we have are internal criteria which can be described and expounded in their own terms but not justified in terms of any external criteria taken from other contexts of life and belief. Against this it has been urged by K. Nielsen (1967, p. 207) and J. Kellenberger, 'that there can be such questions since some modes of life - that centred around belief in trolls and fairies, for instance - have been rejected as irrational' (1985, p. 13). This, no doubt, is true; but it need not contradict Phillips. Rather it may be taken to underline his point that the distinction between the rational and the irrational is always drawn in terms of criteria *internal* to a form of life: if beliefs in trolls are rejected as irrational, then that occurs *within*, for example, a scientific or a Christian form of life, i.e. not in their own sense but in the sense proper to science or the Christian faith; and this is perfectly rational as long as we have reasons to assume that the scientific or Christian criteria of rationality are relevant to the beliefs in question. Thus in order to reject a whole form of life we do not need a specific ('objective') set of more fundamental external criteria of rationality by which we assess not only particular beliefs but whole modes of life. All we need are reasons for believing those beliefs to fall into the province of science or the Christian faith, i.e. some second-order beliefs about the kind and type of belief in question.

Now it is an essential aspect of our cognitive structure as free and rational agents to have second-order beliefs of this sort, and continuously to strive after better ones, because we have to orient ourselves in the multiplicity of forms of life in which we exist. To do this explicitly and to get clear about this process is precisely what rationality is all about. The world surrounding us is so complex, and the information accessible to us so manifold, that we have to reduce its complexity and select the information important for us if we want to survive and act within it. This we do by developing perspectives on the world which select some information and ignore others. We then integrate the information selected into cognitive models of the world which are less complex than the world and precisely for this reason capable of providing orientation and guidance for our actions. This is done in not just one but a multitude of not necessarily homogeneous ways so that we exist simultaneously in a variety of different 'worlds'.

In order to avoid existential schizophrenia we develop second-order beliefs which enable us rationally to select information, build and relate cognitive models, and chose courses of actions. Some of our perspectives on the world surrounding us are partial and so specific that they select only very special information; some are, to a greater or lesser degree, shared by others and enable us to orient ourselves in a common world. But whereas partial perspectives, even when shared by others, can only provide relative orientation, it is the prerogative of religion to offer a total perspective which, even when not shared by others, provides an absolute orientation and helps us to integrate everything into a coherent picture. In short, our various modes of life form a network of mutually interdependent beliefs and practices. Changes in one area will sooner or later have consequences in others - as we all know from experience and history. We apply our criteria across contextual boundaries if we consider them to be relevant to the problem at stake, and we evaluate the internal criteria in the various contexts in the light of what for us are the more basic norms taken from those forms of life which we accept as central to our view of the world and our understanding of our place in it because they involve our entire personalities.

Thus to reject the idea of external criteria beyond such formal requirements as consistency which are generally applicable to all forms of life, and to accept the relativity of rationality, is not necessarily to fall into the trap of an amorphous pluralism and relativism according to which anything goes. Rationality is not tied to one form of life only, but neither are our forms of life isolated from each other or every form of life as central to our individual and common way of life as any other. Instead there is room for option and argument at every level of life. To live reflectively is to be permanently involved in a process of sorting out the sound beliefs and practices from the unsound ones. The basis for this is, on the one hand, the internal criteria of the contexts in question and, on the other, the individual and social requirements of a consistent system of beliefs across the boundaries and a coherent way of life in all the various contexts in which we exist.

It follows that the distinction between internal and external rationality is ambiguous, and the whole debate consequently confused, because to believe something on internal grounds can mean a number of different things, not all of which are equally acceptable. At least three cases are to be distinguished. A believer may hold his or her belief on grounds which are part of the very belief in question (Root, 1962, p. 13); or on grounds which are part of the same system of beliefs or forms of life; or on grounds which are part of the same believer's system of belief or 'noetic structure' (Plantinga, 1979, pp. 12-13). The first case is not a case of rational belief at all because it blurs the vital distinction between a belief and the reasons for a belief: if belief in Christ is the only 'ground' for this belief, it would be an arbitrary, irrational, even trivial belief. This is not so in the second case. It is perfectly rational to accept a belief on the basis of other beliefs which belong to the same forms of life: Christians character-istically believe in the resurrection of the dead on the basis of their belief in the resurrection of Christ, and there is nothing irrational about this. Similarly in the third case, if a belief is supported by the beliefs that form the foundation of one's system of beliefs, it is ratio-nal, as has been shown by Alvin Plantinga (1979; 1981; cf. Gutting, 1982, pp. 79-82). But foundational structures of belief-systems, for all their structural similarities, can and do differ from person to person. If belief in God is basic to my system of beliefs it can provide grounds for my believing in the resurrection of Christ and for my believing that the sun will rise tomorrow. But this will not be the case for one who does not believe in God; whereas he or she may have other reasons for believing in tomorrow's sunrise, this is most likely not so for the resurrection of Christ. Consequently, what is rational for me is not necessarily so for somebody else (Kellenberger, 1985, pp. 102-3), but if it were, it might be for different reasons.

That is to say, rationality is relative not only to a particular system of beliefs and practices but also to a particular person or group of persons; and the two kinds of rationality do not necessarily coincide. Claims to believe something on internal grounds may refer to the criteria of rationality operative within the form of life to which the belief in question belongs, and this is how they are usually understood by Phillips and other Neo-Wittgensteinians. But they may also refer to the criteria of rationality operative within the complex system of beliefs and practices of a particular person or group of persons, and this is something quite different. The difference is that in the first case it is a form of life, in the second a person that has basic beliefs which may be adduced as grounds or evidence for other beliefs. But whereas a form of life comprises a relatively homogeneous set of beliefs so that basic beliefs in a system are not of a completely differ-ent kind from the others, this is not so with persons that exist in a plurality of diverse forms of life. A person may, on the basis of his or her beliefs or noetic structure, have grounds for the belief in the resurrection that are not part of, or even at odds with, those accept-able in the Christian forms of life. So what seems to be an external ground from the Christian perspective can be an internal ground from the personal perspective, and vice versa. Consequently, the internal rationality of a system of beliefs is not to be confused with the internal rationality of a believer's system. The former is made explicit - in the case of religious beliefs - through theological reflection and argument which specifies what is to count as rational and irrational in the religious forms of life in question. The latter is manifest in the critical screening of our beliefs and practices to separate the veridical from the illusory and the legitimate from the illegitimate in all areas of belief and practice relevant to our life. In that this is done by reasoning and argument, both individually and collectively, rationality is intimately linked with argument and reason.

To sum up, there are many forms of rationality, for human life and reasoning is not a monolithic activity. All forms of rationality are relative to reasoning in both contexts of beliefs and practices, and contexts of personal appropriation of beliefs and practices; yet there is no reasoning without reasons, concepts and patterns of inference, and therefore some rudimentary form of rationality. Rationality begins to flourish in an atmosphere of argument and discussion in which we learn to communicate and critically evaluate not only our beliefs but our reasons for and against our beliefs.

III

It is this *argumentative form of rationality* which I hold to be basic to theology. Thus in claiming theology to be a rational enterprise I mean above all this: that it is concerned with argument and with the attempt to solve problems by reasoning, appeal to evidence and conceptual inquiry. Theologians - unless they are very bad theologians - do not revel in pronouncing mystery and paradox, nor do they set out to construct systems of ultimate truths. What they are trying to do is to solve problems by argument and reasons. In this weak but significant sense theology is, and always has been, rational: it presents reasoned beliefs, not non-debatable dogmas for the faithful to believe and the godless to ignore; it proceeds by argument, and it seeks to convince by reasons.

It follows that theology is to be understood in terms of the problems which it attempts to solve, the arguments which it employs and the reasons which it adduces. It is distinguished from other intellectual endeavours by its problems, and related to them by its argumentative procedures. Consequently, we are faced with two fundamental questions: What are the problems which theology seeks to solve? What are the standards which it applies, and the kinds of argument which it uses, in its attempts to solve those problems?

Both questions are such that there is no unique statement of the problems which they express; and therefore no single answer to them. First of all, they may be taken in a *factual* or a *normative* sense. As factual questions they raise (in a broad sense) historical issues: What problems was theology trying to solve at a given time? Which reasons did it offer in tackling those problems? Which standards did it observe in its arguments? Questions of this sort will receive different answers at different times. Although there are recognizable types of problems that recur in different form (e.g. about God, about human existence, about the world and its maker etc.), theology has been concerned with widely differing problems in the course of its history, not all of which would have been accepted as theological problems by theologians of other periods and traditions. And although there are certain common standards which more or less explicitly underly every argumentative endeavour (e.g. the rules of logic or the assumption that rigour, honesty and clarity will ensure that argument will not be a waste of time (Toulmin 1969; Bieri et al., 1979; Apel, 1980; 1982; Kuhlmann and Böhler, 1982)), theology has taken on very different forms when it has insisted on exclusively theological standards ('revelation') or when it has accepted, e.g., tenets of rationalist metaphysics ('reasonableness') or empirical science ('generalizable experience') amongst its standards of rationality.

However, the bewildering variety of answers to the factual questions shows that in order to understand theology we have to move beyond history. History may tell us what was or is the case. It is of no help in deciding what ought to be the case, i.e. which problems are *adequate* to theology and which standards are theologically *appropriate* in tackling them. To answer this we are forced back to normative questions which typically raise systematic issues: What problems ought theology be trying to solve? Which standards ought it to observe in doing so?

Again there are no unique or universally accepted answers to questions of this sort. Every answer, as, e.g., the dispute between Rome and liberation theologians abundantly illustrates, involves the whole conception of the nature and task of theology which is presupposed, and these conceptions vary. But conceptions of the theological enterprise which are a matter of course to theologians within one tradition may be far from self-evident to theologians from another. Whereas it is part of the dogmatic structure of Roman Catholicism 'that the one and true God our creator and Lord can be known through the creation by the natural light of human reason' (Denzinger and Schönmetzer 1967, no. 3026), this has been firmly denied by Karl Barth and other Protestant theologians. Consequently, the answers to the normative questions that have been accepted as normal and satisfactory within the one tradition have been far from convincing and sufficient for those outside it.

This plurality of conceptions and the essential relativity of normative proposals raises new kinds of problems for theology and requires its rationality to become more sophisticated. Theologians who become aware of it cannot simply continue to discuss the problems commonly accepted as theological within their own tradition but have to justify what they do and the way they do it. Besides having to solve theological problems they have to sort out theological from non-theological problems and theologically acceptable from non-acceptable standards; and this requires explanation and justification of the criteria which they apply. Accordingly, theological disputes often concern not only theological problems and their solution (first-order disputes) but questions like whether or not a given problem is a theological one or a given standard theologically acceptable and, even more fundamentally, what it is for a problem to be a theological one or a standard to be theologically acceptable (second-order disputes). Thus a more sophisticated theology typically reflects not only on first-order questions like 'Is the world created by God?', 'What does the Bible tell us about creation?', 'Why is there evil in the world?' but also on second-order questions like 'In what sense, if at all, are these theological questions?', 'What does it mean to say that the world is created?', 'Is the evil in the world compatible with its being created by a good, omniscient and omnipotent God?' etc; and it may even, by way of an academic division of labour, assign specific kinds of problems to specific disciplines (historical, systematic, fundamental theology) which together constitute the body of theology. In short, from being rational in fact, theology becomes self-consciously rational by reflecting not merely on what it receives as theological problems within its tradition but on the theological status, adequacy and appropriateness of its problems, arguments and standards of argumentation.

The emergence of self-conscious rationality in theology has been a historical process intimately linked with the general development of Western culture; and it decisively changed the face of theology. For whereas theology has always been rational, it has not always been self-consciously rational. The more it became so the more it was led to question many of the assumptions taken for granted in traditional theology and the less it could ignore questions of justification which were put permanently and at every level of argument on the theological agenda. This has made life more difficult for the theologian but it has also opened up new areas of theological thought. In particular it accounts for the predominance of methodological reflection in modern theology. And although this development has met with sharp criticism by those who fear theology will become too intellectualist, too much occupied with itself and thus not attentive enough to its primary task (i.e. the reflection of substantial theological problems directly relevant to the religious life of the community), the process from reflection to self-reflection cannot be reversed, nor can the intrinsic logic of argumentative rationality be avoided. If problems are what count, the problem of which problems are to count counts most.

IV

The argument so far has assumed that there are theological problems. But precisely this has been questioned. The problems which theology attempts to solve - as Hegel, Freud and logical empiricists have argued in their different ways - are said either to be unintelligible and thus unsolvable or, if they are intelligible, they are not specifically theological and thus cannot be solved by theology. Under the philosophical microscope they turn out to be the result of conceptual confusion or to dissolve into a set of historical, philosophical, psychological and sociological problems which fall into the domain of those disciplines but do not require any specifically theological treatment. What traditionally has been taken to be a theological problem really is an unanalysed complex of spurious and/or non-theological problems. It follows that theology can be reduced without loss to science and philosophy and, therefore, no longer claim to be an autonomous and intellectually respectable discipline. I shall call this the *reductionist argument*.

This argument has been countered by R. Swinburne (1977), K. Ward (1982) and S. T. Davis (1983), to mention but a few. They argue that theological problems, claims and arguments such as whether (or that) there is a God who is omnipotent, omniscient, perfectly free etc., far from being essentially confused and unintelligible, can (if understood correctly) be shown to be perfectly coherent and intelligible because it makes sense to suppose that reality is such that they are true. But even if we accept that their arguments are successful, this is not enough by itself to refute the reductionist argument. The intelligibility of theological problems and claims is a necessary, not a sufficient, condition for such a refutation. What we also need to show is that those problems are such that they withstand reduction to non-theological problems, i.e. that they raise genuinely *theological* and not merely historical, philosophical, psychological or sociological issues.

This is not to ask for a proof of the inevitability of theology. Theology as an autonomous discipline is presumably no more necessary than any other intellectual endeavour; and it may well disappear, as Barth (1936) envisaged, because all its tasks have been taken over by other disciplines. It is, after all, not the discipline but the problems which count; and long before theology developed into an autonomous discipline there were theological problems and attempts to solve them. Thus what is needed in order to refute the reductionist argument is an account of genuine and intelligible theological problems which resist analysis into more basic non-theological problems of whatever kind; and traditional problems of dogmatics like the existence and goodness of God, creation, revelation, salvation, sin, life after death, last judgement, eternity etc., which have actually been at the centre of theological debates, are genuine candidates for such an account if they prove to be intelligible and to resist reduction.

It is not to be expected that all will live up to this test. But it would be rash to assume from the outset that none of them will. However, if there are some genuine theological problems, there may well be more; and if they are not only of different sorts but fall into different and mutually irreducible sets, theology will turn out to be a much more complex, manifold and less closely knit enterprise than is sometimes appreciated. For different sets of problems define different *types* of theology (e.g. Greek and Christian theology); and the same set of problems but different standards of argument and rationality (e.g. natural reason or revelation) define different *forms* of theology within a type (e.g. natural or revealed theology). And because, as will become apparent, theology has never been of one type or one form only, 'theology' is not the name of a single, simple activity but of a cluster of problems and activities not all of which have always been accepted as equally respectable by all theologians.

From the beginning theology, because of its different roots, has been a complex enterprise, marred by a conflict of origins and prone to develop in quite different sorts of directions. This is also true of Christian theology. There have always existed not only different forms but also different types of theology based on different sets of problems which have not always been happily married and have often been the cause of sharp controversy. If we survey the theological tradition we can, in an admittedly summary fashion, distinguish at least three different sets of problems which have been taken to be genuine theological problems and which have given rise to different types of theology, i.e. philosophical theologies, experiential theologies and revelational theologies:

1   Philosophical theologies characteristically receive their problems via the *metaphysical* route: they concentrate on problems like the origin of the world, the ground of being, the ultimate principle of order, the source of the good and the bad, the reason for the surplus of meaning over meaninglessness, the nature of being itself, a supreme being or absolute subjectivity etc. These not only are more general and more fundamental than anything dealt with in particular sciences but are inherent in the very framework of these and all other human endeavours and therefore constantly recur in different forms. Problems of this sort are understood to be basic, permanent and unavoidable; and consequently they are taken to refute the reductionist argument.

2   Experiential theologies characteristically receive their problems via the *religious* route: they are erected around problems like the nature of the holy, the character of the numinous, the truth of myths, the meaning of rituals, the cognitivity of mysticism, the ground and nature of religious beliefs, practices and institutions, the moral and doctrinal dimensions of religious life etc. These arise from particular, individual or communal religious experiences or configurations of such experiences which are too specific to be adequately and exhaustively dealt with in any other but their own religious terms. Problems of this sort are said to belong to a specific province of human experience and life and therefore to require special treatment beyond that provided by sciences like history, psychology or sociology.

3   Revelational theologies characteristically receive their problems via the *revelational* route: they concentrate on problems which they claim to have been provoked by the self-revelation of God in specific historical and prophetic events like the exodus, the message of prophets or the life of Christ; and they understand these problems to be not only riddles which we may hope sooner or later to be able to solve, but genuine mysteries which, although they engage us totally, we are never in a position to grasp fully. Problems of this sort are said to be irreducible because of their divine origin and content: they are posed by God's own dealings with humanity and cannot adequately be dealt with if this is not appreciated.

The three sets of problems are often combined, as the theologies of Augustine, Thomas Aquinas, the Lutheran divines of the seventeenth century, Schleiermacher, Rahner, Hick, Pannenberg or Lonergan demonstrate in their different ways; they have been the starting-point of widely differing theologies; and none of them has been conceived, determined and described in just one unique way. The metaphysical approach, for example, has been based on conceptions of the problematic set that are ontology-centred (Aristotle,

Hegel, Tillich), cosmology-centred (Plato, Whitehead), subjectivity-centred (Descartes, Fichte), morality-centred (Kant) or sign-centred (Peirce). The religious approach has been based on conceptions of religion that are foundationalist (Schleiermacher), pragmatist (James) or experience-based (Smart). The revelational approach has been based on conceptions of revelation that are exclusively christological (Barth), pneumatological (Calvin), salvation-historical (Rahner) or phenomenological (van der Leeuw, feminist theology). However, for all the differences in the way they are conceived and in the kind of theologies erected on this basis, the three sets together form a network of genuine theological problems which provide sufficient reason to reject the reductionist argument.

The sceptic will not easily be convinced by the three sets of problems mentioned, and certainly not by all in the same way. Revelational theologies, it might be objected, are based not on real but on putative problems. At their worst they are confused or just imagination, at their best mere claims of a divine revelation that fall within the province of the second set. For if there is such a thing as revelation, it must come through human experience, and the religious experience on which such claims are based is all there is as a genuine cause of problems. Experiential theologies, on the other hand, do indeed deal with profound and widespread phenomena in human culture and history, but all they call for is a scientific study of religion, not a specific theological and doctrinal approach. The metaphysical set, finally, insofar as it raises intelligible problems at all, does not raise theological ones. If the world should indeed be such that it requires an ultimate principle of existence or order, it requires just this principle but not God. For God is defined in relation to worship, and it would be perverse to worship a principle, for principles deserve neither loyalty nor praise. 'To say that there is a God is therefore different from saying that there is a Creator or First Cause. God may be Creator: but primarily he is the object of worship.' (Smart, 1971, p. 31) So what is intelligible in the metaphysical set is not (yet) theological, and what is theological is not intelligible.

Even if these arguments were sound and cogent, they would not suffice to show that the three sets described can include no genuine theological problems; and as long as this is not shown, we are justified in presuming that at least some of the problems of traditional theology are innocent of incoherence and reducibility until proven guilty. Nevertheless, the arguments draw attention to an important aspect of the three sets of problems offered by traditional theology, viz. that they are conceived from quite different perspectives. The revelational set comprises problems that arise within the internal perspective of the believers themselves; the religious set problems that pose themselves in the external perspective of a (scientific) observer of religion; the metaphysical set problems which arise not only in religion but in all human endeavours and with respect to everything there is or might be. And it may well be asked whether theology, if it fuses together problems from so different perspectives, is not bound to be inconsistent or at least full of internal tensions and conflict.

If this is the case, it is not an accidental fault easily to be overcome but part of the very nature of theology as it has developed over the centuries. From the beginning it has been a complex enterprise with conflicting elements, and although the elements have been redefined and rearranged (reduced or multiplied) from time to time, the conflicts have remained. They are, to a large extent, the legacy of the peculiar genesis of Western theology and the different roots from which it originated. It is to these that we turn next.

Chapter 2

The Origins of Theology

I

Theology, I have asserted, is a rational enterprise. It presents reasoned beliefs; it proceeds by argument; and it seeks to convince by reasons. Now reasons necessarily favour or disfavour something else (Edgley, 1969), and it requires some level of cultural and intellectual sophistication to grasp clearly the difference between a claim and a reason for or against a claim.

In Western culture this was first achieved and critically observed by the Presocratic philosophers, who thus became the originators of both philosophy and theology. They began to change the world by interpreting it rationally, i.e. by replacing unargued tales by argued theory. Opinions - even widely held, religiously sanctioned or seemingly self-evident opinions - they did not regard as true knowledge. Instead they hoped to attain to the truth not by reverently accepting ancient tales and traditions but by rigorously subordinating assertion to argument and dogma to reason in all areas of human life and thought (J. Barnes, 1982a). Contrary to the mythical polytheism of the time they not merely claimed the apparent chaos of events to conceal an underlying order but followed Thales in arguing this order to be the product of impersonal rather than personal forces; and by supporting their arguments by rational considerations they became the fathers of both philosophy and science. Similarly, they turned their back on the mythical conceptions of popular piety and poetry because of the moral and rational deficiencies of such conceptions. But whereas some, like Democritus and Protagoras, were led to agnosticism or atheism by the new scientific attitude, others, like Xenophanes, paved the way to theological reflection by drawing out the monotheistic implications of their cosmological speculations and by applying their philosophical insights to a forceful moral (practical) and speculative (theoretical) critique of the anthropomorphic polytheism of Homer and Hesiod. Science, they realized, expelled the gods but not god. On the contrary, it provided means for conceptualizing god which made it possible to oust anthropomorphism and to introduce a more abstract notion of divinity; and it required this divinity as a sort of first principle among the explanatory causes of the universe (cf. Aristotle, *Met.* I.3.983a8-9). So for the first time in history it became possible to *think* (i.e. form concepts) of god, and at the same time difficult if not impossible not to think god. This was a momentous move, for now claims about god were not primarily something for which reasons had to be sought, but themselves (necessary) reasons required to explain other claims, sc. the claims of science and, in particular, of cosmology. Whereas the gods ceased to be part of the furniture of the world, god became an explanatory principle which, like all principles, was justified by being required by that which it was designed to explain.

Precisely here, at the transition from tales about gods to explanatory concepts of god, we have the origins of theology. Rational theological argument is impossible without a concept or concepts of god; yet there are no concepts of god without models in terms of which god is conceptualized; and these models are inadequate if they do not provide us with criteria for determining what is true and false in our thinking and speaking about god. It is here that anthropomorphic myths fail most conspicuously. They do not offer such models because - as Xenophanes observed - 'each group of men paints the shape of the gods in a fashion similar to themselves ... the Ethiopians draw them dark and snub-nosed, the Thracians red-haired and blue-eyed' (frag. 125) - that is, they leave us without any criteria of truth and falsity in theological matters. If we want to conceptualize god, we have to find some other starting-point; and Presocratics like Xenophanes were convinced they had discovered this in cosmological science and astronomical speculation: the vastness, order, unity and comprehensiveness of the universe became their model for thinking god and for criticizing the shortcomings of mythical anthropomorphism. Thus theology began its career as a branch and integral part of philosophy; it originated with the cosmological speculations of natural philosophy and the philosophical critique of traditional mythology; and for a long time to come theology and philosophy remained a joint enterprise.

Theology, then, has a rational root, and its main source is not religious tradition but philosophical reflection. Although the term literally means 'god-talk', it is not one of the original ways of talking about gods or god. Before theology there was myth, and only when the spell of mythology was broken by philosophy did theology become possible.

Philosophical reflection, not myth, was the matrix out of which theology arose; its concepts of god were based not on religious experience but on cosmological speculation which provided the models for conceptualizing god; and it always remained at a rational distance from the womb of the unconscious out of which religious myths and their symbols are born.

Contrast (and often conflict) between popular piety and theology were the consequences of its close association with philosophy, whereas contrast and conflict between theology and philosophy only emerged clearly with the rise of Christian theology. From the beginning theological discourse about god (*ho theos*) contrasted with mythical discourse about gods (*theoi*); and the contrast was due not to a critical reduction of the many gods to one but to a philosophical conception of the divine (*to theion*) which not only provided criteria for a critical evaluation of traditional mythology but offered the independent grounds without which the edifice of theology could not have been erected. Theology, as a distinctive intellectual discipline, emerged gradually in the groping for a concept of god which involves both the idea of divine singularity (there is only one god) and of divine transcendence (god is neither part nor the whole of the world). This sophisticated concept, which was never unambiguously formulated in antiquity, presupposes a clear grasp of a twofold difference: the *monotheistic difference* between gods and god which is central to the idea of the singularity of god; and the *cosmological difference* between god and the world which is basic to the idea of the transcendence of god. Both differences took a long time to be grasped clearly, and they were only gradually built into the concept of god. But the process was started by Greek philosophers, who for this reason hold pride of place as the initiators of theology; and even though terminology is not a sure guide in these matters (cf. Stead, 1977, pp. 89-90), the changes from 'gods' (*theoi*) to 'the divine' (*to theion*) and from there to 'god' (*ho theos*) signal the main stages of this important development in Greek thought.

In short, the rise of theology, as distinct from both mythology and cosmology, was due to a twofold change in thinking and talking about deity. On the one hand, polytheistic talk of gods became replaced by monotheistic talk of the divine. On the other hand, the pantheistic tendency of identifying the divine with (part of) the world or the basic principles operating in the world became replaced by a talk of god which was sensitive to his transcendence over the world without jeopardizing his relation to it. Both changes did not take place at once, and both took a long time to come to maturity. The first was initiated by the Presocratics, the second by Plato and Aristotle, to whom we turn next.

II

Plato's philosophy not only manifests the intimate relationship between theology, philosophy and the critique of mythology, it culminates in a theology in which the end of philosophical wisdom coincides with the end of religion (Allen, 1985, chs 1-3). Plato has been called the creator of philosophical theism (A. E. Taylor, 1971, p. 493; but compare the divine philosophy of Xenophanes (J. Barnes, 1982a, pp. 82ff) and other Presocratics (Vlastos, 1952)), and there can be no doubt that his philosophical religion (cf. Charlesworth, 1972, pp. 6ff) decisively changed the meaning of 'theology'. Before Plato it seems to have been more or less equivalent to 'god-talk' as exemplified by the tales of Homer and Hesiod. After Plato - as can be seen from Aristotle (*Met.* III.4.1000a9; XII.5.1071b27; XII.10.1075b26; XIV.4.1091a34) - it came to mean something like 'rational (or theoretical) account of god'. The term *logos* in 'theology' is now understood philosophically in the sense of 'to give account of' (*logon didonai*); and this transformed the meaning and task of theology from talk about gods into a critical reflection about god. For to give an account of x requires some y in terms of which we give an account of x; and to give an account of god requires some model of thought and argument in terms of which we give an account of god. Plato was the first who realized this clearly; and he proposed the philosophical conception of the soul (*psuchê*) as the most adequate model for a rational account of god, i.e. for an argumentative theology.

The term 'theology' is first documented in Plato (*Rep.* 379a1ff), and the context in which it occurs is illuminating (cf. Jaeger, 1947, p. 4; Caird, 1904; Moore, 1921; Solmsen, 1942). For Plato the myths of popular religion and the anthropomorphic, childish and often immoral talk about the gods by the poets have an extremely harmful effect on the education of children. In his *Republic* he therefore requires the poets to follow critical outlines or models of proper talk of god (*tupoi peri theologias*) which present god as he truly is. That is to say, since god is good, he cannot be the cause of evil; since he is perfect, he cannot change; since he is true, he cannot deceive. In short, whatever is said about god has to follow the basic maxim that all the good is due to god, everything evil, however, is due to anything else but god.

This is not a self-evident truth. On the contrary, Homer (and not only he) gives every reason to suspect it to be false. But for Plato the views of poets and popular piety are of little value in theological matters. What counts is not pious opinions about gods but true knowledge of god; and this is open only to the philosopher. The mythical theology of the poets is of no evidential value as long as it is not purified in terms of the rational theology of the philosopher. For the truth which myths contain, if indeed they contain any, can only be discerned by those who know what god truly is. But then this knowledge cannot be derived from a critical reduction of traditional myths to a rationally acceptable core through historical or allegorical interpretation (cf. *Phaedrus*, 228dff). Rather it is already to be presupposed if we want to perform the hermeneutical task successfully. It follows that the philosophical account of god has to be worked out independently of the mythical tradition; and it was the achievement of the Presocratics to realise this. Yet although they were right in principle, they failed in practice by confounding metaphysics with meteorology in their account of the divine. Fascinated by the new empirical science, they were led to confuse the divine with the physical universe as a whole (or the basic stuff out of which they believed it was made) by not distinguishing the specious knowledge of the sensible world of becoming from the true knowledge of the intelligible world of being.

Plato corrected this lack of philosophical sophistication. He did so by invoking the Socratic doctrine of the soul, with its fundamental distinction between mind and body. For Plato, mind, not body, is what we have to start with. There is no knowledge worthy of that name which is not knowledge of the immutable, universal and archetypal objects of pure intelligence, the eternal forms or ideas which make up the intelligible world of true being; and this world is accessible only through the soul, by way of contemplation and by the ascent of the mind from the world of sense to the world of ideas. For truth is inherent in the human soul; it is available through a process of recollection (*anamnesis*) whereby the soul recalls the forms it knew before it was joined to a body, by moving from the realm of sense perception to the intelligible realm of dianoetic (figurative or mathematical) and noetic (conceptual or dialectical) knowledge of the archetypal forms; and at the apex of the forms there is the Good, the supreme reality and the highest value upon which all other intelligible realities depend. For all 'objects of knowledge derive from the Good . . . their very existence and being; and the Good is not the same thing as being, but even beyond being, surpassing it in dignity and power' (*Rep.* 509b). Plato refuses to say more of it, for what is beyond being is also beyond knowledge and the powers of human reason. All we can know is that there is something 'that every soul pursues as the end of all its actions, dimly divining its existence, but perplexed and unable to grasp its nature' (505).

It is not altogether clear whether Plato identifies the Good with god. But it is clear that there are close similarities between the two. For if there is a god - and Plato is one of the first explicitly to argue for this (*Laws* X) - he cannot belong to the sensible world but must belong to the realm of the eternal and immutable. On the other hand, he cannot be a form amongst others if the cosmological difference between god and the world, the one and the many, is not to be obscured. Although not a sensible reality, he is neither a member of the class of forms nor simply identical with the totality of forms. Indeed - and here we hit upon the specific Platonic model for conceptualizing god - he is not a form at all, but a *soul*: the soul of the world. This becomes clear from Plato's arguments against atheism, i.e. the belief that there are no gods or no god and that the world is the product of purely mechanical motions of corporeal elements. There are, he argues in the *Laws*, many different kinds of motions in the world but all motions belong to one of two classes. They are either causally communicated motions (things moved by something else) or spontaneous motions (things moved by themselves). Yet all causally communicated motions presuppose some spontaneous motion as their source (894c-895b), and the only things capable of self-motion are things alive, i.e. things with a mind or soul (*psuchê*). For only souls have wishes, plans and purposes, only souls are good, and while some souls are better than others, there is one perfectly good soul (*ariste psuchê*) at their head. It follows that since no physical movement is spontaneous (896d), all cosmic movements must be due to a soul or souls. The argument disregards the question whether there is one god or many but it is clear that there may be more than one such soul, and that there must at least be two. For there is regular and irregular motion, order and disorder in the world, so that besides the best soul there must be other souls which are not wholly good (896e-898d). On the other hand, the prevalence of order over disorder shows that there is a supreme cause, i.e. the good god who, as ruler of the world, is both a transcendent and an immanent deity: he participates in the immutability of the forms which he transcends both as their principle of being and as the immanent ground of the participation of the sensible world in the forms.

It is precisely this which places god beyond intelligence and being (*Rep.* 509b) - not because he is unintelligible but because he is super-intelligible. For the principle of being cannot itself be said to be (at least not in the same sense), and the ground of everything intelligible cannot itself be one of the intelligible things. 'Just as we cannot look directly at the sun, which is the source of the light by which we see other things, so also we cannot look directly at the source of intelligibility by which we understand everything else' (Charlesworth,

1972, p. 9). Theological knowledge is essentially imperfect knowledge of the suprarational; and god is only inadequately accessible to philosophical reason not because he is irrational but because of the limitations of our intelligence. But what in principle cannot be fully known, not even by dialectical reason, 'cannot be put into words like other objects of knowledge' (*Seventh Letter* 341c-402). Thus at the highest point of his metaphysics Plato's philosophy passes over into a theology which is expressed not in rational but in, on the one hand, *apophatic* and, on the other, *mythical* discourse, both of which proved fateful for the further development of theology (cf. McLelland, 1976, pp. 8ff). In talking about god, we can choose to confine ourselves to negations: he is without parts, beginning or end, shape, position, motion or rest, identity or difference, indeed, he 'in no sense *is*', he is 'not named or spoken of, not an object of opinion or of knowledge, not perceived by any creature' (*Parmenides* 137c-142a). Alternatively we must have recourse to myth, which is the closest approximation to a subject that is beyond full comprehension and defies rational expression in terms of mathematics and dialectics. This is not a plea for a return to traditional mythology and its totally inadequate ways of talking about the gods. Rather it is a plea for a 'new mythology of god' which elaborates the concept of the world-soul in the light of the philosophical insight into the Good in the way exemplified by Plato's own great myths.

Plato's theology is the first fully worked out example of a rational, i.e. argumentative, account of god based on a philosophical model, the model of the soul; and it clearly demonstrates both the strengths and weaknesses of this approach. Within the limits of this model Plato offers arguments for a particular understanding of god, as the divine soul ruling the world, which have decisively influenced Western philosphy and theology. But the arguments carry weight only as far as the soul-model goes and whatever cannot be answered on the basis of it is left tantalizingly without explanation. How, for example, is the divine mind related to the world which it rules? How is the world-ruler related to the Good or to other forms which exist independently of himself and which he contemplates? Where does matter come from which again appears to exist independently of the forms and of god? Where does the Demiurge come from who in Plato's *Timaeus* shapes matter according to the forms as best as he can? Is he inferior to or identical with the ruler of the world? How does he relate to 'the father and maker of all this universe' who is said to be 'past finding out and, even if we found him, to tell of him to all men would be impossible' (*Timaeus* 28c)? These and other questions are left wholly obscure because the model of the world-soul as such does not suggest any specific or even possible answers to them.

This manifests a principal problem of theological reflection. It can only offer a rational, i.e. argumentative, account of god by being based on a model; but not every idea or complex of ideas is good for a model of god, and every model of god not only answers problems but raises new ones because of its intrinsic limitations. So theology is faced with two fundamental tasks: it has to justify the models which it uses for conceptualizing god; and it has to delineate the limits of its models in order not to confuse the mystery of god with the limitations of our model-bound concepts of god. Now different forms of theology will use different models and delineate their limits in different ways; and different types of theology will offer different kinds of justifications, because what is offered and accepted as justification will depend on the problems which a theology is designed to solve. This explains both the unity of the Greek type of theology and the differences within it. Because they started from cosmological problems, Greek philosophers all sought to offer justifications for their theological models in terms of the explanatory function of god for (aspects of) the universe as a whole; but because they disagreed about which models best conceptualized this function they developed different forms of cosmo-theology. The pattern was set by the Presocratics, who applied their scientifically successful quest for rational explanation in terms of causes and principles to cosmological problems; and classical Greek philosophy followed their lead.

III

The Presocratics used the universe and what they took to be its basic principles as a model for conceptualizing god and adumbrated a theology virtually indistinguishable from cosmology. Plato criticized this as confused, and suggested psychology as a better basis for theology and the soul as a more adequate model for god. For Aristotle this was a wrong step in the right direction: not psychology but a better physics was what was needed to ground theology; and this required Plato's speculations to be replaced by a more adequate account of science, logic and god (cf. J. Barnes, 1982b).

Aristotle achieved this by rejecting the Platonic theory of an independently existing world of forms, replacing it by an account of the existence of forms *in* things, and supporting this by a theory of inductive knowledge according to which we start from sense experience and derive the general from the particular by a process of abstraction. Whiteness is neither ontologically nor epistemologically prior to white things but a matter of there being white things from which we can by way of abstraction come to know that they are white. However, to know this to be true or false is not to know a thing of a particular kind (as Plato's theory of knowledge as vision suggested) but a proposition; and we know a proposition if we know whether its predicate term is rightly or wrongly affirmed or denied of its subject term. This can be done in a variety of ways first codified by Aristotle who (in his *Analytics*) worked out a sophisticated logic of terms and deductive inference which strongly emphasized the subject-predicate form of propositions. To this he added (in his *Physics*) a theory of causality originally extracted from the model of human action, i.e. the work of a craftsman who, for producing a statue for some purpose (final cause), uses some material (material cause), works on it (efficient cause) and changes it into some new form (formal cause). Generalizing this from human action to physical events and combining it with his subject-predicate logic led Aristotle to offer a metaphysical account of substances as irreducibly basic individuals of hylemorphic structure, i.e. something which can be designated by a demonstrative phrase ('this'), whose existence is not parasitic on something else ('this statue'), and which is a composite of matter and form ('a marble Hermes'). Substances of this sort are the ontologically basic units of reality and the ultimate referents of all knowledge; we know them if we are able to explain why they are what they are and not something else (their essence); and it is the task of scientific knowledge to find out the essence of things in order to be able to explain why they cannot be otherwise. Applying all this to cosmological problems, Aristotle was led to replace Plato's philosophical religion by a scientific theology whose task is to explain why the cosmos is what it is and cannot be otherwise, and to substitute intelligence (*nous*) for soul (*psuchê*) in his attempt to find a scientifically adequate model for god. In short, he founded theology as a science - the supreme theoretical science. This needs explaining.

For Aristotle all science is either practical, productive or theoretical. Practical sciences like ethics or politics are concerned with action; productive sciences like farming, engineering or poetics with the making of things; theoretical sciences, which are superior to the others, with explanation and the discovery of truth. The theoretical sciences again subdivide into three species - natural science, mathematics and theology - for there are three basic types of objects about which we can have true knowledge and which can be marked off from each other by different combinations of the two characteristics 'being capable of change' and 'existing in its own right'. So the objects of natural science like natural bodies (e.g. animals or stars) and artefacts like houses or statues are capable of change or motion and exist separately, i.e. as substances in their own right. The objects of mathematics, on the other hand, like numbers, and universals like whiteness are changeless but - and here Aristotle departs from Plato - do not exist separately, i.e. apart from particular white things or particular groups of things; and therefore they are not substances themselves but exist only as modifications of substances. It follows that 'if there are no substances apart from natural substances, natural science will be the primary science' (*Met.* VI.1.1026a18-19). Yet objects of the two sorts described are not all there is. We can envisage a third type of object which exhibits both the excellencies of the objects of natural science (existence in its own right) and of the objects of mathematics (changelessness). For what is changeless is superior to what is capable of change because knowledge of it will always be true; and what exists in its own right is superior to what does not exist separately because it is not parasitic upon some other existent. Therefore what is changeless and exists in its own right is superior to everything else, indeed, is divine; and divine substances of this sort are the subject-matter of theology.

But are there substances of this sort? Are they not merely conceptual constructions without a basis in reality? It is hardly an argument for their existence that theology as a theoretical science is impossible without them. But this is only the first step of Aristotle's argument. The second is that theoretical science is impossible without theology. More exactly, as mathematics is impossible without the changeable objects of natural science, so natural science is impossible without the changeless objects of theology: the existence of divine substances is necessarily required by natural science and mathematics because it is impossible for theoretical science to exist and theology not to exist. His arguments to this effect are well known and can be found in Book VIII of his *Physics* and Book XII of his *Metaphysics* where he argues for the existence of an unmoved mover, a changeless source of change. If there is to be any change in the universe - and 'change' is Aristotle's term for every motion on earth and in the heavens from becoming and perishing through qualitative and quantitative change to change of place, including the eternal circular movement of the stars - it must be due to some original source which imparts change to other things without changing itself and whose very essence is to act and to move the fixed stars in their concentric celestial spheres. For all change is a form of causality as specified in this theory of causes; all change, therefore, is to be explained in terms of either extrinsic (*A* is changed by *B*) or intrinsic (*A* changes itself) causes which are co-present or simultaneous with the change they cause; but in either case we have an infinite series of (external or internal) causes and therefore no explanation at all if there is not a first uncaused cause of all subsequent change. So if there is change at all, there must be a changeless source of change; and if there is to be a satisfactory explanation of change, there must be a self-explanatory cause of change. Aristotle did not suppose this argument to establish the singularity of just one changeless source of change. There are, he believed, more than one such changeless substance, and perhaps as many as 47 or 55 for 'there must be as many such substances as there are motions of the stars' (*Met.* XII 8, 1073a36-8). But they are principles of immutable and eternal circular movements within the universe, and therefore moving divinities which initiate change by changing themselves. Yet beyond them and transcending the universe, though as its cause and therefore the most exalted and excellent substance not outside it, there is the ultimate principle of the world, the one prime unmoved mover.

This primary divinity is conceived by Aristotle in terms of three intimately related models of thought: the model of substance, the model of mind or intelligence (*nous*) and the model of causality. The first is used to develop the characteristic of 'existing in its own right' (which god must have if it is to be a cause), and results in the conception of god as the highest being or most divine substance. The second is used to capture the characteristic of 'changelessness', and leads to the conception of god as the *noesis noeseos*, the permanent thinking of thinking. For 'it is the function of what is most divine to think and to use its intellect' (*Parts of Animals* IV 10, 686a29) and there is nothing more divine to think of than the divine intellect itself. The third is used to show that the highest being cannot fail to exist because it is required as the ultimate principle of every change in the universe, and that it is precisely by permanently contemplating its own essence that it performs the function of this principle; and this results in the conception of god as the unmoved mover. For on the one hand the primary divinity does not in any respect depend on anything different from itself for its existence and nature (it is *unmoved* and *unmoving*), otherwise it would not be the *self-explanatory* cause of all change; on the other hand there can be nothing which does not depend on it (is *moved* by it), otherwise it would not be the *cause of all change*. But how can a changeless (unchanged and unchanging) substance be the cause of all change? Aristotle answers in terms of the second model: by being conceived as pure intelligence (*nous*), i.e. as the permanent act of self-contemplation in which the act and the object of contemplation coincide. For contemplative life is the noblest and happiest that can be lived, and as perfect contemplation god changelessly 'initiates change' as the ultimate 'object of love' and desire by which everything less perfect is drawn towards this divine perfection (*Met.* XII 7, 1072b3-4).

Once more it is easy to see where the models break down. God, conceived as the First Principle in this way, cannot be said to be the efficient cause of the universe; matter and forms owe neither their nature nor existence to it but are ungenerated (*Met.* XII 3, 1069b35); and even when considered as the final cause of the world it remains obscure how inanimate beings can be drawn by love towards it. Second, the model of substance breaks down because god, as conceived by Aristotle, cannot be identified independently of the universe and does not seem to be separable from the universe. Further, the model of mind is made incoherent by turning mind into something that exists in its own right and unaffected by anything different from it; used theologically this model leads to a totally self-contained divinity which perpetually actualizes its essence independently of any relations to anything outside itself; it is without concern for anything but itself; the course of the world is neither initiated nor in any way providentially modified by it; and the perfection and happiness which it enjoys are in principle beyond anything worldly beings can hope to achieve (cf. Ward, 1982, pp. 213-14). Fourth, the model of causality cannot be developed in a way that leads to a self-explanatory cause; the notion of an ultimate cause is incoherent because causes are not themselves capable of producing an effect but are 'means through which something else produces an occurence' so that an 'infinite regress of causes faces us in every case' (Macmurray, 1956, p. 153); if, therefore, the universe requires a self-explanatory principle, it cannot be a cause but only an (intentional) action: for whereas causes require explanation in terms of other causes, the ascription of an action to an agent is self-explanatory (cf. Farrer, 1967, pp. 134ff). Finally, the problematic notions of a changeless source of change and a perpetually self-contemplating contemplation underline that the Aristotelian god is conceived and conceptualized as an ultimate principle of cosmology; that it is the most exalted being of the universe inferred from the changes we observe in the universe; that this view of god is based not on religious considerations, or the demands of worship, but on the postulates of a particular view of the intelligibility of the world and its scientific explanation in terms of a specific theory of causality; and that theology is a science precisely in so far as it is the science of the metaphysical principle(s) of physics or natural science.

Yet for all its shortcomings, Aristotelian theology amounts to a clear counter-proposal to traditional mythology. It conceptualizes god not as a mythological person, but as a metaphysical principle; and it takes this to be the only rationally defensible and scientifically acceptable core of popular religion and mythology. God is to be understood as the ultimate self-explanatory principle of the world; anthropomorphism and all 'the rest has been added by way of myth to persuade the vulgar and for the use of the laws and of expediency' (*Met.* XII 8, 1074b1-10). The vulgar may enjoy it. The philosopher has no need for it.

IV

Aristotle's conception of theology as the metaphysical queen of theoretical sciences, its cosmological grounding, and the framework of causality in which it was developed became philosophical commonplaces even where his specific theory of causes and conception of theoretical sciences were modified or rejected. Stoic philosophers, who distinguished their own kinds of theoretical sciences, sc. logic, ethics and natural science, followed Aristotle in placing theology together with pure physics in the third category but differed from him by rejecting mind (*nous*) as model for conceptualizing god, and replacing it by their model of *logos* or spirit (*pneuma*). Contrary to the Aristotelian *nous* the Stoic *logos* was not conceived as an unchangeable substance existing in its own right, but as a dynamic force that permeates all parts of the universe and organizes it teleologically. This force (or field of force) was identified with the structure of matter and believed to be of a specific pneumatic quality; but it was held to be neither a substance itself nor a quality reducible to some other substance. Rather, all substances were understood to be abstractions from this ontologically prior pneumatic field. Consequently, Stoic ontology placed relations over substances; Stoic logic concentrated on propositions rather than on terms; and Stoic theology used the *logos*-force as a model for divinity precisely because it was taken to be the one true reality, the omnipresent principle of creativity that underlies all being and becoming and directs everything to its specific end. Accordingly, god is conceived to be the omnipresent field of creative force that organizes all matter and teleologically structures the whole of the universe.

   This dynamic model of divinity allowed Stoic theology to relate much more positively to traditional mythology than either the Platonic or the Aristotelian tradition. There is only one god, the omnipresent divine *logos*; but it appears in many different forms and has become named in many different ways. So the gods of popular piety are but different names for, or ways of talking about, the one god. To see this we have only to learn to use the right methods of hermeneutics which allow us to penetrate beyond the surface meaning of myths to their true meaning; and the Stoics ingeniously elaborated and employed *etymological* and *allegorical* interpretation as the most appropriate means to discover the cosmological and moral insights enshrined in the tales of traditional religion. Cosmos-centred philosophical theology and religion-centred mythology were thus joined in a way that appealed to many who had lost faith in traditional beliefs but were still under the spell of religion; and precisely this made Stoicism one of the most popular philosophical movements in the Hellenistic age.

It was presumably Middle Stoicism (Panaitios of Rhodes 180-110 BC and Varro 116-27 BC) which developed the threefold pattern of mythical (or poetical), physical (or natural) and political theology that found its way into Tertullian's *Ad nationes*, Eusebius' *Preparatio evangelica* and Augustine's *De civitate Dei*. The first type belongs to the poets and to the cults of popular religion; the second to the philosophers and their theoretical explanation of the cosmos; the third to the constitution of cities and countries. None of them, as Augustine shows, provides an appropriate starting-point for Christian theology. It requires a framework of thought that allows us to conceptualize the Christian God without compromising his universal claim to be the ultimate truth and to be worshipped by everyone. Political theologies are inappropriate for this because they are too particular, being restricted in their validity to certain cities or countries; mythical theologies are superstitious follies which debase the divine by their crude anthropomorphism and their shameful presentation of the gods; and natural theologies waver between being theological physiologies of the cosmos or rational attempts to interpret the deeper meaning of religious myths. Nevertheless, although natural theology is not identical with the 'true theology' (*vera theologia*) of the Christian faith, it is at least a faint pagan analogue to it: the other types of theology are nothing but human inventions and of a purely conventional understanding of god, whereas natural theology, for all its inadequacy, deals with god and not merely human conceptions of god. It is the only one among the pagan types of theology with a universal scope, because it concentrates on the principles of the cosmos and is an essential part of the scientific and philosphical quest for truth; and it is this which allows Christian theology to relate positively to it.

Its placement in the context of natural theology decisively influenced the emerging character of Christian theology. In its attempt to define itself relative to the pattern of contemporary theological thought, Christian theology chose in a careful and critical (but nonetheless unmistakable) way to side with the theoretical science of the philosophers, rather than with the mythical piety of poets and people or with the religious ideology of the state. Neither the religious experience enshrined in the myths and cults of traditional religion nor the ultimate systems of value and meaning operative in human societies were the primary frame of reference for the working out of Christian theology, but, rather, the philosophers' theoretical quest for truth and insight into the intelligible structure of the universe. Christian theology thus followed philosophy in its attempt to find its way, between the Scylla of religious mythology and the Charybdis of ideological idolatry, to the safe shores of a scientific study of ultimate truth. It chose to become academic rather than popular or political; and this decision has remained determinative of its character ever since.

The decision has had immense importance for Western culture, but also grave if not (as some would argue) disastrous consequences for Christian theology itself. It seems to be wrong even to try to fit Christian theology into the tripartite pattern of Hellenistic theologies; and Augustine had good reasons to hesitate. For has Christian theology really more in common with the theoretical theology of (e.g.) Aristotle than with the mythical theologies of Homer or Hesiod? Did it not, by relating itself to the natural theology of cosmic order, forfeit the chance of coming to grips with the biblical experience of God acting in history? Was the philosophical account of true knowledge as knowledge of eternal, changeless and necessary being, which is accessible only to *theoria* or detached contemplation, not incompatible with the eschatological experience of something wholly new and of its totally involving character? Was there not a priority of becoming over being in this experience which did not fit the conceptual structures of traditional thought, and a rupture of all given structures by God's acting in Jesus Christ that did not merely enlighten but wholly transformed reality as normally experienced? Would not the narrative patterns of mythical thought have been more appropriate than the conceptual structures of philosophical reflection for a rational account of the God of the Bible, who is not a principle to be inferred but a person to be worshipped? In short, perhaps Tertullian was right after all with his rhetorical question: 'What has Athens to do with Jerusalem?'.

Before we see in the following chapters what and why it has to do with it, let us pause to digest the main points made so far.

Theology was a Greek discovery. It originated with the philosophical quest for reasons for anything and everything and, more particularly, with the systematic search for reasons for the structure and character of the cosmos, the ordered universe. This cosmological pattern of Greek theology was set by the Presocratics, and all later philosophers followed it. So the development of theology from Plato's *psuchê*-theology of a world-soul through Aristotle's *nous*-theology of a changeless source of change to the Stoic *logos*-theology of an omnipresent field of force that teleologically orders the cosmos can be described as a series of attempts to offer models for conceptualizing god as a principle of cosmic order, each seeking to improve on the shortcomings of the former ones. For all their differences, however, they agreed that theology is marked off from the mythology of popular piety and the religious ideology of state-cults by being a *theoretical* discipline, indispensable within the circle of theoretical sciences and an essential part of the human quest for true knowledge.

Precisely here we have the source of a deep-seated conflict between religious life and theological thought that has troubled theology from the beginning. Whereas myths are expressions of religious life and tradition which manifest the religious experiences of individuals and groups in a given society, theology sought to provide a rational account of god which was based not on religious experience and life but on cosmological reflection. Not religious practice but cosmological theory was the matrix out of which its talk of god arose; and this led to a permanent ambiguity in the notion of god. For mythical talk of gods and philosophical talk of god differ not only in origin but also in problematic orientation. The former has experiental roots in life, the latter intellectual roots in reflection; on the other hand, theology is not the critical reflection of religious life but an attempt to explain the intelligibility of the cosmos in terms of ultimate principles. Thus their notions of god differ because they correspond to different kinds of problems. Whereas the god of theology is a metaphysical principle designed to solve intellectual problems of cosmology, the gods of religion are worshipped because of their manifestations in religious experience; but whereas cosmological explanation offers an account of god stripped of all traces of personal deity, religious worship seems to require a personal account of god. The ideas of divine person and of divine principle, therefore, are not simply identical, and they cannot be combined without conflict. They may be used to refer to something different; then what is called 'god' in religion and in theology is not the same. Alternatively they are used to refer to the same; then we have somehow to combine the two descriptions, and are faced with a potentially inconsistent notion of god which has to answer at the same time to the demands of cosmological explanation and of religious worship. Or the god of theology is taken to be the true god of religion and the mythical account of god accordingly demythologized; this is bound to lead to a conflict of internal and external perspectives on the god(s) of religion if what the philosopher takes to be irrelevant accessories in the religious notion of god are central to the worshipper, and what is suggested to be the central core of religion from without is of minor or no importance within. Precisely this seems to be unavoidable where the worshipper's religious understanding of god arises out of religious experience and practice, whereas the philosopher's theological understanding of god is based on cosmological reflection and theory. Yet there is a further possibility. It is a type of theology which is not based on cosmology and its external perspective on the god(s) of religion, but which critically unfolds the internal perspective of the religious understanding of god(s) by reflecting religious life from within. As an *intellectual pursuit* it contrasts with mythology; and as an intellectual pursuit *within religion* it contrasts with philosophical theology. But it is a reflective endeavour like the latter, and it is based on the same religious experiences as the former. It is what may be called a *religious theology*, and one manifestation of it is Christian theology.

Chapter 3

Christian Theology

I

Christian theology began its career as a contradiction in terms; it spent its youth trying to overcome it; and it achieved this eventually by redefining the meaning of 'theology' in a way that identified it with ecclesiastical or trinitarian theology and reduced all other theologies to mere pseudo-theologies.

In the Roman world of pluralistic beliefs, religions and philosophies the meaning of 'theology' was specified in terms of the tripartite system of political, mythical and natural theologies; and Christian faith, argument and reflection was not theological in any of these senses.

1   It was not a local cult tied to a particular country; it made exclusivist claims about the risen Christ; Christians refused to fulfil the religious duties required of every citizen; and therefore they were considered atheists inimical to the political and religious order of the state (Harnack, 1905). In short, Christian faith, at least during the first centuries, was not the civil religion of a particular society, and Christian theology not the religious ideology of a state or country.

2   Christian faith also differed from traditional myths and their syncretist successors in Gnosticism by insisting on the singularity, unity and universality of God, by rejecting the pagan cults and deities as the veneration of idols and pseudo-gods, and by making exclusivist claims about the risen Christ and the God who raised him. In short, Christian theology was not a particular kind of mythology alongside other mythologies.

3   Christians propagated a faith which offended philosophical minds in more than one way. It was new and what was new could not be true for what was true must be old (cf. Osborne, 1981, pp. 2-3); it insisted on God as personal and acting not only as creator and ruler of

the world but also in the history of the Jewish people and, above all, in the life, death and resurrection of Jesus Christ; it proclaimed his resurrection to be the beginning of a new eschatological life and hope in the resurrection and life everlasting of all who have faith in Christ; and it was for all this considered by contemporary philosophers to differ from myths only by being even more irrational and incredible, attractive only to the credulous, and not worthy of serious consideration. In short, Christian theology was not a philosophical theology and never managed to become philosophically a fully respectable discipline.

Thus none of the Hellenistic types of theology provided a proper framework for Christian theology; but neither did the prophetic theology of the Hebrew tradition or its combination with the Greek traditions in Hellenistic Judaism (Philo). True, because the latter understood the one and only God not as final cause but as free creator, and because it relied on divine intervention and revelation in particular historical events, it was a more appropriate paradigm for Christian theology than any of the other theologies outlined. It was a revelational theology; in it the term 'theologian' denoted not the person who speaks about God but the person through whom God himself speaks (the prophet); it was practical knowledge of God's will as divinely revealed in the law rather than theoretical knowledge of God's being as accessible to human speculation; and it conceived God as acting in the history of his people and therefore as person and not merely as principle. But the Christian faith moved beyond even this. It conceived itself to be no longer a quest, but an achievement, not a preliminary, but the perfect knowledge of God; it understood God's nature, will and person on the basis of the eschatological event of the life, death and resurrection of Christ; and by explicating the personhood of God in relation to the fate of this particular person, it was led to conceive Jesus Christ as divine person, and the one God as internally differentiated.

From the beginning, therefore, Christian theology had to define itself in contrast not only to the mythologies of the Graeco-Roman world, but also to the natural theology of Hellenistic philosophies and the prophetic theology of the Jewish tradition. It had to conceive God in personal terms, and as acting in history, without relapsing into myth; it had to conceive him as creator and ruler of the universe without reducing him to a metaphysical principle of the cosmos; and it had to conceive him as the eschatological saviour who had acted in Jesus Christ in a definite way, universally valid and relevant not only for the Jews but for everyone. None of the contemporary theological paradigms could combine all this in a convincing and consistent way.

Thus Christian thinkers were forced to develop a new theological paradigm: *christology.*

The term 'christology' has a number of meanings. Frequently it is confined to the doctrine of the Person of Christ. But this obscures its foundational import for all Christian theology. In its fundamental sense christology is not merely one of the Christian doctrines but the frame for all of them; it provides the overall pattern and conceptual resources for understanding God, world, human existence and everything else in relation to God's final self-revelation in Jesus Christ; and it requires everything in Christian theology to be considered in this relation. To see the point of this normative proposal two things should be noted. First, the relation in question is a multiple relation which necessarily involves more than two *relata.* For example, if theology considers human existence in relation to Jesus Christ there are not two but three *relata* to be taken into account, viz. human existence, Jesus Christ and God. Second, the *relata* of this relation are complex and internally differentiated. They consist of interrelated aspects or dimensions which compose the *relatum* in question only when taken together, and which require to be spelled out in dialectical descriptions. For example, theology considers not the world *tout court* but the fallen creation of God on its way to final redemption; not human existence *tout court* but the existence of the sinner justified by God; not God *tout court* but the divine love revealed in Jesus Christ through the working of the Spirit, and the inscrutable and ambivalent presence of God in nature and history; not Jesus *tout court* but Jesus Christ, i.e. the first of all who by being raised from the dead finally revealed the loving will of God. Thus 'Christ' is a title which Christians apply to Jesus in order to confess him to be the decisive act of God for the salvation of his creation; 'Jesus' is the proper name of a particular human being with a specific history in the context of the history of Israel and the world; but the combination of that title and this name in the foundational Christian confession 'Jesus (is the) Christ' includes in its scope not only the historical facts about Jesus's life, personality, teaching and death in the context of the history of Israel, but also the response to Jesus by those who call him Christ and their consequent belief in his resurrection and in the divine reality disclosed by that event. This complex 'Christ-event' is the point of reference for all Christian thinking about God, Jesus, the world and human existence; it is summarized in the credal confession 'Jesus (is the) Christ' and explicated by the whole range of Christian doctrines; and it is the task of fundamental christology to map out the grammar of these doctrinal explications of the faith in Jesus Christ which requires it to distinguish and relate the irreducibly different dimensions of the 'Christ-event', i.e. the *historical dimension* (the history of Jesus and Israel), the *soteriological dimension* (the faith of the Christian community in Jesus as the Christ) and the *theological dimension* (the working of God in all this for the salvation of his creation).

The christological paradigm of Christian theology was worked out in numerous and sometimes highly problematic ways in a long and complicated process culminating in the trinitarian and christological doctrines of Nicaea and Chalcedon; and it opened the way towards a proper *Christian theology* when it became systematically and critically related to the various theological endeavours of the time. The mythical theology of poetry and of popular piety was the religious context *against* which it was defined; the philosophical theology of the metaphysical tradition provided the conceptual framework *in terms of* which it was defined; and the revelational theology of the prophets remained the background *on the basis of* which it was defined. Relative to these different contexts Christian thinkers gradually worked out a christocentric theology whose basis was the New Testament Gospel, and whose basic task was the conceptual self-explication of faith in Christ as the definitive revelation of God's saving love for his creation.

Christian theology, then, was (and is) essentially *christology*; and this further complicated the already complicated relationship between theology and philosophy. Christology is too mythical for the philosopher and too philosophical for the mythologist. It differs from mythology in its conceptual structure, historical anchorage and eschatological orientation; and it differs from philosophical theology in its concentration on the universal relevance of a singular eschatological event as opposed to the general metaphysical structure of the cosmos, its interest in the contingent and practical as opposed to the necessary and theoretical, and its irreducibly metaphorical, symbolical and parabolical character. Accordingly, the relationship between theology and philosophy changes from being primarily a problem for philosophy to being a problem for theology. The rationality of christology is the touchstone of theological rationality, and throughout the history of Christian theology both in its eastern (Orthodox) and western (Roman Catholic and Protestant) forms christology has been at the centre of all attempts to clarify the relationship between theology and philosophy.

II

This was a new conception of theology, and the christological emphasis has been of paramount importance in the shaping of Christian theology. It is still a rational (i.e. argumentative and discursive) enterprise. But it is one which takes the Christian faith in the redemptive revelation of God in Jesus Christ as the central clue for its outlook. Its basic problems arise not from religious experience, tradition or metaphysical inquiry, but from revelation and faith; and when it does take up problems of religious experience and metaphysics, these remain secondary or preliminary to those posed by *faith* and *revelation.*

Some theologians, notably Karl Barth, have concluded from this that in a systematic exposition of Christian dogmatics methodological priority is to be assigned to the doctrine of revelation. But God's salvific revelation in Christ has always been central to Christian theology whereas the *doctrine* of revelation has become prominent only in modern theology, under the pressure of epistemological questions raised in the seventeenth century. Barth consummates this tradition of modernity but tries, in his own trinitarian development of the doctrine of revelation, to overcome the shortcomings of those accounts which consider it primarily or exclusively in epistemological contexts. As a theological category 'revelation' is used to refer not merely to a special source of knowledge alongside other ('natural') sources, but to the primordial eschatological event of Jesus Christ's life, death and resurrection which for Christians rupture all common experiential contexts and force an irreversible transition from the old life to the new. In this comprehensive sense, theology refers to God's revelation in Christ as the fundamental principle of Christian life, thought and theology by which all beliefs and actions are to be judged, but which cannot itself be judged by anything more fundamental. Revelation is the final court of appeal not because what is revealed is an axiomatic truth to be accepted by everyone on insight or authority, but because it is the self-revealing activity of the sovereign God who has freely chosen to make himself known to us in Jesus Christ in such a way that we are free to acknowledge him as our God.

Of course, before we can *appeal* to revelation we must have reasons to believe that what we are appealing to *is* the revelation of God (Locke, 1690, IV.xix.14). Christians have such reasons. But they themselves are grounded in revelation. For Christians the decisive reason to believe in the life, death and resurrection of Christ as God's revelation is *faith*; they are prepared to give reasons for their faith; but because faith knows of nothing more fundamental than God's self-revelation in Jesus Christ, this is their final court of appeal in all theological matters. In short, the concept of revelation in Christian theology is used to summarize its conviction that the foundational experience of faith is entirely due to God both in its non-contingent content and in its contingent actuality. Hence Christian theology is a theology of faith as much as of revelation; and to understand it we must briefly elucidate the concepts of revelation and faith.

'Revelation' in its Christian use is a complex concept referring to God's self-revelation in Jesus Christ in which he communicates his loving will and inner self to us. Revelation is a complex communicative act which comprises historical, soteriological and theological dimensions. It is first of all a *historical act*, a series of events associated with Jesus and his followers who confess him to be the Christ which is open to historical description and exploration. Theologically, this historical act is the worldly means of an *expressive act* in and through which God communicates his loving will to us. But soteriologically this expressive act is only *potentially* revelatory. It becomes a *revelatory act* only when it is received and interpreted by someone as the revelation of God's will to him or her. Without the acknowledged working of the Spirit in the receiver it is not a revelation; and this is acknowledged only when Jesus is confessed to be the Christ. There is no revelation without reception in faith; yet reception and faith do not make Jesus God's self-revelation to us. To see how the two are related, we need a phenomenological analysis of revelation.

1   Structurally revelation is an activity that is (1) *relational*, (2) *directed* and (3) *effective*. (1) It is *relational* because in it God reveals himself *to someone*. (2) It is *directed* because this relation is asymmetrical (the revealer is logically prior to the receiver of the revelation), irreflexive (the revealer and receiver of the revelation cannot be identical), and intransitive (if A reveals himself to B and B to C, A has not revealed himself to C).

Those who think that revelation can be communicated to others by those who have received it will dispute this last point. But the revelation cannot be reduced to a peculiar source of information or a peculiar way of receiving it. The idea of communicating revelation (*revelatio mediata*) is confused: revelation is divine self-communication, and a human communication of that is not revelation but a report of it. The result is at best second-hand knowledge got *from* the revealer, or *about* the revealer; it is never first-hand knowledge *of* the revealer. Furthermore, in Christian usage *God* and nobody else is revealer: we may witness to his revelation, but we cannot be its agents. Consequently, to avoid confusion, it is useful to distinguish between *revelation* (which is solely due to God) and *proclamation* (which is the Christian witness to God's revelation before others).

(3) Finally, revelation (but not proclamation) is *effective*, because it occurs only when it is received, and is known to have occurred, by at least one person. It is more than an activity of the revealer directed to someone: it must be intelligible as such (or it fails in principle), and someone must be aware of it (or it fails in fact). A merely intended revelation is not a revelation at all; in its Christian sense, at least, 'revelation' is an achievement-word: the receiving (not the accepting!) of it is as necessary to it as its giving (Penelhum, 1971, p. 103).

2   Pragmatically revelation is (1) *inter-personal*, (2) *direct* and (3) *particular*. (1) It is *inter-personal* because it is a communicative activity between persons who act as revealer and receiver. Communication, however, is a contingent activity. It may be impossible for us not to communicate at all, but any particular communication could be otherwise, or could fail to occur. In particular, we may fail to respond to communications which we receive. Thus to conceive God as a revealer is to conceive him as a person; and to conceive revelation as a communication is to allow that it may be rejected. (2) Revelation is *direct* in that it is a communicative act, not a record or report of such an act. The divine self-communication takes place only in the co-presence of the revealing God and the human receiver of his revelation, not in merely human communications about revelation. Reports of revelation, and information based on it, are mere claims about it or due to it, and such claims are always open to question as to their adequacy and truth. (3) Revelation is *particular* because it is addressed to particular individuals, even though what is communicated concerns the whole of mankind.

3   Semantically revelation is *mediated* and involves *interpretation*: it is a communicating activity performed in and through Jesus Christ. It is tied to a specific series of events which are open to historical description (historical acts). But these events are invested with a significance beyond the historical: they are claimed by Christians to reveal the redemptive activity of God (expressive and revelatory acts). But these events do not carry this import on their face. They are *signs*, used to communicate a specific meaning, which can only be grasped by interpreting them. And signs require triadic relations of signification between a signifier (the sign in the narrow sense), a *significatum* (its meaning), and an interpreter (the user of the sign).

Signs, in short, do not exist independently of being constituted, used and interpreted as signs. They are interpretative actions, or the results of such actions.

Now actions are distinguished from other events by being governed by intentions and conventions; intentions and conventions involve beliefs; and these form the background against which an action is to be understood. Accordingly events can only function as signs if they are actively interpreted as such, which requires them to be governed by conventions or intentions that in turn determine their specific meaning. The events of Jesus's life and death can only be God's revelation if they can be interpreted as divine actions, i.e. as governed not merely by human conventions but by divine intentions - and we cannot interpret them as such unless those divine intentions are somehow known to us. But if they were known to us apart from these events, the events would not be revelatory in the sense claimed for them. It must be in and through the very events of Jesus's life and death that the divine intentions governing them come to be known. But only linguistic phenomena have this self-interpreting character: non-linguistic events have to be independently interpreted, and are always open to differing interpretations, because the relation between event and interpretation is a contingent one. Actions indeed are generally and necessarily determined by the intentions that govern them, but only linguistic ones explicitly *manifest* those intentions.

It follows that the events of Jesus's life and death are revelatory only if (1) they become intelligible as *divine actions* and (2) their significance becomes intelligible in terms of the *divine intentions* governing these actions; and this is impossible if they are not explicitly interpreted to us in this way. Now Christians claim that precisely this has been the case in Jesus's own teaching and, above all, in the apostolic witness to the significance of his life, death and resurrection. But these interpretations, like all human interpretations, may be misconceived; even if they are possible they are arbitrary if they do not correspond to divine self-interpretations; and merely possible interpretations cannot be authoritative. If, therefore, Christians accept them as adequate and authoritative they must do so because of the divine corroboration of Jesus's teaching in the resurrection, and the divine authorization of the apostolic witness to this in the working of the Spirit. Without this divine corroboration and authorization all we have are claims by Jesus, the Apostles and the Christians that what they proclaim is indeed the true significance of the events involved. Divine authorization here cannot be replaced by Christian claims about the divine authorization of Christian claims, the inerrancy of scriptures or the infallibility of the teaching office of the church: it can only be provided by God himself, who corroborates the Christian message freely through the illuminating working of the Spirit. Thus although revelation is not illumination, illumination is the only sufficient reason to accept the Christian message of the divine revelation in Jesus Christ; and as illumination is the God-given insight that this message is true, the proclamation of the Gospel is a necessary condition for the illumination to occur.

To sum up, Jesus's life and death are revelatory of God's redemptive activity because they are part of the specific divine actions whose intentions are made known to us by the divinely authorized interpretations of the Christian Gospel. They have a significance beyond that accessible to the historian because they function as signs in the wider context of specific divine actions; this significance can be known by everyone because it is made explicit in the interpretation of these events and actions in the Gospel, and communicated in the proclamation of the church; and these interpretations become intelligible as divinely given by being corroborated by the Spirit.

4 Theologically revelation is (1) *divine*, (2) *definitive* and (3) *correlative with faith*. (1) It is *divine* because it is a communicative activity of *God*: there is only one revealer, namely God himself. (2) It is *definitive* because it is God's *self*-revelation which, because it reveals his true character, innermost being and unchanging will, cannot be superseded although we may never be able fully to understand it. (3) It is *correlative with faith* because the revelation of God has been received in faith by some who not only have interpreted the events of Christ's life and death in terms of the divine action of his resurrection into the everlasting community with God, but have accepted this interpretation as true and freely acknowledged God on the basis of it. That this has happened is part of the very content of revelation. For if God reveals himself because he intends to save us, if what he intends he achieves, and if it is by faith that we are saved, it is hardly surprising that his revelation has not met with no faith whatsoever. Not only is there no faith without revelation, there is also no revelation without (not necessarily my, but someone's) faith. Thus although revelation is person-relative and we must therefore distinguish its reception from its acceptance, it is also divine and therefore achieves, in at least some cases, what it intends: to be received and accepted in faith.

5 Epistemologically revelation is (1) *belief-invoking* and (2) *inexhaustible*. (1) It is *belief-invoking* not because what is revealed

are propositions about God but because it cannot occur without yielding propositional beliefs about, amongst other things, God. If God's revelation is received in faith it will lead the receiver to hold certain beliefs about God, the world and his or her own existence in particular and human life in general, which form the content of the Christian confessions of faith. (2) It is *inexhaustible* because no belief held on the basis of faith can comprehend the richness of the divine revelation: there is no Christian belief about God, the world or human existence that could not be improved.

This, in rough outline, is what I mean when I call Christian theology a theology of revelation. But getting clear on the concept of revelation is not enough to show that Jesus Christ is the self-revelation of God. To establish this, we need evidence, and the only evidence sufficient to establish it, according to traditional theology, is faith and the testimony of the Spirit. Hence Christian theology, just because it claims to be a theology of revelation and not merely of the possibility of revelation, is also a *theology of faith*. For the revelation of God in Christ is, by its very nature, neither a public datum open to inspection to everybody nor merely a private experience of some communicated to others. We can transmit records of this event to others, but not the event itself. For it is a divine communicative activity given only in and through the faith in Christ in which it achieves its end. Revelation and faith are co-dependants; they are internally and mutually related; but revelation (the productive activity) is prior to faith (the receptive activity), logically, ontologically and theologically.

Epistemologically both faith and revelation are accessible to us only insofar as they become manifest, articulated and communicated in human *beliefs*. They are divine activities which operate in, with and under worldly phenomena; and human beliefs and actions are the phenomena in and through which faith manifests itself. Thus as there is no faith without revelation, so there is no faith without some beliefs, and no awareness of faith without some conscious beliefs about faith. Yet faith is not identical with our conscious or unconscious beliefs about or based on faith, for (1) belief and awareness of faith (or faith-consciousness) does come in degrees, but faith in Christ does not; (2) belief and awareness of faith differ from believer to believer, but if this were also true of faith, they would not have the same faith; (3) the beginning of faith is fixed once and for all with the revelation of God in Jesus and his reception in faith as Christ, whereas the beginning of Christian beliefs and of the awareness of faith depends on each individual's encountering, understanding and accepting the message of the Gospel; (4) our becoming aware of faith and our beliefs about faith do not constitute faith but bring to mind that faith constitutes us as sinners saved by the redeeming love of God; (5) faith in Christ is a gift of God, not a function of our beliefs or awareness of our faith: whereas the latter vary with our states of consciousness and degrees of knowledge, the former does not; (6) we are justified by faith (not because of faith), but we are not justified by our consciousness of faith, the degree of our awareness of faith or our beliefs about and based on faith; (7) death will put an end to our awareness of and beliefs about faith but not, so Christians believe, to our faith: on the contrary, it is precisely the faith in Christ by which we shall live although we shall die. In short, Christians agree in their faith in Christ but they differ in their awareness of this faith and, accordingly, in their beliefs and the ways in which they express, present and understand them.

Now if faith in Christ, and the revelation to which it responds, become accessible to us through our own beliefs or the beliefs of others communicated to us, we come to know about faith, broadly speaking, either by acquaintance (i.e. at first hand) or by description (i.e. at second hand). In the first case we become aware of our own beliefs and convictions in matters of faith, in the second case of the beliefs and convictions of others. The first provokes us to find reasons for (or against) what we discover ourselves to hold to be true, the second to find reasons for accepting or rejecting what others hold to be true. In both cases, however, we need *criteria of identity* of the faith, and of the revelation expressed in so many different beliefs. Without such criteria we cannot just assume an identity of faith underlying the great variety of Christian beliefs, for in matters of faith it is not self-evident how to distinguish between right and wrong beliefs, or between more or less adequate forms of belief.

All criteria of faith are based on experience; they are relative to the consensus of the Christian community; and they are the result of critical hermeneutical processes in this community. For neither our own faith nor the faith of others is given to us as an unalloyed datum. Both become accessible to us only in the form of beliefs, and normally in the form of second-hand beliefs communicated to us. Communication, however, presupposes signs; signs are context-sensitive; and contexts may and do change. Thus our faith-beliefs are always interwoven with our particular experiences; and because what is given to us is not faith as such, but faith as articulated in beliefs and communicated by signs in particular contexts, we can come to identify our faith only through a hermeneutical process of distinguishing the essential common faith in our variety of beliefs.

Believers, therefore, have access to their faith only if they are aware of it; and they are aware only of what they have articulated cognitively. Their articulation is always filtered through their conscious beliefs, alloyed with their experiences, structured with their knowledge and infected with their superstition and errors. To others, however, faith becomes accessible only indirectly through the multifarious (individual and common) expressions of Christian beliefs in confessions, proclamations, prayers and actions. But these, being tainted with the subjectivity and historical particularity of believers, are not the faith itself: it may always be questioned whether they adequately express the Christian faith, and whether what they express is true. And both questions have been a driving force in the formation of a system of Christian beliefs. The first required it to specify criteria of identity of faith: and it is the function of scriptures, creeds and confessions to provide such criteria for the Christian community. The second requires critical reflection on the character, ground and genesis of Christian faith and beliefs, and the adequacy of the criteria of faith accepted and operative in the Christian community; and this now is the task of *theology*.

III

Theological reflection differs from both faith and philosophy. From the first by being essentially discursive or argumentative in character. From the second by starting from within faith and Christian beliefs and aiming at nothing but an ever better understanding of faith through a critical reconstruction of these beliefs in the light of God's revelation in Jesus Christ. Whereas philosophical theology is developed from the standpoint of the human experience in general, Christian theology is developed from the standpoint of the faith and experience of the Christian community (cf. Hartshorne, 1964, p. 73).

For the Christian theologian, therefore, the main problem is not faith and revelation but their adequate, i.e. error-free, expression in word and action. For the philosopher, on the other hand, it is precisely faith and revelation itself. What do Christians refer to and what do they claim, when they talk of revelation and faith? Are they justified in thinking that there actually has been a revelation? What is revealed in revelation? What are the credentials of faith? Are the credentials external or internal to revelation and faith?

These are philosophical questions. But they also arise in theology. Yet whereas philosophy judges questions of meaning and justification by general standards of *reason* which are applicable more widely than merely to Christian beliefs and expressions of faith, theology judges questions about them by standards internal to the Christian community and derived from *revelation*. It elucidates expressions of faith by critically distinguishing the faith they express from the (perhaps inadequate) way they express it. It does this by appealing to the biblical and credal criteria commonly accepted in the Christian community; and it justifies these criteria by reference to God's revelation in Jesus Christ. Thus elucidation and exposition, not justification, is its primary task. For before we can examine reasons for Christian beliefs we must be clear about their content. Theology, then, is a permanent process of 'faith seeking understanding' of itself, and of everything else, in the light of faith. It is no longer a function of a philosophy that tries to elucidate the metaphysical principles and presuppositions of scientific accounts of the world; it is a function of faith which aims at elucidating the content, implications, character and act of faith in Christ.

Precisely this character of the theological process poses two permanent problems at the very heart of Christian theology. The first is the *problem of reflection* or, more precisely, of the *relationship between faith and reflection*; the second is the *problem of perspectives* or, for our purposes, of the *relationship between theological and philosophical perspectives on Christian beliefs*. Both problems have, in various and often combined ways, dominated the history of the relationship between Christian theology and philosophy; and we have to distinguish them as clearly as possible if we want to disentangle and clarify some of the many issues raised by it.

The problem of reflection

I use 'reflection' as a summary term for those cognitive activities by which we control our cognitive and non-cognitive states, operations and ways of relating to our environment. If we call 'mind' the system of our cognitive states and operations (perceiving, imagining, judging, memorizing, learning, thinking etc.) as distinct from our volitional, emotional, affective and other non-cognitive states and processes, then reflection is that self-referential mental activity by which we become aware of the distinction between, on one hand, our organism as the whole of our psychological and physiological states (mind and body) and, on the other, its place in its environment - the inside/outside distinction.

We are organisms with complex emotional, volitional and cognitive capacities, and we exist in complex causal interdependence with the environments which we influence, and by which we are being influenced in a multitude of ways. When we influenced our environment through behaviour guided by intention or convention, we *act* on it. But actions presuppose beliefs, and beliefs are a particular kind of propositional attitude. On the one hand propositional attitudes like beliefs, desires, hopes or fears differ from sensations like pain in that they have a content: they do not merely present themselves to us but are ways in which we represent something to ourselves. The contents of propositional attitudes are propositions (cognitive constructions) by which we represent possible states of affairs to ourselves which we believe, desire, hope or fear to obtain. And beliefs, as opposed to desires, hopes and fears, embody propositions *as true*: rightly or wrongly, they embody *information*.

Beliefs come by degrees, which are subjective probabilities relative to alternatives (Mellor, 1980; Swinburne 1981). And every belief belongs to a *system* of beliefs, which in turn belongs to the wider network of propositional attitudes, emotions, evaluations and volitions which explicitly or implicitly guide our actions. For without emotions and evaluations we cannot believe, and without the cognitive constructions (propositions) embodied in our beliefs we could only respond to sensations but not act on them. Of course, the world is more complex than any of our cognitive constructions of it, and by producing a variety of models of it we cognitively reduce its complexity. We achieve this through the mental operations like perception, interpretation, classification (comparison, abstraction and comprehension), conceptualization and judgement by which we gather and process information, and by those - imagination, speculation and creative invention of alternative states of affairs - that together guide our actions in and on our environments. Reflection is that self-referential component of our mental activities by which we critically control our cognitive operations and their results in the context of our beliefs, desires and actions.

The information embodied in our beliefs is gathered through perception and communication, and stored in our memory. This acquisition of beliefs is a causal process which relates events to certain propositions, and because we exist in continuous causal and communicative interaction with our environment, we are always reweaving our systems of belief. However, we not only acquire information, we also process it; and while the processing relations internal to our systems of belief are causal, the relations between the propositions are discursive. Thus we justify beliefs by reference to other beliefs which are reasons for it; we infer new beliefs from old ones; we criticize beliefs on the basis of others; and we retain or change beliefs because of others. This is not to say that all our beliefs are conscious beliefs. On the contrary, most of the beliefs on which we act are tacit beliefs disposing us to certain kinds of actions rather than others. They form the background knowledge to the more sophisticated cognitive states of conscious beliefs (i.e. the believing that we believe a certain proposition (Mellor, 1980, pp. 146ff)) and rational beliefs (i.e. those based in the right way on the right sort of evidence (Swinburne, 1981, ch. 2)). But justification, inference and criticism are, as relations, non-causal relations between beliefs and, as activities, conscious ways of processing beliefs which are open to us because we are capable of reflecting, i.e. controlling our cognitive operations conceptually.

As a self-referential cognitive process reflection involves a distinction between what is reflected on (information) and the way it is reflected on (conceptual processing). Now information is true or false; it differs from matter by being constituted by the propositions embodied in (e.g.) beliefs; and we gather, store, process and transmit information in a variety of ways characteristic of human persons. Thus we gather information primarily, if not exclusively, through *perception* and *communication*, and these two modes of information-acquiring transactions require us to perform the different cognitive tasks of, on the one hand, constituting information and, on the other, interpreting already constituted information. Thus the senses used in perception yield non-conceptual information constituted by ourselves, whereas the (linguistic) signs used in communication convey conceptual and non-conceptual information constituted by others, which we can only receive if we know how to interpret these signs and their use in the light of the intentions and conventions governing them (Evans, 1982, pp. 124ff). However, the processing and reflection of either kind of information is possible only on the basis of its transformation into our own informational system; and this always involves a re-structuring of the information received which allows for misconception, error and illusion.

If this is true of belief and reflection in general, it is also true of theological belief and reflection. It follows that the self-critical awareness of the difference between its own reflections (theology) and what it reflects on (faith) is an essential part of the theological process. Theology is permanently faced with the problem of distinguishing and relating the faith in Christ which it attempts to reflect on and its conceptual reflection on this faith; the existential 'logic' of faith and the conceptual 'logic' of theology; the first-order expressions of faith (e.g. the narratives of the gospels or the metaphorical and parabolical language of prayer, proclamation and confession) in and through which it receives its information and the conceptual self-explication of faith in the second-order theological reflections on Christian beliefs. This is the fundamental methodological problem *intrinsic* to the theological enterprise. It is posed by the irreducible difference between:

faith as the divinely given receptive mode of God's self-revelation in
   Jesus Christ and its peculiar theological character;
the manifestations of faith in the experiences, beliefs, actions and
   speech-acts that characterize the human *life of faith* and its peculiar existential rationality;
amongst these in particular the *discourse of belief*, i.e. the (individual
   or communal) verbal expressions of faith and their peculiar self-
   involving linguistic character; and
the *discourse of theology*, i.e. critical reflection on the life of faith and,
   in particular, the discourse of belief in the light of revelation and
   faith, and its specific conceptual structure.

Hence the central intrinsic task of theology is to work out the proper relationship between the existential structure of faith in Christ, the experiential structure of Christian beliefs and (verbal and non-verbal) actions, and the conceptual structure of Christian theology.

The problem of perspectives

The second set of problems arises from two closely related facts. On the one hand, all reflection is perspectival. Our discursive thinking is in terms of opposites and contrasts, determinations, negations and the exclusion of alternatives; and the beliefs which we reflect select only certain aspects of reality and are relative to particular stand-points of individual persons or of groups of persons. On the other hand, there is always more than one perspective in which something may be perceived and reflected. For a 'perspective', in Russell's defi-nition, is 'the view of the world from a given place' (Russell, 1921 p. 101); there is more than one place from which to view the world (although some places may provide a more illuminating perspective on it than others); places may be shared with others (to some extent, at least), and so may be perspectives; yet difference of point of view will always cause differences, however slight, between perspectives which claim to be perspectives on the same from different places.

   The perspectivity of all our believing, knowing and reflecting has been explored intensively in recent years (Wisdom, 1944; 1953; 1965; Wittgenstein, 1967; 1968; 1969; Hick, 1969; 1984; Barbour 1974; King, 1974; Kaufman, 1960; 1968; 1972; van Buren, 1972; Ritschl and Jones,

1976; Ritschl, 1984; Jones, 1985), especially in the wake of Wittgenstein's reflections on 'seeing', 'seeing-as', and 'interpreting' (cf. Budd, 1987). This is a natural starting-point and confirmed by the historical fact that the notion of perspective has been derived from visual perception and has gained philosophical importance in accordance with the traditional Western attempt to model thinking on vision and its application to the problem of history in the philosophical tradition of Leibniz (Chladenius, 1742). However, the dangers of this epistemological model are well known, and if the notion of perspective is not to fall prey to them, it has to be generalized and developed in a way that makes seeing and other sensory perceptions particular determinations of the more general structure 'perspective'. One way to do this is by elaborating Russell's preliminary definition in the following manner:

1   Perspectives are one-many relations with the following characteristics: they are relative to places (I shall call this the *standpoint* of a perspective); they focus on one or more things in a wider context or world (I shall call this the *range* of a perspective); they are, because of their twofold relativity, selective and concentrate only on some and not on all possible aspects of that on which they focus (I shall call this the *content* of a perspective). The standpoint of a perspective may be shared (common perspective) or not (individual perspective); the content of perspectives may be more abstract or more concrete depending on the (number of) aspects of things in their range on which they focus; the range of perspectives may be partial (if they focus on some things) or universal (if they focus on everything); and whereas partial perspectives may be reflexive, universal perspectives are self-reflexive because they include their own standpoints within their range.

2   Perspectives are real relations in the sense that the standpoint from which they proceed and the range of places to which they relate have some existential independence of the perspective itself; they have an existence of their own if independently of the perspective in question they can belong to the ranges or worlds of other perspectives. Hence a perspective is only putative if its range, or items in its range, cannot belong to the range of some other perspective; and a perspective is non-existent if its standpoint cannot belong to the range of other perspectives.

3   Perspectives are cognitive relations which establish states of information or systems of beliefs in living organisms. Each perspective 'contains its own space' or 'private world' (Russell, 1972, pp. 95ff) which can be spelled out as the network of beliefs of the organism in question; each perspective, because it is focused on some things rather than on everything, establishes what Polanyi has described as

the difference between 'focal' and 'subsidiary awareness' (1962, pp. 55ff) by placing some focal beliefs against a background of tacit beliefs which constitute the context of plausibility of the former; and because of its selectivity each perspective contains a content of cognitive constructions which, in more sophisticated cases, can be elaborated into symbolic models of its world.

4 Perspectives involve interpretation, common perspectives share cognitive means of interpretation, and universal perspectives provide comprehensive frames of interpretation. Interpretation is a relation between an interpreter, an addressee of the interpretation (who may be identical with the interpreter), an *interpretandum* (the referent of the interpretation) and an *interpretans* in terms of which the *interpretandum* is interpreted. If I interpret the speck in the sky to you as a hawk, I point to something in the sky and describe it in terms of a complex of concepts (thing, animal, bird, hawk) which must be shared by both of us if the interpretation is to be successful. And the same is true when we interpret passages from Mark's Gospel or sonnets from Shakespeare, although in a more complex and compli-cated way because it involves the interpretation not of non-conceptual but of conceptual information: we have to identify the text in question, understand and explicate its world of meaning and 'fuse' it with our, or the addressee's, world of meaning in terms of concepts which enable us to translate or transfer meaning from the world of the text to the world of the addressee of the interpretation; and as this world of meaning is as much an *interpretandum* for us as the world of the text, interpreting a text consists in relating two *inter-pretanda* by means of concepts which lead, in Gadamer's phrase, to a 'fusion of horizons'. In short, interpretation always involves the iden-tification of the *interpretandum* (in the case of texts, the under-standing of their meaning at a linguistic level: what do they say?), its description (in the case of texts, the explication of their meaning: what do they mean?), and therefore presupposes shared means of identification and shared means of description between the inter-preter and the addressee (or, in the case of texts, between the text, the interpreter and the addressee). Shared means of identification and description, however, presuppose common frames of reference, meaning and interpretation; these involve systems of concepts, norms and beliefs which are transmitted through the language and traditions ('stories') of the community in question; hence there is no common perspective without a common language, tradition and way of life, and no universal perspective without a comprehensive, coherent and self-referential frame of interpretation grounded in a particular form of life and practice.

Because the notion of interpretation has played an important role in recent debates about perspectives, stories and forms of life, let me briefly add the following. Wittgenstein distinguished between 'seeing' in the sense of seeing something (e.g. lines on a paper), 'seeing-as' in the sense of seeing the lines on the paper as a cross, and 'interpreting' in the sense of interpreting the cross as a symbol of the Christian faith. He understood 'interpreting' to be an activity which involves the making of a conjecture or entertaining of a supposition about what we see. 'Seeing', on the other hand, is a state, the visual experience of something present. And 'seeing-as' lies between the two other concepts, each of which it resembles in different respects (cf. Budd, 1987).

John Hick has generalized this analysis. He expands the concept of seeing-as to the comprehensive notion of experiencing-as and claims that 'all human experiencing is experiencing-as' (1984, p. 19) and involves the interpretation of what we experience in terms of the system of concepts which constitute our world of meaning. This, however, implies a different understanding of interpretation, and Hick distinguishes two senses. In the implicit or 'first-order sense we are interpreting what is before us when we experience this as a fork'. This subsuming something under a specific concept 'is normally an unconscious and habitual process' which depends on the system of concepts that we use in our linguistic community. The explicit or second-order sense, on the other hand, is 'a matter of conscious theory-construction', as is the case when a historian interprets the data or a metaphysician interprets the universe (pp. 23ff). It is the interpretation of something already conceptually determined which integrates it in a wider and, in the case of religious interpretations, all-comprehensive and ultimate context of meaning; and as this may be done in different (religious or secular, or different religious) ways, higher-order interpretations will be more contested than first-order ones. Thus there is a 'hierarchy of interpretation' which ranges from, for example, the experience of Jesus as a living organism (physical description) through his experience as a Jew in the Palestinian society of his day (historical description) to the experience of Jesus as Christ (Christian description); and (pp. 24ff) the higher up the interpretation, the greater are the possible alternatives (Jesus may religiously be experienced not only as Christ but as a prophet, a rabbi, the Messiah etc.). In short, there are different levels of implicit and explicit interpretation, but there is no form of experiencing-as devoid of interpretation or cognitive choices. Some of these choices (e.g. to experience this as a fork) are uncontroversial because they have a high plausibility in our linguistic community and language in terms of which we think and behave. Others, like experiencing Jesus as Christ or the universe as God's creation are highly controversial because their context of plausibility is restricted to the Christian community.

It has been objected to Hick's account that it does not allow us to distinguish between religious belief and a set of hallucinations. Often, as in the case of Jesus's resurrection, the difference between believer and unbeliever is not that they agree on the event but disagree on the significance of it but differ about whether such an event took place at all (Helm, 1973, pp. 158ff). Hence it is required that before we can begin to apply a hierarchy of interpretations to something 'it must be possible to identify what is being denoted independently of the higher-level ways of denoting it' (p. 160). But this is not necessarily the case. The idea of levels of denoting and interpretation is misleading and a basic inconsistency in Hick's account of interpretation due to the empiricist left-overs of his philosophy. He thinks that while historical interpretations of Jesus are acceptable to all insofar as they correspond, and can be shown to correspond, to the facts, religious interpretations are at best an admissible interpretation of basically ambiguous phenomena and will only, if at all, be vindicated eschatologically when all the facts and their ultimate significance are on the table. Yet on his own account there can be no facts apart from interpretation and therefore no situation in which we agree on the facts but disagree about the interpretation: whenever we agree and disagree, whether in this life or another, it is about interpretations. Similarly, if *all* experiencing involves interpretation, it is misleading to speak of levels or a hierarchy of interpretations: there are only different interpretations some of which are more widely accepted than others because they pertain to areas like science or history in which we have accepted decision-procedures for cases of disagreement. But religious interpretations of Jesus, for example, are not based on physical and historical ones, they are not interpretations of historical interpretations of Jesus but different, viz. religious interpretations of Jesus. And while it is true that they must be consistent with historical interpretations of Jesus if they are to refer to the same entity, it is not true that it is the historical or physical descriptions which fix the reference of our religious descriptions. The resurrection of Jesus is not a Christian interpretation of the empty tomb but, if it is what the Christian faith confesses it to be, an act of God which can be denoted only in the perspective of Faith. Thus resurrection-language is indeed interpretative language. But the *interpretandum* is not a historical event but a divine action, and the criteria of identification accordingly not external but internal to the Christian perspective. In short, historical and religious interpretations are not related as levels of interpretation but as different interpretative perspectives with different contents and only partially overlapping ranges. They offer not only different interpretations of the same entity but provide different frames of interpretation for everything in their range. But the religious frame is more comprehensive than the historical one because everything interpreted in the historical frame can also be interpreted in the religious frame but not vice versa.

Frames of interpretations are systems of concepts, language, beliefs and practices. They are confirmed or modified by permanent application; they coexist synchronically with a plurality of other frames of interpretations not all of which are compatible with one another; and they are carried diachronically from generation to generation in the way of life of a linguistic community, or subcommunity, like the scientific or religious communities. All interpretations, therefore, are relative to frames provided by particular perspectives whose bearers are specific communities with their particular languages, ways of life and systems of belief. And as we commonly participate in more than one such group and community, we share more than one perspective with others. We can enter into the viewpoint of these different perspectives by engaging in the relevant activities and by learning about their standpoints, ranges and contents through participation. For perspectives are not something we use but something - in Polanyi's phrase - in which we dwell. We neither observe nor handle them but live in them (Polanyi, 1962, pp. 195ff). Yet although we can enter into perspectives and leave one perspective for another, we cannot step outside every perspective altogether. Similarly, whereas we can prefer one perspective to another in terms of internal coherence, consistency with other perspectives, illuminating power and orientational capacity, what is acceptable in one perspective depends on criteria internal to it. What is acceptable as a historical description is not decided by criteria operative in physics; and what is acceptable in the religious perspective does not depend on historical or empirical criteria. We can, because of our self-reflexive capacities, question and examine the criteria in our perspective by developing philosophical meta-perspectives on them; and we can trace links between perspectives and their internal criteria by a variety of techniques for establishing co-referentiality across perspectives and their different standpoints, contents and ranges. But there exists no absolutely privileged or 'master'-perspective which dominates all others and which decides on what is ultimately acceptable or unacceptable in other perspectives. Even universal and self-referential perspectives like religious perspectives with their all-embracing interpretative powers are not without alternatives; and nobody in our pluriform cultures can dwell in a religious perspective without being aware of the fact of alternative all-comprehensive religious and non-religious frames of interpretation. Accordingly religious perspectives and the whole way of life and network of beliefs which go with them cannot be justified by external but only by internal criteria. They provide the ultimate frame of meaning and interpretation for those who dwell in them. But they do not offer ultimate security nor are they immune to criticism and questioning. They may (and often are) misleading; and they may (and often do) respond to outside criticism in a variety of ways ranging from apologetic rejoinders to dogmatic demarcation. Yet every criticism will be from some (internal or external) standpoint and perspective or another: there is no neutral view of the matter, only a variety of not always compatible views on it from different angles. Thus it 'could be that the religions are all experiencing erroneously, projecting different illusions upon the universe. And it could on the other hand be that they are each responding to an infinite divine reality which exceeds our human conceptualities and which is capable of being humanly thought and experienced in these fascinatingly divergent ways' (Hick, 1984, p. 26). There is no neutral answer to this problem but more than one perspective in which it may be answered.

The possibility of a variety of differing perspectives on the same thing is particularly obvious in the case of cultural phenomena which involve human activities and their results (actions and artefacts). They all can be reflected upon under two types of complementary descriptions from different points of view and within different frames of reference: the *internal perspective of the participants* (or, in our case, the *perspective of Faith*) and the *external perspective of the observer* (or, for our purpose, the *perspective of Reason*). Neither of these and their respective descriptions can be reduced to the other, can replace the other or can be taken absolutely by itself without distorting a proper understanding of Christian faith and its historical objectifications. Thus they can only claim to be about the same thing by conceiving their common point of reference as an irreducible unity-in-difference and difference-in-unity of internal and external aspects.

Now if we understand theology to be the critical and systematic exposition of the internal perspective of Faith, then a theology which simply ignores the external perspective is weaker than one that does not and a theology which unfolds the internal perspective in such a way that it reconstructs the external perspective within the perspective of Faith is stronger than one that does not. And the same is true of the external perspectives of Reason. But although both types of

perspectives may be of different complexity and internal differentiation, there exists an irreducible difference between Faith's view
of itself and everything else and Reason's view of faith and everything else; between the internal perspectives of Christian beliefs and
theology and the external perspectives of philosophy, history and
science; between theological self-explications of faith in Christ, which
unfold a very specific particular in its universal significance from the
standpoint of the Christian experience, and philosophical or scientific
explanations of the fact, form and content of Christian beliefs in
terms of metaphysical accounts of the cosmos or critical accounts of
religion. This is the fundamental methodological problem of the
extrinsic relation of the theological enterprise to other disciplines. It
has accompanied Christian theology from the beginning and has
taken on a number of typical forms which reflect the major changes in
our understanding of reason. To mention but five:

1 *Faith and nature* (natural reason): For many centuries the problem
  has taken the form of the relationship between theological and
  non-theological or natural perspectives on Christian beliefs or,
  within theology, of the relationship between nature and grace.
2 *Faith and reason* (rational reason): In the Enlightenment this was
  replaced by, or combined with, the relationship between theological and philosophical or metaphysical perspectives on Christian
  beliefs or, within theology, by the relationship between natural
  and revealed theology.
3 *Faith and history* (historical reason): When not only the historical
  particularity of revelation but also the historicity of reason came
  to be appreciated, the relationship was reformulated in terms of
  theological and historical perspectives on Christian beliefs or,
  within theology, in terms of the relationship between history and
  dogmatics.
4 *Faith and experience* (experiential reason): The rise of psychology
  in the late nineteenth century has augmented this by the relationship between theological and psychological perspectives on Christian beliefs or, within theology, by the relationship between
  accounts of faith based on religious experience and on revelation.
5 *Faith and communication* (communicative reason): In our century
  the dominant constellation - at least in the continental tradition -
  has become the relationship between theological and sociological
  perspectives on Christian beliefs and practices or, within theology,
  the relationship between the empirical and social orientation of
  practical theology and the exegetical and dogmatical orientation of
  systematic theology.

In each of these constellations 'faith', 'reason', 'revelation', 'experience' etc. take on different (shades of) meanings and, accordingly, pose different kinds of problems. Each has provoked characteristic answers from both sides of the debate. But none has been definitive or satisfactory, not only because the answers given in one paradigmatic constellation do not solve the problem posed by the others, but above all because each reproduces but cannot overcome the basic difference of perspectives and the irreducible duality of factors which it involves.

The problem of reflection and the problem of perspectives have been the major sources of conflict in the long and problematic relationship between Christian theology and philosophy. They have frequently been combined because the same language, and in addition often the same conceptuality as well, is used in the internal reflections of theology and the external reflections of philosophy. The difference between faith and reflection within theology is then linked or even identified with the difference between internal and external perspectives on theology. The result is that theological reconstructions and explications are no longer distinguished from philosophical constructions and explanations. This is a permanent source of confusion for a number of reasons. First, it relates theological answers to non-theological problems and vice versa. For it is one thing to explicate a phrase like 'God is love' theologically as summarizing the specific Christian experiences of the God who has raised the crucified Christ from the dead, quite another to explain it philosophically as a description of 'the ideal companion who transmutes what has been lost into a living fact within his own nature' (Whitehead, 1926, p. 154); and confusion is bound to result from uncritically combining the two. Second, theological self-explications of Christian beliefs have frequently been distorted by views which are foreign to them but were brought in via the language and conceptuality used to analyse and rationally reconstruct them. For example, there are good reasons to consider the widely held theistic belief in the existence of a supreme and beneficent Being to be a philosophical distortion of the proper Christian understanding of God which, because it does not know God apart from his self-revelation in Jesus Christ, is to be construed in trinitarian rather than theistic terms.

It is clear that theologians are unable to control alleged distortions like this without criteria for critically distinguishing proper from improper reconstructions of the Christian faith; and these criteria have to accord with the common experience of the Christian community. Thus, in order to avoid some of the worst distortions, confusions and misunderstandings which endangered the very existence and unity of the Christian community in the first centuries, the churches agreed on three basic standards for Christian beliefs and theology. In their systematic function, though not necessarily in their particular historical form, these continue to govern theological reflection:

1 They accepted a canon of exemplary scriptures which enshrined the foundational experiences of their common faith in Christ and their paradigmatic expression as the source and norm of all theological reflection (*Bible*).
2 They agreed on a summary outline of the faith expressed in the Bible which served as a rule of interpreting the Bible in accordance with the faith as lived, experienced, confessed and taught in the Christian community throughout history (*Creed*).
3 They developed, on the basis of this, a christological grammar of Christian talk of God, the world and human existence which is encapsulated in the trinitarian and christological doctrines of Nicaea and Chalcedon (*Dogma*).

All three standards - and this is what is important about them - witness in their different ways to the *centrality of Jesus Christ* for Christian faith and theology: the story of Jesus Christ is the unifying principle of the Christian Bible including the Old Testament scriptures; the second article is the centre of the Creed; Dogma establishes Christology to be the grammar of Christian belief, doctrine and theology; and Christology safeguards the centrality of Jesus Christ for all Christian thinking about God, world and human existence. From the beginning, therefore, Christian faith, life and reflection have been christocentric. Christological reflection has been the origin of Christian theology. It was here where the relations to traditional mythology, philosophical theology and Jewish monotheistic faith had to be clarified; and christological issues have remained at the centre of the differences between philosophy and theology, history and dogma, experience and revelation, action and reflection.

PART II

FAITH AND REASON

Chapter 4

Perspectives and the Quest for Harmony

The first major source of problems in the relationship between Christian theology and philosophy is the difference between internal and external perspectives on faith and its manifestations, between (as I shall say briefly) *Faith* and *Reason*. (The capital letters indicate that I refer to the perspectives, not to items within the perspectives.) It has taken on many forms in the history of Western theology. On the one hand, Christians have differed widely in their self-understanding and understanding of faith and revelation, as is manifest in the different confessional traditions. Accordingly, the internal perspective of Faith has been elaborated in different ways and led to a great number of differing theological positions. On the other hand, there have been different conceptions of reason; the external perspective of Reason has been developed in philosophical, historical, psychological or sociological terms; and they have provoked a wide variety of theological reactions. But even if we concentrate solely on philosophical perspectives and the particular issues raised by them we find not one but a whole cluster of problems and a great variety of theological attempts to come to grips with them. Some such attempts have been particularly influential; and in what follows I shall delineate and discuss some of the most important of them.

If I concentrate primarily on *theological* attempts, the reason is simple. The problem of perspectives is a genuine theological problem not merely a (philosophical) problem about theology. Theology cannot unfold the internal perspective of Faith in a critical and systematic way while ignoring the external perspectives. It is not a completely self-sufficient intellectual enterprise, and the christological concentration of Christian theology was never meant to restrict the universal scope of its claims. It referred to a particular revelation but it claimed that it revealed the ultimate truth about God, world and human existence. This claim was bound to conflict with other claims to (ultimate) truth. There were, after all, other religions and faiths with similar claims; and there was a considerable body of human knowledge apparently achieved without divine revelation or grace and with obvious implications for theology. Theology had to take up this challenge. It could not rationally expound the Christian faith without attempting to relate the achievements of human reason to the Christian revelation. And there were at least four options open to it, all of which have been championed at one time or another:

1   The *exclusivist position* claims Christianity to be the only path to truth. Salvation and knowledge of truth is through Jesus Christ alone who, according to John's Gospel, said 'I am the way, and the truth, and the life; no one comes to the Father, but by me' (John 14:6). Accordingly, other claims to salvation and truth have to be rejected as wrong or mere pseudo-claims. The position is obviously difficult to sustain for theological and philosophical reasons. Philosophically we cannot both insist on the unity and universality of truth and simply reject what is true outside Christianity as wrong and illegitimate. Theologically we cannot ignore that the very point of the Christian revelation is that God desires all humankind to be saved including those who have never heard of Christ. But then, given his love, mercy and power, it is difficult to imagine that he has not provided the means for them to come to know the salvific truth.

2   The *dualist position* reacts to these problems by dropping both universalist axioms. It assumes a theory of double truth: what is true in the perspective of Faith need not be true in the perspective of Reason, and vice versa (cf. Maywald, 1871; Betzendörfer, 1924). And it accepts a restriction of the universal scope of salvation: God desires the salvation of all humankind, but only those who have faith in Christ will in fact be saved. But the first reaction dissolves the very idea of truth that is necessarily bound up with the idea of universal validity. Truth is not relative to given frames: for example, we cannot hold theologically that God created the world, and philosophically (or scientifically) that the world has not been created but simply is. This idea that one and the same proposition viewed from different standpoints can be both true and false is entirely at odds with the idea of truth. It does not help to argue with Rescher that this is only seemingly so because 'once we assume the "internal" perspective of a particular one of them, the truth-theoretical situation is, presumably, restored to a classical order' (Rescher, 1973, p. 151), for then we should conclude not 'that a proposition can be *both* true and false' (p. 150) but that what is viewed as true and false from distinct standpoints are different propositions. (This raises further problems about what is, or can be, identical between different standpoints and perspectives; we shall have to return to this.) On the other hand, the

second reaction undermines trust in the love and salvific will of God and leads into the perils of a doctrine of double predestination: how can a good and loving God consign the majority of human beings to perdition without even offering them a chance to know him? If he wills their damnation how can he be good? And if he does not will it but cannot prevent it, how can even those who have faith trust that he will be able to save them?

3   The *pluralist position* is an epistemological variant of the dualist position. There may be more than one way to truth and salvation. If they seem to be incompatible to us this is because we do not fully know and comprehend the truth. Accordingly, the problem is not an alleged incompatibility of different 'truths' but the imperfection of our knowledge of truth: we know enough about God to recognize him at work everywhere in nature and history, but we do not know enough about him to recognize him not to be at work in events and actions seemingly incompatible with what we believe to be true. The problem with this approach is that it implicitly or explicitly denies the normative and definitive character of God's revelation in Christ: God may turn out to be quite different from what faith believes him to be; and we cannot be sure that what we believe about him on the basis of revelation and faith will not have to be drastically modified in the course of further growth of our knowledge.

4   The *inclusivist position*, finally, tries to escape the perils of relativism by claiming Christ, (1) to be the definitive revelation of God; (2) to be the revelation of an inexhaustible mystery and source of wisdom; and (3) to be the final crown and fulfilment not only of the Old Testament hopes and aspirations but of all approaches to truth and salvation wherever they may occur. Every truth contributes in a perhaps imperfect and preliminary way to the absolute truth revealed in Christ; every claim to truth, from whatever quarter, has therefore to be tested as to its compatibility and consistency with the Christian revelation. The mystery revealed in Christ does not resist reason, but invites exploration in the light of all knowledge available. Truth is not confined to Christ, although it is best defined in Christ, so that even if some knowledge of truth comes without God's revelation in Christ, it must be compatible with and contribute to a better understanding of this revelation and its universal implications.

The inclusivist position and its quest for harmony has been favoured by Christian theologians since the days of the apologists. They were the first explicitly to claim every true insight to be a preliminary contribution to the truth finally revealed in Christ. Abraham and Socrates alike they considered to be Christians before Christ. For, as they argued (by combining Stoic, Platonic and Christian ideas) the divine *Logos* has implanted seeds of truth in many places, and inspired both prophets and philosophers, before it became entirely present in Jesus Christ. This *Logos*-doctrine was the beginning of Christian argument for the inclusivist position. But although it defined the issue and offered broad outlines of a solution, it took some time before viable theological models emerged from its tentative suggestions. One of the first was delineated by Augustine, and the Augustinian tradition has kept it alive for more than a thousand years.

Chapter 5

The Two-Books Model

Books are wholes; they are meaningful; and they have authors. To understand the world as a book, or a library of books, must have been a tempting idea to a thinker educated in a culture which assumed the study of classical texts to be the proper way to gain knowledge about the world; and to conceive nature as God's other book must have been natural to a theologian devoted to the study of the Bible and yet not ignorant of the beauties of the world. Augustine did not coin the metaphor of the two books (Blumenberg, 1983): but he was the first to use it as a theological model to integrate the internal and external perspectives on faith. In his exposition of the creation story (*De genesi ad litteram*, in Migne, *Patrologiae cursus completus. Series Latina* 32, pp. 219ff) he insists against gnostic spiritualism and neo-Platonist emanationism that God has written not only the Book of Scriptures (*liber scripturae*) but also, and before that, the Book of Nature (*liber naturae*). The books are different but both Nature and Revelation have one and the same author (*unum esse auctorem*). Thus philosophical cosmologies based on metaphysical accounts of Nature cannot, if true, contradict Revelation: all truth is grounded in God who creates everything *ex nihilo*. Three points should be noted here.

1   Books are meaningful wholes. Thus by describing nature (or the world) as a book, Augustine conceives it in all its natural, historical and cultural dimensions, with their infinite details and inexhaustible perspectives, as a meaningful whole and ordered cosmos which can, in principle at least, be understood. The unity and intelligibility of the world (including its history, as he undertook to show in his *De civitate Dei*) is presupposed in all our dealings with it, not derived from them. In experience and action we assume the world to be a unity, and all its infinite detail to belong to one coherent pattern; and we suppose it to be intelligible so that if we fail to understand it it is our fault, not nature's.

2   However, books disclose their meaning to those who are able to read them. But - as Augustine argues in his *Enarratio in psalmum* (XLV 6-7) - whereas the Bible can be read only by the educated few with the appropriate linguistic capacities (*qui litteras noverunt*), the study of Nature is open even to the illiterate (*idiota*). Yet, looked at more closely, this turns out to be an ambiguous advantage which does not cancel the epistemic prerogative of the Bible. Because Nature is not couched in linguistic idiom, with its self-interpreting capacity, its greater availability goes with a greater obscurity: the Book of Nature allows for many interpretations and requires the interpretative key of the Scriptures to be understood correctly.

3   This key is required not only for the correct interpretation but even for the correct identification of the world. A book is an obvious unity, but the unity and intelligibility of the world is not self-evident. It is neither one of the physical facts about the world which we could discover, nor a metaphysical fact inferrable from such facts. The idea of the world as an intelligible unity transcends everything that could be derived from a study of worldly events and facts. It is a regulative idea, an *a priori* decision to place all facts in a common frame of reference, and to call the frame of all these common frames the world. For the Christian this fundamental frame of frames is the *creation*: he does not know of the world apart from knowing it as creation.

But this is not a self-evident thought. It took a long time, heated theological debates and centuries of religious education before the two terms *world* and *creation* became virtually interchangeable in Western culture. Augustine's use of the Two-Books Model no doubt contributed to this development. But it is based on presuppositions which are far from self-evident. To identify and interpret the world as an intelligible unity, as the book model demands, we must see nature as a creation that points to the true nature of its maker. But to do this clearly and unambiguously is impossible unless we know its creator in the first place. Without that knowledge we can have no clear knowledge of the world as creation, and hence no knowledge of its unity and intelligibility. For the singularity of God is what guarantees the world's unity, and his revealed will its intelligibility; and revelation is what guarantees a single author of the Book of Revelation and the Book of Nature, by revealing the God who saves to be the God who creates.

The Augustinian tradition, and notably Bonaventura, has systematized these ideas. The *liber mundi*, originally a fully sufficient source of knowledge, became unintelligible to us because of our sin and fall; but God in his mercy has given us the *liber scripturae* which shows us the meaning of everything written in the Book of Nature and thus allows us to regain the knowledge which we have lost (*Collationes in hexameron* XIII.12). So the Book of Scriptures is the key to the Book of Nature; the internal perspective of faith reveals the full meaning and truth of what, because of our sin, can only inadequately be grasped in the external perspective of natural reason.

The model of the Two Books suggested a specifically theological perspective on the world and its knowledge. It co-ordinated the internal perspective of Faith and the external perspective of Reason by reference to the common author of Nature and Revelation: God. But the functioning of the model depended on the epistemic priority of the Book of Scripture over the Book of Nature, and it broke down when the focus of interest changed from their common author to their different languages. For the Book of Nature, as Galileo pointed out (1623, p. 232) is 'written in the language of mathematics' ('scritto in lingua matematica') and the Book of Scriptures is obviously of little use in deciphering that language. It has to be studied on its own - independently of the Book of Scriptures. Only so can we hope to arrive at a proper understanding of it. Hence Descartes's decision, according to his *Discours de la méthode*, to give up 'l'étude des lettres' (including theology) in order to devote himself totally to the study of himself (*moi-même*) and of the 'grand livre du monde' (1637, p. 9). This independent study of the Book of Nature by calculation and experiment was the beginning of modern science; and the independent study of the self and its capacities by critical self-reflection the beginning of modern philosophy. Thus, ironically, the Two-Books Model achieved precisely the opposite of what it set out to achieve: it began as an attempt to integrate nature, and the natural knowledge of the world, into the theological perspective, and it ended by freeing the study of the Book of Nature from domination by the Book of Scripture.

However, what was undoubtedly a gain for modern science posed profound problems for modern philosophy. The scientific study of the Book of Nature continued to operate on the assumption that nature was a unity and the world an ordered whole. But it had lost the traditional theological justification for these fundamental assumptions, i.e. the revelation of God the Saviour as God the Creator, and of the world as creation, thus establishing the unity and intelligibility of the world by contrasting it as creation with its creator. Parallel to the rise of modern science, therefore, philosophy sought to provide new justifications for its fundamental assumptions. This was done first in terms of *natural theologies* independent of, and increasingly in contrast to, the revelational theology of the Christian tradition which were based on ontological, cosmological and teleological analyses of the structure of the world and the self. And when these attempts broke down under the impact of Hume's and Kant's critical philosophies, it was done by deriving constitutive and/or regulative *principles of human mind and knowledge* from a transcendental analysis of the capacities and presuppositions of human understanding and reason. During the first period the metaphor of the Two Books was still widely used but with an important change of emphasis. Nature now illuminates Revelation, and not vice versa; the Book of Nature is the key to the Book of Scriptures: reason, not revelation, is the final arbiter. In the early nineteenth century, after Hume's and Kant's philosophies had effectively undermined the theological foundations of the scientific study of nature and history, even this use of the Two-Books Model began to fade. But for much of the formative period of modern culture the idea of an independent study of the Book of Nature promoted the rise not only of science but also of philosophical natural theologies outside traditional theology of revelation. These independent ways of revelation and nature, of faith's internal perspective and reason's external perspective, led equally to knowledge of God. And even this twofold way broke down when the attempt to find philosophico-theological foundations for science finally ended. What theology began as an inclusivist programme developed into a pluralist position, and ended in a philosophical and scientific position excluding theology altogether.

Chapter 6

The Nature-Grace Model

The Augustinian model of the two books was heavily indebted to the *Logos*-centred metaphysics and hermeneutics of Stoic and neo-Platonist philosophies. As their distinctive focus was not the sensible world but the intelligible reason behind it, so it emphasized not the Book of Nature as such but its divine author. Hence it did not flourish readily in the sober, empirical, and *cosmos*-centred atmosphere of Aristotelian philosophy. Thus when the schoolmen took Aristotle rather than Plato as the paradigm of human knowledge achieved by natural reason, they followed Thomas Aquinas (1224-74) in replacing it by another version of the inclusivist programme: the model of Nature and Grace. This drew the boundary between philosophy and theology differently, by relating the natural knowledge of philosophy, including philosophical theology (*theologia philosophica* (*Super librum Boethii de Trinitate* 5.4.c)), to revealed theology (*sacra doctrina* (*Summa theologiae* I.2.*proem.*)) as imperfect to perfect knowledge of God and world. Unlike the Two-Books Model it involved an explicit grading of the perspectives in a hierarchical order. It imposed on the perspectives of Reason and Faith the rule that grace perfects nature, and that by means of analogy we can intelligibly move from the external perspective of nature to the internal perspective of grace. Although no likeness can be discerned between the two perspectives without a greater unlikeness having to be discerned as well, there is an ultimate harmony between philosophy and theology. Thus some philosophical insights, e.g. into the structure of the act of understanding, provide natural analogies for theological truths like the trinity (Lonergan, 1967a; Burrell, 1979, ch. 12), which transcend reason but have been disclosed by God through Christ and the prophets, transmitted through scripture and tradition, and preserved in the church. And some theological truths, like God's existence, singularity, unity, goodness and perfection are demonstrable by philosophical reason, as Aquinas undertakes to show in his much-discussed *quinque viae* and demonstration of the divine perfections. Thus the evidence of change in the world leads to a First Cause of all effects; the order and design in nature to the idea of an intelligent Designer; the contingency of the world to its necessary ground. But all this, although important, is only a preamble to faith because the most important theological truths are not accessible to reason. In short, philosophy is an indispensible handmaid to theology, and natural knowledge of Reason is not only valid within its limits, but a perfectible preamble to the revealed knowledge of Faith.

The Nature-Grace Model co-ordinates two complementary perspectives on an infinite and homgeneous range of truths grounded in God, the Primal Truth. It is a much more powerful version of the inclusivist position, compatible not only with the dynamics of the growth of knowledge in either field but, even more importantly, critically aware of the essential partiality and intrinsic limitation of all human knowledge and the always greater ignorance surrounding it. The insights of Reason are infinitely inferior to the insights of Faith, and even these hardly scratch the surface of the infinite mystery of God. On the other hand, philosophical and theological knowledge, in their graded but complementary way, form a coherent whole that can be ordered in a deductive system of knowledge after the manner of Aristotelian science. The unity of knowledge thus corresponds to the unity of truth and the difference of perspectives ultimately turns out to be negligible.

This model is a remarkable theological and philosophical achievement, but the following points need emphasizing:

1   Though ontologically truth is one, epistemologically there are different realms of truth distinguished by the way in which we gather and justify knowledge of them. On the one hand there is the natural realm of what is rationally knowable, on the other the suprarational realm of what surpasses human reason and is merely credible on faith. Propositions which are either self-evident or can be derived from self-evident propositions are *knowable*; propositions revealed by God and believed not on evidence but on his authority are *credible*. The difference between the perspective of Reason and the perspective of Faith is thus recast as a difference between two sources of knowledge (nature and grace) and two sorts of knowledge (demonstrable and credible). This additive co-ordination deactivates the tension between the two perspectives and is the first step towards their harmonization.

2   These two realms of truth are distinct but continuous. The truths disclosed by reason are not contrary to the truths disclosed by revelation. The former are believed because they are evidently or

demonstrably true; the latter because of the trustworthiness of God who reveals them. But God is the Primal Truth from which all truth is derived. Therefore the truths accessible to natural reason cannot contradict the truth of the Christian faith (*Summa contra gentiles* I.7.42): they are preliminary and partial insights into what is fully made known in revelation. In short, the additive co-ordination of two sources and sorts of knowledge is strengthened by showing them to be complementary and non-contradictory. This is the second step towards harmonization.

3 To the different realms of truth correspond different modes of knowledge. Reason assents to the truth of propositions on evidence or demonstration; but it is fallible and may err. Faith, on the other hand, although it is the most imperfect act of the intellect considered as knowledge, is infinitely superior to reason because of its infallible object (*Summa contra gentiles* III.40). It is intellectual assent to truths about God not on evidence but on authority. For although it cannot, in this life, appreciate the evidence for what it believes to be true, it believes it to be true because it has been revealed by God whom it believes to be the Truth. Its assent is motivated not by evidence but by belief in God: it trusts that the author of revelation also guarantees its truth. Thus the co-ordination of the two sources and sorts of knowledge is further strengthened by introducing a hierarchical asymmetry in their relationship: grace is superior to nature as a source of knowledge, and faith, although inferior to reason as a mode of knowledge, is superior to it with respect to what it knows. This is the third step towards harmonization.

4 Besides truths accessible only to reason (the natural, including some theological truths like the existence of God) and truth accessible only to faith (e.g. the trinity or the incarnation) there are also - for grace does not contradict but perfects and elevates the natural - truths which may be known either way (*Summa theologiae* II.ii.2.4 ad 2). For as not all men are philosophers, or have the time, leisure and intellectual capacity to inquire into the ultimate truths of the world, God in his grace has made even those truths which can be known philosophically more readily available to the average man through Christ and the teaching of the church (*Summa contra gentiles* I.5). Thus both philosophical theology and revealed theology can hold the same truths about God. But they arrive at it in different ways. Whereas philosophical considerations start from creation and end with God, theological considerations start from God and only then arrive at creation (II.4). But this requires that the principles of revealed theology are received directly from God through his revelation as imparted through Christ's teaching and transmitted by the

church. As such they cannot be demonstrated, and need no justification (*Summa theologiae* I.1.5 ad 2). The principles of philosophical
theology, on the other hand, must be justified, and are only justified if
they are so self-evidently true that they cannot even be thought to be
false (*Summa contra gentiles* I.7.43). But this is only a preliminary and
partial knowledge of their truth. For what reason finds to be self-
evidently true (*naturaliter nota*), faith knows to be ultimately
grounded in God himself: we know the self-evident principles of
natural reason only because they are made known to us by God our
creator who has endowed us with their knowledge (I.7.44). The idea of
creation, therefore, is the basic albeit unexplicated theological
presupposition of both philosophical and revealed theology (cf. Pieper,
1953, pp. 17,19); and it underlines the ultimately theological (not
philosophical) character of the whole enterprise. Thus the harmony
between the two sources and sorts of knowledge is finally achieved by
showing philosophical theology to be a domain in which nature and
grace, reason and faith partly overlap without, however, endangering
the ultimate priority of grace over nature and faith over reason.

The Nature-Grace Model has, in one way or other, become the
standard way of describing the relationship between theology and
philosophy in the Roman Catholic tradition. But its integrating power
depends on three presuppositions which are far from self-evident: the
idea of creation as the common frame of reference for both
philosophical and theological knowledge; the God-given unity and
identity of truth despite irreducibly different realms of truth and
ways of coming to know the truth; the validity of the use of analogy to
move intelligibly from the order of nature to the order of grace without either mystifying reason or rationalizing revelation.

Criticism of the model has concentrated on all three presuppositions. The first was a matter of controversy between Aristotelian
philosophy and Christian theology throughout the middle ages
(witness the debate about the eternity of the world); and it became
even less self-evident in the modern period, when philosophy and
science ceased to refer to God in their explanations of the world. The
second and third became increasingly problematic in late medieval
nominalism. The *via moderna* (the Occamist way of thought) attacked
the *via antiqua* of Thomist intellectualism for its uneasy mixture of an
Aristotelian ontology of being with its idea of a science of necessary
and evident knowledge, with the intrinsically dynamic, historical and
contingent nature of the Christian faith. In a strictly Aristotelian
sense, theology failed to qualify as a science, since it could not live up
to the standards of necessary and evident knowledge (cf. Lohse, 1958,
pp. 27-8). God in his *potentia absoluta* could well have ordained

everything in a different way, and it was only because of his *potentia ordinata* that things were as they were. This was not only difficult to accommodate in a science of necessary knowledge, it placed theology squarely outside the realms of science and philosophy, i.e. of the natural knowledge obtainable by the human faculties of sensual experience and reason. Consequently, the *via moderna* had to give up the metaphysical attempt at a unified and comprehensive system of philosophical and theological knowledge. It could only avoid making theological matters utterly incomprehensible by proposing an epistemological dualism between philosophy and theology, couched in terms of a double logic, a double truth and a double mode of knowing (Lohse, 1958, pp. 43ff). Thus although it still juxtaposed the two orders of nature and grace, it no longer managed to show how they complement each other. This allowed reason to move more freely in the natural order, but undermined its capacity to move by analogy to the order of grace, for it reduced the hierarchical integration of the two orders to a mere additive co-ordination of two sources and sorts of knowledge, without inquiring into their formal compatibility. Used in this way, however, the model of nature and grace merely restated the different sorts of knowledge which it was originally meant to integrate theologically. It had thus lost its point; and it became replaced by a completely different model in the Protestant Reformation.

Chapter 7

The Law-Gospel Model

Reformation theology dismissed the 'mixo-philosophico-theological' model of Nature and Grace of scholasticism and replaced it by the purely theological model of Law and Gospel. The difference may be described as the transition from an additive co-ordination of the two perspectives of Faith and Reason to an internal reconstruction of the perspective of Reason within the perspective of Faith. What used to be an external contrast between Nature and Grace is now re-created as an internal differentiation of the perspective of Faith in terms of Law (*lex*) and Gospel (*evangelium*), viz. the knowledge of God, world and human existence *extra Christum* and *in Christo*. This is a purely theological distinction. But by relating two theological perspectives, not a theological and a non-theological one, the theological perspective is universalized and made independent of the philosophical perspective. Theology is seen strictly in the service of the explication of faith in Christ and its vision of reality. Its christocentric orientation and, at the same time, encompassing approach manifests the Christian conviction that God's revelation in Christ has disclosed the fundamental character of reality and illuminates the totality of experience. Hence it constitutes the decisive point of reference for interpreting the totality of reality, and requires all theological thinking about God, the world, and human existence to be christologically determined.

The idea of such a universal and all-comprehensive but strictly christological theology was first realized by Luther; I propose to consider his approach in more detail.

Luther was trained in the Occamist way of thought, and accepted its criticism of scholastic attempts at a comprehensive theory of both theological and philosophical knowledge. But he did not follow the *via moderna* in compartmentalizing theology and philosophy. Instead he offered a christological reworking of this dualism in a distinctive *theological* approach to philosophy, science and history by dividing

all human knowledge into knowledge of God, world and human existence *extra Christum* and *in Christo*. The result is a conception of
theology, couched in dialectical rather than analogical terms, with
two distinctive features: the contrast between philosophy and theology is heightened; and theology becomes a universal and all-
comprehensive enterprise.

According to Luther, philosophy and theology are fundamentally
different, yet they neither contradict nor complement each other
(*Weimarer Ausgabe* 39/2, 27, 31-2). Philosophy has the world for its
field and whatever it talks about, even in metaphysics, must make
itself felt in the present and experienced world. Theology, on the
other hand, has 'the invisible things as subject' (WA 39/2, 15, 8-9),
i.e. those 'which are believed, i.e. which are apprehended by faith'
(WA 39/2, 6, 26-8; Dalferth, 1982). This looks like the traditional distinction between the knowable and the (merely) credible. But it is not.
Philosophy and theology are neither different stages in our knowledge
of things nor knowledge about different sorts of things. They are
different kinds of knowledge of the same things, placed in different
perspectives and different frames of reference: viz. the *coram mundo*-
perspective of its relations to things in the world and the *coram
deo*-perspective of its relations to God. Both perspectives are necessary for an adequate understanding of reality; both allow for growth
of knowledge and a perfecting of our understanding of God, world and
human existence; but there is no transition from knowledge in the
first perspective to knowledge in the second, and thus no direct combination of knowledge achieved in the one frame with knowledge
achieved in the second. Confusion is bound to result from mixing
philosophical discourse about things *coram mundo* with theological
discourse about things *coram deo*; and precisely this mixing of discourses Luther diagnoses as having been the endemic evil of scholastic theology.

One of his ways of stating this point is in terms of the Aristotelian
theory of causes. Originally derived from the model of human action,
it became depersonalized when applied to physical objects, and then
used metaphysically to explain the world in terms of a First Cause,
which perpetually actualizes its essence independently of any relations to anything outside itself. Luther rejects this as a theologically
inadequate conception of God unable to make sense of creation and
eschatology. These problems are beyond the grasp of philosophy,
which can acquire knowledge about things in the world in terms of
their formal and material causes, but not in terms of their ultimate
efficient and final cause: the creaturehood and final destiny of things
are beyond the limits of philosophical insight (*De homine*, prop.

11-15). They cannot be read off natural phenomena accessible to reason *coram mundo*, for they characterize their existence *coram deo*. This relation, however, is not open to philosophical scrutiny because its main term (God) is not a natural phenomenon, nor the totality of natural phenomena, but invisibly present in them. It grounds everything that exists *coram mundo*, but is not one of the things that exist *coram mundo*. It is not a relation in the world, but the relation which defines the world; and it can only be read into the world if known from somewhere else.

Luther's contention is an extrapolation from the paradigmatic case of our knowledge of ourselves as human beings, and we may illustrate his point by considering the final cause of the human being. Luther does not deny that Aristotelian philosophy presents a teleological picture of human beings in terms of the ends of their actions. But he rejects the scholastic attempt to combine Aristotelian teleology with biblical eschatology by speaking of a 'duplex finis hominis', viz. a natural and a supernatural end ('finis proximus seu naturalis' and 'finis ultimus seu supranaturalis') related according to the principle 'finis proximus non excludit finem ultimum' (Thomas Aquinas, *Summa theologiae* I.65.2). Taken in its strict eschatological sense there is only one end of human beings: the reconciliation of the sinner with God; and this end can be achieved neither by degrees nor by divine-human co-operation, because although we are rational agents *coram mundo*, we are sinners *coram deo* and, as such, unwilling and unable to co-operate with God. Theology knows the human being not as 'animal rationale' but as 'homo justificandus' (WA 39/1, 84, 2), i.e. as the sinner who needs to be saved, because considering us *coram deo* it must differentiate the perspectives of Law and Gospel and allow for the eschatological difference between what we are now (sinners) and what we will be then (justified sinners). Because it considers human beings in their relations to God (and God in his relations to them) and because it can only do this by emphasizing the difference between what this relation is like now and how it might and should be, it must translate all non-theological statements about human beings into statements about the sinner and/or the saved sinner. Only in this dialectical way can it speak of the human being; and only on the basis of this dialectical understanding can theology proceed to speak analogically about God.

Luther proposes, therefore, to replace the scholastic two-stage teleology with its emphasis on analogy and its mixing of philosophical and theological discourse with a two-relations eschatology worked out in strictly theological discourse, giving priority in its vision of reality to the dialectics between protology and eschatology over the analogical ordering of finite and infinite reality. Thus theology neither includes nor merely adds to philosophical knowledge of human beings (and of everything else) but reworks it in terms of the eschatological contrast between sin and salvation. Its operative principle is the difference-in-unity of dialectics, not the unity-in-difference of analogy.

What is true of the final cause is also true of the efficient cause. The predicate '- is created' is a relational one which locates the subject of which it is truly predicated *coram deo* by stating its very existence to be effected by God's action (Farrer, 1967, p. 22). It does not contribute towards defining what things are (their essence) or describing how they are (their factual existence). Philosophically it is uninformative, for if it is true of anything accessible to our experience and reason, it is true of everything. But it does not follow from everything being grounded in God that some apprehension of God belongs to us by nature. To know a thing which is created is not to know that it is created, and Luther denies that philosophy does or can know about creation and the creaturehood of things. It may come to know the world to be governed (WA 44, 591, 34ff) and to have a 'primum movens et summum ens'; it may affirm the direction of nature and the existence of a first, total and sufficient cause. But all this is knowledge of the 'gubernatio mundi', not of the 'creatio mundi', the creation of everything 'per verbum ex nihilo' (WA 39/2, 345, 24-346, 23; WA 42, 292, 15-22), which must be meaningless to a philosophy which holds *ex nihilo nihil fit*. Yet philosophical theology of the scholastic type presupposes precisely this meaningless idea. It fails in its inferential reasoning from the world to God because this reasoning presupposes that the world is the creation of God, and wordly events are the effects of divine activity. Cosmological inference is the inverse form of the doctrine of creation; but 'to believe the article of the creation of things from nothing is more difficult than to believe the article of the incarnation' (WA 39/2, 340, 21-3); and there is no Christian doctrine of creation apart from faith in Christ. For 'created' is no more a simple descriptive predicate of the world than 'sinner' is of man. Both predicates locate whatever they apply to in a specific relation to God; both thus presuppose the identification of God in relation to whom all things are located. But there is no adequate identification of God apart from his self-identification to us in Jesus Christ, and our identification of him in and through faith in Jesus Christ. In short, because it tacitly depends on the location of the world in the *coram deo*-perspective, on its identification as creation, and on the identity of its creator with the God revealed in Christ, philosophical theology is a hybrid enterprise and as such unable to bridge the gap between the perspectives of Faith and Reason.

It follows that the philosophical proofs of the existence and attributes of God are theologically worthless. They not only depend on the identification of the world as creation in their starting-point, but also on the identity of the First Cause, End and God in their conclusion. But they provide us with no convincing grounds for these identifications, or for concluding that 'world' and 'creation' refer to the same thing, or that the First Cause and End in the perspective of Reason and the Creator and Saviour in the perspective of Faith are identical. Thus they do not succeed in fixing the reference of Christian talk of God. At their best they tell us that the First Cause and End of all things is different from everything else and that we cannot know what it is, but only what it is not. However, identifying knowledge of God can only be derived from faith, not from the world. For God is a unique being which has to be known by acquaintance, not by inference and description. He is apprehended in faith, not by a reason which discerns an unchanging world of divine ideas behind the flux of visible things; and our conceptions of him are true in as much as they conceptualize what is apprehended in the experience of faith. Faith, however, is not a supernatural cognitive act. It is faith *in Christ* and, as such, an eschatological relationship of communication with Christ through the Spirit; and it is the Spirit of Christ and therefore God himself who effects it. Thus only when we come to experience Christ through his Spirit do we apprehend our relation to God in faith; and we experience Christ only in situations in which he is communicated and understood, i.e. in which (as Luther puts it) the Gospel is proclaimed and received in faith; and because faith is God's communicative act in us, it is the threefold act of God in Christ for us, God the Son with us and God the Spirit in us which together fixes the reference point of Christian talk of God the Father, Son and Spirit.

However, fixing the reference of our talk of God is not the same as conceptualizing that to which we refer; and whereas faith in Christ fixes the referent it is theology's task to conceptualize it. Now Luther agrees with the tradition that our conceptions of God cannot be descriptive, but must be imaginative constructions; that all apprehension involves interpretation; and that our imaginative constructions will inevitably be coloured by our experiences, including our preconceived ideas of God and the world. But he insists that these constructions must be couched in christological rather than cosmological terms and proceed along the lines of an *analogia Christi* rather than an *analogia entis* or *operantis*. Neither our experience of the world nor the theological tradition yield adequate concepts of God, but only the experience of faith in Christ as recorded in the Bible. Faith and the Bible are the guidelines of theological reflection.

If philosophical ideas guide theological inquiry, confusion is bound to result; and unless theological doctrines are checked against the biblical witness, confusion cannot be detected. Jesus Christ is the key for discerning the activity of God not only *extra Christum* but also *in Christo*; and only because we can read it off here can we read it into nature and history.

'Reading into' is not a subjectivist interpretation, but a discerning of God's hidden reality in nature and history in the light of faith. Luther agrees with the tradition that the Christian faith must see God everywhere at work and that it will always be an inscrutable mystery how God is at work in everything. But he does not simply contrast God's hiddenness in nature with his revelation in Christ. Rather he affirms a twofold hiddenness of God. First, God is hidden in nature and history: he is not made manifest by them; not even the fact that they are created can be affirmed without faith. But God is also hidden in the cross of Christ in a precise sense: namely 'under the contrary' (*sub contrario*) as Luther says. For although faith can read God's presence off the cross, even Christ's suffering and cross do not manifest it *tout simple*. It must be read into them: it is manifest, in other words, only to faith (WA 7, 585, 16-587, 22). Yet if faith is characterized by the dialectics of 'reading off' and 'reading into' how can it avoid being reduced to an arbitrary subjectivist interpretation of the cross? How can Jesus Christ be the key for discerning God's activity in him and everything else if we cannot know him as Christ apart from knowing God? Does this not beg the question, as many have argued (cf. Hepburn, 1958, ch. 5)?

To avoid this epistemological impasse, Luther appeals to the self-explanatory character of God's revelation in Christ, and its reception in faith. Because faith in Christ is the work of the Spirit who assures us of God's revelation in Jesus Christ, 'reading off' and 'reading into' coincide with the faith in Jesus as the Christ. The eschatological situation, in which God's act in the believer (faith) interprets God's act in Christ (revelation) in a way that reveals the character and purpose of God's acting in creation as his love for us, is thus characterized by a strict correlation of *sola fide* and *solus Christus*. In faith in Christ God brings us to know who he is - both our saviour and the creator of everything - and identifies himself as hidden but present even when we cannot recognize him. This fixes the reference of our talk of God so that trinitarian talk of God the Father, Son and Spirit becomes inevitable; and it provides the christological criteria we need to guide our imaginative constructions of God and of our relations to him.

Luther's explanation of the manner of God's interaction with us, in

Christ and through the Spirit, is purely theological. This is where his theology departs most significantly from the scholastic theologies with their use of analogy to relate the realms of nature and the realm of grace by the rule that 'no likeness can be discerned without a greater unlikeness having to be discerned as well'. For Luther, to speak about God's relation to us is not to speak analogically about God but non-analogically about us. Rather we extend analogical discourse to everything we consider in theology. For Luther it is beyond doubt that 'omnia vocabula in Christo novam significationem accipere in eadem re significata' (WA 39/2, 94, 17-18; cf. Työrinoja, 1987, pp. 232ff). When we speak theologically about the world (including ourselves) we do not merely add a new aspect to our non-theological knowledge of it. We speak about it in a different frame of reference by considering its eschatological relations to God; and this involves a shift from how *we* conceive the world to how the world is conceived *by God*. But Luther is not arguing, as did Aquinas, that in theology everything is to be considered *sub ratione Dei*, i.e. in its relation to God 'ut ad principium et finem' (*Summa theologiae* I,1, 7). He is suggesting that in theology everything is to be considered not as we see it, in its relation to what we conceive to be God, but as God's *intuitus originarius* sees it; and because we can only do this if God allows us to participate in his view of creation as disclosed in Christ, the *modus loquendi theologicus* is intrinsically christological.

The basic distinction for Luther, therefore, is not between analogical and non-analogical discourse within theology but between theological discourse and non-theological (or philosophical) discourse. This involves a transformation of the problem of analogy from a doctrine of analogical predication to a hermeneutical theory about the functioning of words of the same language (e.g. Latin or English) in two different universes of discourse, viz. philosophy and theology. The two universes have different grammars and even when they speak about the same subject-matter, they present it from different points of view, i.e. as we know it by our ordinary means of apprehension and reflection, and as God knows it and communicates to us by conforming us to Christ in faith. But although philosophy and theology have different grammars and use the same terms differently, they are not mutually unintelligible. We can understand the meanings of terms like 'God', 'man', 'world', 'free' or 'just' from their use in either universe of discourse by paying close attention to their grammar, their linguistic environment and the situations and contexts of their employment. Grammatical analysis, therefore, not philosophical speculation, is the key to theological insight. Luther replaces the metaphysical enterprise of scholastic theology and its doctrine of analogy by the idea of (what he calls) a *grammatica theologica* (WA 5, 32, 19; cf. Raeder, 1977, pp. 34ff, 55, 305): theology is the grammar of Christian discourse and, above all, of the biblical writings which disclose the paradigmatic structures of the Christian experience of God's relationship to the world.

Luther's theology of strictly theological discourse can only contrast with philosophical discourse in this way because of its peculiar internal structure and mode of operation. It replaces analogy by dialectics and becomes all-comprehensive by turning the problem of theology's external relation to other branches of knowledge into a problem within theology. The opposition *between* theology and philosophy becomes an opposition *within* theology worked out in terms of the dialectics of Law and Gospel. This is what makes Luther's theology so powerful. Because it internalizes problems of external relationship, it can remain remarkably independent of changes in science and history, while making a strong claim to see the whole of reality as the field of God's action. The neo-Protestant gulf between nature as a closed continuum of worldly events and the action of God, experienced only in the personal life of the believer, is foreign to Luther's thinking. God's activity permeates everything; he is *semper ubique actuosus*. But he is involved in two quite different ways. Corresponding to his twofold hiddenness, in creation and cross, theology has to acknowledge his two modes of acting - in Christ and outside Christ: the *Law* and the *Gospel*. In the *coram deo*-perspective, therefore, all happenings in the world have to be interpreted in the light of this fundamental distinction, i.e. God's *natural* and his *spiritual* presence in Law and Gospel.

God is *naturally* present but hidden everywhere and in everything; if he were not, everything would simply stop being (WA 46, 558ff). Besides this, however, he is *spiritually* present in particular occasions where he makes his presence known in such a way that we are provoked to acknowledge him in faith. It is the self-explicatory character, and strict correlation to faith, which distinguishes his spiritual presence in his promises, in Christ, and in the Gospel, from his natural presence in all things. And whereas his natural presence, even when recognized, remains ambiguous as to the character of his will, his spiritual presence reveals his will to be that of a loving father who cares for his creation.

For Luther God's spiritual presence is not simply that by which we come to recognize his natural presence. We can know him to be naturally present without knowing about his spiritual presence (WA. *Tischreden* 5, 368, 21ff). This natural knowledge of God is the *cognitio Dei legalis* which 'the philosophers have had as well, but which is not the right knowledge of God' (WA 46, 668, 9-12; WA 46, 657-74, esp. 667, 8-9). Right knowledge of God is the *cognitio Dei evangelica*, the knowledge of God's spiritual presence in Christ and his word. Only here do we apprehend him directly and recognize unambiguously his character and will. However, even here he is still naturally present and hidden as well. To recognize his natural presence is thus always a matter of 'reading into', and so a case of indirect apprehension. And this, as faith becomes painfully aware of in the face of evil, is often difficult if not impossible because we cannot directly recognize his natural presence but must maintain it contrary to what all experience and reason may seem to suggest.

The different modes of God's presence correspond to different modes of his divine and creative activity. On the one hand he acts in all things by acting through all things (WA 18, 710, 1-711, 19). This is the way of the Law, which for Luther symbolizes God's acting in the realm of creation according to his inscrutable almighty will; and even though he does not act directly but co-operates with the secondary causes which he has created *ex nihilo* (WA 43, 71, 7-9), he is not simply the uniform power of action in all acting but remains the free agent who 'can and does everything that he wills' (WA 18, 636, 29-30).

But God acts in and with particular things which he has ordained as vessels of his grace. This is the mode of the Gospel, i.e. of God's merciful action in the realm of grace, in which he makes himself known as saving love by adapting himself to the mode of receptivity of his creatures (WA 43, 179, 11-19). Here he does not co-operate with his created activity although he does not act without its natural means (WA 7, 588, 10-15). He is the sole author of acts of grace and, at the same time, the co-author of the created means in and with which he performs his acts of grace. The realms of creation and grace are therefore not related as two stages of a monolithic creative activity of God. They are constituted by the two fundamental ways in which God acts *in Christo* and *extra Christum*. The result is a *paradox of divine double agency*, i.e. of God acting at once, and not necessarily harmoniously, in both realms; and a corresponding *paradox of human double existence*, viz. of existing either (as sinner) *simul creatura et peccator* or (as saved sinner) *simul iustus et peccator*. Thus Luther's theological discourse is dominated not by the analogy between human and divine agency across the difference of the realms of Nature and Grace but by the dialectics of both divine and human agency in the perspectives of Law and Gospel.

All this restructuring of theological discourse comes from the strictly christological concentration of Luther's theology. But for the cross, we might ignore the dialectical structure of God's hidden activity in and through all created things and his revealed activity in and with particular created things. For at the cross these two activities actually run contrary to each other: the one resulting in Christ's death, the other in his and our life. The cross therefore marks a difference between God and God (WA 40/2, 342, 28-30), between the inscrutable will of the almighty God who wills both life and death alike, and the revealed will that shows God to be love, and to be willing our life.

The dialectics of divine activity at the cross led Luther to affirm the difference-in-unity between the *deus absconditus* and the *deus revelatus* to be the irreducible mark of every adequate conception of God. This is not the contrast between God as he is in himself and God as related to us, but a difference in God's relation to his creation. Of God in himself we can have 'nulla scientia et cognitione nulla', for 'quae supra nos nihil ad nos' (WA 43, 458-9). God in his relation to us, however, has to be conceived in terms of the contrast between sin and salvation and thus differentiated into his relation to the sinner (*deus absconditus*) and to the saved sinner (*deus revelatus*). Without this distinction we either fail to acknowledge God at work in everything, good or bad, or we fail to safeguard the identity of God who acts both *extra Christum* and *in Christo*. No theology which construes God's action by the dialectics of his saving act at the cross can bypass his twofold action in Law and Gospel and the dynamic tension between the world as old creation and as new that goes with it. If it does it will fail to note the eschatological difference between 'that which is the case' ('id quod res est') and 'that which is not yet but will be the case' ('id quod futura nondum est') and conflate the world as it is with the world as it should be as God's creation (WA 56, 371, 28-31). Thus we cannot fully understand creation if we abstract protology from soteriology, i.e. from christology and eschatology; and we cannot avoid this abstract approach unless we interpret everything not only *coram deo* but in the differentiating perspectives of Law and Gospel.

The theological programme emerging from Luther's considerations can be summarized as follows:

1   Everything that is can be identified and described in the perspective of its worldly relations (*coram mundo*), including its relations to itself (*coram seipso*), and in the perspective of its relations to God (*coram deo*).

2   To place something in relation to something else requires both terms of the relation to be identified. We know how to identify things that stand in worldly relations (e.g. by reference to their time and place), but we cannot so identify God. Identification-procedures appropriate in the *coram mundo*-perspective do not help us to

determine who he is. We can only identify him by his revelation, i.e. his self-identification in Christ; and as this cannot be appreciated apart from faith, God is unambiguously identified only by faith. Thus whereas reason can identify and describe things in the *coram mundo*-perspective, only faith can identify and describe things in the *coram deo*-perspective.

3   Philosophy construes everything, including God, in the light of the *coram mundo*-perspective because it does not know God apart from the world. Thus philosophical theology argues from the intelligibility of the world to the intelligibility of God; its conceptions of God are designed to explain the intelligibility of the world; and in order to establish the possibility of such perfect intelligibility it conceives God's existence to be necessary. Theology, on the other hand, construes everything, including the world, in the light of the *coram deo*-perspective because it does not know the world apart from God as revealed in Christ. It argues from the mystery of God revealed in Christ to God as the mystery of the world; it construes the world to be the realm of the creative activity of God; and it conceives the existence of the world to be not necessary, but ultimately intelligible only in terms of God's free decision to create and sustain it.

4   The difference between the two perspectives is conceived differently by philosophy and theology. In the *coram mundo*-perspective of philosophy the two perspectives are distinguished by the relations which things can have either to some or all others or to themselves (the world), or which they all can have to something else (God). In the *coram deo*-perspective of theology, on the other hand, they are distinguished by God's creative relations to what is different from him (creator) and by the relations amongst those to which God relates in these ways (creation).

5   The *coram mundo*-perspective is complex and includes relations to oneself (*coram seipso*), relations to some others (*environment*), and relations to all others (the totality of environments or *world*). Reality conceived *coram mundo* is relative to these different sets of relations and can accordingly be identified and described in an irreducible variety of ways.

6   The *coram deo*-perspective is also complex. It includes relations of God to himself (*theologia* in the traditional sense of the doctrine of the *trinity*), and relations of God to others (*oikonomia* in the sense explicated by the doctrines of creation and redemption). These latter relations, which tradition has conceived as communicative activities in terms of the divine word, are irreducibly twofold in mode (*lex* and *evangelium*) and require the *coram deo*-perspective to be distinguished into the perspectives of *Law* and *Gospel*.

7 Everything in the *coram deo*-perspective (including God, worldly events and human existence) is to be placed in the two perspectives of Law and Gospel. They are differentiated, not by the things placed in them but by the dialectics in God's relations to his creation as revealed in Christ and experienced by faith: Law and Gospel are the two fundamental and irreducible modes of divine activity *ad extra*; and to place things in the perspectives of Law and Gospel is to locate and characterize them relative to these modes of divine activity.

8 These two *coram deo*-perspectives are not just different but dialectically related. Because everything is placed in both of them, there exist two descriptions for everything: Law-descriptions of God (*deus absconditus*), world (fallen creation) and human existence (sinner), and Gospel-descriptions of God (*deus revelatus*), world (creation and new creation) and human existence (saved sinner). But these two descriptions are not simply juxtaposed. The Gospel presupposes, consummates and transcends the Law because it not only shows what is but what should and will be the case. Hence the perspective of Gospel is superior to the perspective of Law. It reveals more about God and reality because it is what determines the identity of the common referent of both Law-descriptions and Gospel-descriptions in the sense of bringing us to know who or what this referent truly is.

9 Whereas the *coram mundo/coram deo*-difference can be construed in both philosophical and theological terms, knowledge of the difference between Law and Gospel is based on revelation and faith, and the distinction between the two perspectives is specific to theology.

10 Neither of the two sets of perspectives (*coram mundo/coram deo* and Law/Gospel) is partially or wholly dispensable, mutually exclusive or merely additive. They are grounded in the structure of reality as disclosed by God's revelation in Christ and perceived by faith: the Law/Gospel-perspectives manifest the structure of the reality of God's relations to his creation, the *coram mundo/coram deo*-perspectives the structure of the reality of his creation.

11 Neither of the two sets of perspectives is related by analogy. Everything is identified and described in an irreducible plurality of ways. But to relate a plurality of irreducibly different identifications and descriptions so as to bring out their common point of reference is the characteristic task of dialectics. Hence dialectics takes the place of analogy as the operative principle of theology.

12 Philosophy generates knowledge of the nature of things *coram mundo*; but it is unable to assess its full import because it lacks an

adequate interpretative framework for evaluating what it knows. Theology provides that framework. It explicates a vision of reality given by faith and rooted in the self-manifestation of the ground of reality itself. It starts from the reality of God as revealed in Christ; and it inquires into the nature of things *coram deo* by placing everything we (can) know in the twofold perspective of Law and Gospel. Philosophical knowledge then appears as knowledge of the sinner, falling under the Law. It may be true, but it is not fully intelligible. We are unable to see whether and how it contributes to what is ultimately helpful or harmful for creaturely existence and the perfecting of God's purpose for his creation. To find this out we must valuate it theologically by placing it in the context of the perspective of Gospel and its clarification of the will of God, and thus critically transform it into orientational knowledge. This is the permanent task of theology *vis-à-vis* philosophical knowledge.

Theology which operates according to the programme outlined becomes all-comprehensive: there is no external aspect which it cannot reproduce internally in terms of Law and Gospel. It unfolds a universal perspective defined not by its external contrasts but by the internal distinctions and modes of operation, through which it attempts to integrate the manifold plurality of our external experience of the world into theology.

The obvious danger of this sort of approach is theological totalitarianism or absolutism stemming from uncritical uses of the universal perspective of Faith as an absolute frame of reference. Where differences about this are fought out not by argument but by the use of ecclesiastical and political power, we have the situation of Europe during the wars of religion in the sixteenth and seventeenth centuries. The all-encompassing approach of theology produced conflict because it could not cope with the plurality of ways in which the perspective of Faith can be developed, nor the perspective of Reason reconstructed within it. The consensus between faith and reason which it suggested failed because it was not grounded in a theological consensus about faith. So the whole approach was abandoned by the Enlightenment, which continued the quest for harmony with a different model altogether.

Chapter 8

The Reason-Revelation Model

The Enlightenment reacted to the disastrous results of theological absolutism by rejecting the internal perspectives of faith and theology, and taking the external perspective of reason and history to be the only rationally acceptable universal perspective. Religious and theological claims must be vindicated by reason, not by the zeal of those who hold them; and reasons must conform to standards of reasonableness established independently of religious commitments.

Standards of reasonableness were not new: Aristotle's principles of logic specify formal standards for reasoning in all areas; and all disciplines, including theology, develop material standards germane to their specific subject-matter. What is new in Enlightenment philosophy is the attempt to specify universally valid principles other than those of logic: the epistemological principles of sound knowledge. Only what conforms to the standards of both logic *and* epistemology is knowledge: the universally valid standards of reasonableness comprise not only the canons of formal logic and argument (*reason*) but also the canons of epistemology (*experience*). The valid ways of justifying beliefs include ways of sorting out the veridical from the illusory, the true from the false and the probable from the unlikely. Only those beliefs can lay claim to knowledge which are both *true* and *justified*. They are true if they cannot not be true (necessarily true) or if they correspond to the facts (actually true); and they are justified to a greater or lesser degree if they can be shown to be necessarily true (necessary knowledge) or to conform to the facts (direct knowledge) or to be entailed by what we know to be true (indirect knowledge) or by what we have reason to believe to be true (probable knowledge). In short, what cannot be proved, or made probable, by reason and experience is not knowledge.,

This conception of knowledge fits a variety of philosophical positions depending on the understanding of 'reason' and 'experience'. The Enlightenment fitted it to a foundationalist epistemology, demanding ultimate grounds of certainty. This is the legacy of Descartes. Mathematics, with its self-evident principles and deductive demonstrations, was the paradigm of all knowledge, including metaphysics (the study of first principles) and physics (natural philosophy). This posed the foundationalist problem: our beliefs may or may not be true; and it is for philosophical reasoning to find out if they are true. Now a belief is true if it can validly be derived from true premises. But the transmission of truth from premises to validly derived conclusions must start somewhere: valid derivation cannot establish the truth of our first premises. Moreover, even truth is not enough for knowledge: we must be certain that what we believe is true. Hence we need criteria of certainty, beyond derivability, to establish the truth of our premises. To specify such criteria is the task of epistemology, the ultimate criterion, according to Descartes, being *evidential experience*. We can accept as true what we can grasp clearly and distinctly (*clare et distincte*): that, and only that, is the foundation of our knowledge.

Descartes's rigorous application of this criterion showed two things. First, this quest for certainty leads unavoidably back to the knowing subject and the primacy of first-person knowledge. Second, this egocentric foundation risks undermining itself by collapsing into cognitive solipsism and epistemological absolutism. For clearly first-person evidence is not enough. Competing claims to have evidence, especially in religious matters, have always been a major source of religious dispute. If what is evident to me is to yield knowledge, it must be communicable to and acceptable by others according to agreed criteria. Evidence that is egocentric and person-relative cannot be the basis for knowledge, which is a social product and intrinsically inter-personal. Hence philosophy after Descartes broadens its approach from an egocentric to a reason-centred epistemology. It inquires into the rational foundations of beliefs by specifying standards of reasonableness in terms of a normative conception of *common human reason*.

'Reason' here does not mean the rational faculty of human persons, but criteria of meaning, truth and certainty valid for all of us in all areas of human knowledge. Now beliefs in different areas are held in widely differing ways. Scientific beliefs are (or should be) held as hypotheses, whereas religious beliefs express commitments or affirmations of trust. Yet there are respects in which all these beliefs can be treated alike. Just as the shapes of bodies of all kinds admit of a common geometrical treatment, so beliefs admit of a common philosophical treatment of two aspects: their *propositional content*, which may be tested for its coherence and plausibility; and their *grounds*, which may be tested for their adequacy. To suggest a homogeneous treatment of these aspects of beliefs is the point of the Enlightenment conception of common reason.

This of course presupposes that we can intelligibly abstract those aspects of beliefs. We must be able to concentrate solely on the propositional content and grounds of beliefs and ignore everything else about them. In particular, to assess faith and theology in this way we must be able to restate them from the outside in terms of their propositional contents and grounds for holding them. That is the point of the theories of *revelation* proposed by Enlightenment philosophers and assimilated by theology: they restate the internal perspective of faith as a set of revelation-based beliefs acquired through divine-human communication in natural or supernatural ways. 'Natural revelation' means a set of true beliefs given through our natural intellectual and moral faculties. 'Special' or 'supernatural' revelation means a set of true beliefs given through extraordinary channels, attested by external credentials and internal evidence, and comprising both things not known before and a 'republication' of things already before us but not fully comprehended. The re-description of Christian faith in these terms replaces the authoritative Word of God with revealed 'articles of faith', and the self-verifying activity of the Spirit with infallible Scripture. Christian faith is transformed into a set or system of Christian beliefs; the rationality of Christian faith into the reasonableness of these beliefs; and their justification into the existence of natural and supernatural sources of relevant information and the reliability of human reports about information so received. In short, from its conceptions of *reason* Enlightenment philosophy develops corresponding conceptions of *revelation*. If 'reason' is a summary term for the criteria of reasonable knowledge, 'revelation' is a summary term for the divine sources of religious beliefs. By combining the two conceptions it answers the problem of perspectives in terms of a comprehensive model of *Reason and Revelation*.

Theology soon participated in this perspective, and elaborated it apologetically. It thus had a major share in confusing the model of Reason and Revelation with the model of Nature and Grace. But this is a mistake. The medievals respected reason quite as much as the Enlightenment did. But they stopped short of rationalism by staying within the internal perspective of Faith, and they yoked reason to the service of faith. They knew that the use of reason must be adapted to the requirements of the domain to which it is applied. By contrast, the Enlightenment, assigning priority to the external perspective, subordinated revelation to the demands of a universal reason, and developed canonical forms of knowledge and argument to which beliefs of all sorts had to conform to qualify as knowledge. Different beliefs may need different reasons, but not different standards of reason. Reason is one, and the standard of reasonableness the same in all areas.

However, this did not prevent the age of reason from developing different, and conflicting, conceptions of reason, notably the *rationalist* and the *empiricist* conceptions. Their differences derive partly from the contrast between *informational* and merely *instrumental* ideas of reason and partly from different paradigms of the instrumental use of reason. Rationalists like Descartes, Spinoza and Leibniz conceive reason to be a special source of information giving us access to indubitable and self-evident truths. These truths are innate and common to all human beings; we can gain certain knowledge if we proceed from them to conclusions which they logically entail: this is the standard form of argument in mathematics, the rationalist paradigm of reasonableness. Empiricists like Locke, on the other hand, deny that we have innate ideas. All our knowledge is acquired in experience, and is only processed by reason. Thus the inductive route of empirical science, with its stress on probability, becomes the empiricist paradigm of knowledge. Reason is restricted to its instrumental use as a judge and guide in everything.

These different conceptions of reason go with different conceptions of revelation, and lead to different models of Reason and Revelation. Reason, for Locke, 'is *natural revelation*, whereby the eternal Father ... communicates to mankind that portion of truth which he has laid within the reach of their natural faculties: *revelation* is *natural reason enlarged* by a new set of discoveries communicated by God immediately' (1690, IV.xix). Thus the instrumental account of reason goes with an account of revelation as a special source of information. For the religious rationalist, however, reason is a source of information about God, world and human existence which, in the extreme case, is sufficient as it stands and can dispense with revelation. Lord Herbert of Cherbury, for example, claimed that the existence of God, the obligation to worship him, the necessity of virtue, the need for repentance from sin, and the prospect of rewards and punishments in this life and the life to come are the five fundamental truths known by everyone and sufficient for salvation. Rationalists, accordingly, concentrate on the ontological argument and *a priori* versions of the cosmological argument, and develop a *rational theology* based on the informative principles of reason. Empiricists, on the other hand, concentrate on *a posteriori* versions of the cosmological argument and on the arguments from design, and develop a *natural theology* based on the information derivable from nature by the use of reason. But their differences notwithstanding, they have a number of important aspects in common:

1   Both rational and natural theologies are rooted in the external philosophical perspective on faith; and both are based on general theories of natural and supernatural revelation.

2   Both accept reason as our last judge and guide in everything, not necessarily in the strong sense of showing revelation to be true but at least in the weaker sense of showing it to be truly a revelation from God.

3   Both understand revelation in epistemological terms as a source of information about God, world and human existence which does not go beyond what is or can be known by reason (strict rationalists like Spinoza), or of additional information which may partly go beyond but can never be contrary to reason (empiricists like Locke).

4   Both seek to solve the problems of perspectives in terms of the model of Reason and Revelation. Some understand it as correlating two sets of beliefs, the first (reason) comprising the universally valid kernel of all religion, the second (revelation) additional beliefs peculiar to individual confessions and religions. Others take it to correlate two approaches to the same information: reason is the supreme judge of all knowledge, including religious knowledge, but its competent use is difficult and possible only for the intelligent few; salvation, on the other hand, is for everyone. Therefore God has revealed all the truths necessary for salvation in ways accessible to those to whom they have been addressed. Revelation accommodates the divinely given information about God, world and human existence to the capacities of the uneducated many. But only reason can grasp clearly and distinctly what is of permanent value in what has been received as revelation; and it is the task of rational and natural theologies to work out what this is.

5   Both types of philosophical theology manifest the conception of God known as Enlightenment *theism*. It provides the point of contact between philosophical perspectives on faith and theological perspectives of faith; and it enables (or misleads) theology to adopt the model of Reason and Revelation. Because we have become so used to this model that we tend to identify theism with the kernel of the Christian doctrine of God, this must briefly be elaborated.

Theism, the belief in the existence of a supreme and beneficient being who is the creator and sustainer of the universe, has become the favourite topic of debate amongst philosophers of religion, especially in the Anglo-Saxon traditions. Although sometimes elaborated in complicated ways, it is basically a simple doctrine - whether in its more traditional forms represented today, e.g., by Keith Ward, Richard Swinburne or John Hick, or in its neoclassical forms exemplified by

Charles Hartshorne or John Cobb. In bare outlines it has three main components:

1   It elaborates and defends a concept of God succinctly summarized by Swinburne: By 'God' a theist understands something like a 'person without a body (i.e. a spirit) who is eternal, free, able to do anything, knows everything, is perfectly good, is the proper object of human worship and obedience, the creator and sustainer of the universe' (Swinburne, 1977, p. 1). This concept of God results from two basic motifs of theism. There is the *cosmological motif*, which makes God the ultimate cause and explanation of the world. Thus rational theology explains the intelligibility of the world by appealing to a self-explanatory being 'whose sheer nature explains its existence, as well as the existence of everything else' (Ward, 1982, p. 8). Natural theology similarly seeks to explain order and harmony in the world by appealing to a purposive mind behind it. Then there is the *religious motif*, which takes God to be a personal being worthy of worship, able to act and free to respond to prayers (Brümmer, 1984). Both motifs use models to conceptualize God and his relationship to the world: the models of *Personal Explanation*, in terms of actions and intentions, and of *Mind and Body*; the models of *Mind, Subject* and the *Elusive Self*; the models of *Personal Agency* and the *Personal Communicator*. Both motifs, and the models of God based on them, are usually combined, because theism is thought to be defensible only if it can meet both world-explaining and religious requirements. Consequently the analogy between human persons as finite but free and creative moral agents and God as the Supreme Creative and Beneficient Agent becomes the key element in theistic conceptions of God.

2   The coherence of this concept of God is required for the second major component of theism: its arguments for the existence of God. To show a Supreme Creative and Beneficent Agent to be possible is not enough; there must be good reasons for asserting the existence of such a being. Thus arguments for and against the existence of God have become a major topic of philosophical argument since the Enlightenment. Without reasons for belief in the existence of God, neither nature- nor revelation-based beliefs can be reasonable. Of the numerous rational bases proposed for belief in God, the ontological and cosmological arguments, and the arguments from design, are especially important. They all argue

1   that the concept of God is coherent and the existence of such a supreme being is possible (arguments for the possibility of God);
2   that such a being actually exists either because it absolutely has to (ontological arguments for the necessity of God) or has to, given the

existence and character of the world (cosmological arguments and arguments from design for the actuality of God);

3 that there can only be one such being, because the unity and singularity of the world allows for only one creator and providential lord of nature and history (arguments for the singularity of God).

The three sets of problems of the *possibility*, *necessity* and/or *actuality*, and *singularity* of God are central to theism and have remained at the focus of debates in Anglophone philosophy of religion up to the present. For the question of the possibility of God implies fundamental questions about meaning, the coherence of concepts and the use of words; the question of the necessity and/or actuality of God implies fundamental questions about logic, ontology, cosmology and the character of the world; and the question of the singularity of God implies fundamental questions about the unity and plurality of worlds, the difference between actual and possible worlds, and the identity of individuals in different worlds. Thus theism is a philosophical construction which places the problem of God at the centre of philosophical debate with intimate links to virtually every philosophical topic. Consequently it is particularly sensitive to changes in these areas.

3 The theoretical nature of theism and its dependence on particular views about the nature and character of the world are manifest in its preoccupation with the problem of theodicy. There has always been evil, pain, suffering and injustice in the world; they have been a major driving force in the formation of religious convictions. In religious rather than philosophical contexts they have usually inspired belief and trust in God, deepened our understanding of him and generated hope for a better reality to come. For theism, however, they constitute a fundamental threat and insurmountable stumbling-block, because they lead us to question the nature and reality of God rather than the nature and reality of the world. In Epicurus' old questions rephrased by Hume: 'Is God willing to prevent evil, but not able? Then he is impotent. Is he able, but not willing? Then he is malevolent. Is he both able and willing? Whence then is evil?' (1779, pt X). Posed in this way the problem of evil is transformed into a problem of the logical compatibility of certain beliefs about God and the world, i.e. the beliefs that

1 God exists;
2 God is omnipotent;
3 God is omniscient;
4 God is wholly good;
5 There exists evil in the world.

This is a theoretical problem (cf. Dalferth, 1981, pp. 538ff), and it has a number of theoretical solutions. If we drop (1) or (5) the problem does not arise; if we give up the idea of infinity in (2) to (4) the problem disappears. Less radical solutions attempt to reject the alleged incompatibility in various ways. It may be argued - e.g. by Plantinga (1965; 1967, chs 5 and 6; 1974, ch. 9; 1975) - that beliefs (1) to (4) do not entail that God does not create, or has no reason to create, beings who perform evil deeds; that the existence of some evil is necessary for the existence of certain sorts of values and second-order goods; that the existence of morally free agents necessarily entails the possibility of moral evil ('Free Will Defence'); or that an infinite number of actions and interactions both between agents in the world and between wordly agents and God necessarily produce effects beyond the control of any individual agent, including God (Hartshorne).

None of these solutions is uncontested; but the theoretical way the problem is posed leaves all the suggested solutions with a ring of practical insignificance: even if belief in God in the face of evil and suffering could be made plausible, it would still not tell the believer how to cope with it, or how to establish the truth of (1) to (4). The alleged incompatibility of (1) to (5) only matters if they are all true; which is not at all obvious in the case of (1) to (4). All theoretical reflection can hope to show is 'that no amount of evil will contradict the existence of a perfect God, as long as the requirement is met, that it is necessarily implied in the existence of a world which leads to overwhelming good' (Ward, 1982, pp. 206-7). But how can this be supported by our actual experience of the world? The world gives little or no reason to suppose that it leads to overwhelming good. Similarly, if we had reason to believe in the existence, power, wisdom and goodness of God, we could agree with Leibniz that this is compatible with the evil and suffering in the world. But Hume has shown that we have little or no reason to infer these beliefs from our ambiguous experiences of the world; and Kant has shown that (1) to (4) are not the sort of beliefs whose truth could even in principle be established by theoretical reason.

So theism faces a dilemma. The compatibility of belief in God with our experience of the world is not enough to justify belief in God: we need independent arguments for this belief. But the arguments of rational and natural theology for the existence of God do not stand up to examination. The *a posteriori* arguments of natural theology from the actual world to God cannot justify asserting the perfect existence, power, wisdom and goodness of God in the face of evil, pain and suffering. Thus the argument of design, based on our experience of order and disorder in our world, participates in its ambiguity; and the cosmological argument cannot justify the assumed intelligibility of the world independently of its inference to a self-explanatory being who makes it intelligible. The *a priori* arguments of rational theology, which conceive God to be either impossible or necessary, either cannot justify the premiss (1) 'It is possible that God exists' rather than (2) 'It is possible that God does not exist' and thus can no more prove the necessary existence of God than it can prove his necessary non-existence, or must rely on *a posteriori* arguments for (1) rather than (2) which - because all the evidence available is as compatible with (2) as with (1) - only manifest a question-begging religious perspective on the world. In short, without convincing arguments for the existence of God the theoretical enterprise of theism fails. Natural theology breaks down because, given the facts of evil, it cannot prove that our world is intelligible in a way that unambiguously points to God; and rational theology breaks down because it cannot make plausible why God should necessarily exist rather than necessarily not exist.

Theism stands or falls with its arguments for the existence of God. The importance of these arguments follows from its external reformulation of the Christian faith in terms of beliefs acquired through and justified by reason and revelation. But are the beliefs examined in the external perspective of philosophy justified in claiming to be about the same as the internal views of faith? Theism insists that it conceptualizes the very God addressed in faith and reflected upon in theology, and that this is borne out both by its concept of God as a perfect personal being and by its arguments for the existence of this God. For both faith and theology talk to and about God in particular ways, and both presuppose him to exist. But then the theistic reformulation cannot restrict its conceptualization to the semantical dimension of the understanding of 'God' which emerges from faith and theology. It must also take into account that they presuppose God to exist; and this is the function of its arguments for the existence of God. Thus just as its concept of God conceptualizes (part of) the semantics of the Christian use of 'God', so its arguments for the existence of God conceptualize (part of) its pragmatics. But it fails in both respects. 'God has now become "a personal being" where before God was absolute Being (not *a* being) in three persons (not *a* person)' (Jennings, 1985, p. 19); and belief in his existence has now become a separate topic of discussion where before it was the inseparable presupposition of the Christian doctrine of God and all other doctrines. No Christian doctrine is (or should be) without foundation in experience. But this is not to say that each doctrine by itself reflects a separate kind of experience. Only the whole system of doctrines together expresses the Christian experience of reality. The theistic concentration upon God and his existence in isolation is bound to distort the integrating view of faith; and to conceptualize beliefs about God irrespective of their wider experiential and doctrinal contexts can only result in misconceptions.

This is borne out by the theistic arguments for the existence of God, which represent, under misleading disguises, isolated aspects of the internal views of faith, but distort the overall picture. For example, the ontological argument represents the Christian experience of the reality, singularity and unsurpassable sovereignty of God in terms of ontological necessity; but it breaks down (amongst other things) because it fails to provide adequate means for determining God's identity in the sense of bringing us to know who God is (cf. Hintikka, 1986). The cosmological argument represents the Christian experience of total dependence on the sovereign will of God as the metaphysical dependence of the contingent on the necessary, and breaks down because it confuses different understandings of contingency (Mackie, 1982, p. 84). And the argument from design represents the Christian experience of the caring guidance of God as an underlying purposive order of nature and history, and breaks down because all this can be explained without reference to God (Dalferth, 1981, pp. 532ff). In short, theism breaks down because it begins with abstractions and ends by committing what Whitehead has called the 'fallacy of misplaced concreteness'.

This is true of the whole Enlightenment approach. It fails because it is too abstract, and defines reasonableness solely in the external perspective. But by insisting on the model of Reason and Revelation as an absolute frame of reference, and on the external perspective of reason as the sole perspective appropriate in matters of truth and certainty, it commits the same absolutist mistake against which it originally reacted. Commitment to the internal perspective of Faith becomes irrelevant or is considered to be a hindrance to the quest for truth and certainty; accordingly theology is faced with the choice of either justifying its claims philosophically or being assigned to the realm of the irrational. Naturally many theologians have opted for the first way out and sought to demonstrate the rationality of theology by accommodating its internal perspective on apologetic grounds to the model of Reason and Revelation. But this was a mistake. They should have rejected the whole dilemma presented by the absolutist distortion of the external perspective. Faith allows for more than one perspective on it; and there exists more than one form of reasonableness.

Chapter 9

The Difference-in-Unity Model

The deadlock between an all-comprehensive theological model, of Law and Gospel, and an equally all-comprehensive philosophical model, of Reason and Revelation, was only broken when, towards the end of the eighteenth century, enlightened absolutism was replaced by democratic liberalism not only in the world of action but also in the world of ideas. People learned to distinguish between *universal* and *absolute* claims and began to realize not only the possibility but the rightness and fruitfulness of many universal perspectives on the same thing, none of which has the privileged status of an absolute perspective. Theology thus came to see the essential reciprocity of internal and external perspectives on the Christian faith; and responded by co-ordinating internal (theological) and external (philosophical) points of view in handling the external perspective. The conceptual machinery for this twofold approach in terms of the difference-in-unity of philosophical and theological perspectives on the Christian faith was provided by Schleiermacher's combination of a theory of human religiosity, a sociological theory of the genesis and structure of religious communities, and a doctrinal exposition of the Christian faith. The upshot of this was that theology conceived the Christian faith to be both one religion amongst others and a comprehensive view of reality as a whole. External and internal perspectives were combined by integrating two universal perspectives (not merely particular and partial perspectives as in the Nature-Grace Model) in a uniform consciousness of truth which united the concern for religion and the scientific spirit of the age. This *Difference-in-Unity Model* dominated neo-Protestant theology throughout the nineteenth century and beyond, and merits a fuller analysis.

Theology reacted to the emergence of the model of Reason and Revelation in Enlightenment philosophy in three different ways. The *orthodox reaction* was to cut itself off from the new spirit of the Enlightenment. It insisted dogmatically on the absoluteness of the internal perspective of Faith, and its all-comprehensive view of reality developed in terms of the Law-Gospel Model. And it denied any theological relevance to the external philosophical perspectives on faith.

The neologist or *rationalist reaction* was to compromise with the spirit of the age. It took over the model of Reason and Revelation, and reformulated the Christian faith in terms of beliefs that could be sustained on the basis of reason, experience and history. Reason required belief in God to be justified in terms of natural reason and religious experience, not scripture and church doctrine; and Revelation required the study of the documents of the Christian faith in a historical and not a doctrinal spirit. This ironing out of the differences between the perspectives of Faith and Reason prompted a dissolution of theological reflection into either philosophical speculation or historical study which remains an endemic danger in modern theology.

The *supranaturalist reaction* emphasized the other side of the rationalist position, i.e. the suprarational strand of the external perspective of Enlightenment Reason on faith. It also accepted the Reason-Revelation Model. But it confined itself to the additional truths claimed to have been received through revelation and to be not contrary to but above reason. It abandoned the whole idea of epistemic justification, replaced it by the commitment to a suprarational revelation, and rested theology exclusively on what in the external perspective was termed 'special revelation'. That is to say, it did not return to an elaboration of the internal perspective of Faith, but based theology misleadingly on only one strand of the external perspective of Reason. The resulting position was only superficially similar to the Nature-Grace Model. It lacked that model's solution to the problem of perspectives, because it lacked the idea that grace perfects nature, and so left the two realms virtually unrelated. Instead of integrating the perspectives of Reason and of Faith from within, it simply replaced the difference between the internal perspective of Faith and the external perspective of Reason by the distinction of a rational and a suprarational component in the perspective of Reason. This only accelerated the growing separation of the realm of theology from that of science and philosophy in the nineteenth century and beyond.

It was Schleiermacher (Neuenschwandner, 1977, pp. 228ff; Williams, 1978; Christian, 1979; Wagner, 1986, pp. 59ff) who overcame both the orthodox denial of the theological relevance of the external perspective of Reason and the rationalist and suprarationalist dissolutions of the internal perspective of Faith. Against rationalist and suprarationalist theology he insisted that Christian theology must be developed from the standpoint of Faith; against orthodox theology, that the external perspective of Reason is the necessary correlate of the internal perspective of Faith. He therefore proposed to integrate the internal and external perspectives on faith in terms of the difference-in-unity of two universal perspectives on the same thing by co-ordinating theological and philosophical descriptions of matters of faith and matters of reason in a carefully balanced way. Although irreducibly different because of their different starting-points and contexts of plausibility, theology and philosophy perfectly correspond to each other.

Schleiermacher undertook to show this in an approach with basically three components. First he develops the external perspective of Reason as a general *theory of religion*, with the Christian faith as one case amongst others. Next he elaborates the internal perspective of Faith in a comprehensive *doctrinal exposition of the Christian faith* which bases the Christian view of God, the world and human existence on the fundamental difference between sin and grace. Finally he tries to show that both perspectives refer to the same thing by grounding their common reference to God, the world and human existence in a *theory of human piety* developed as a specific component of a fundamental philosophical *theory of immediate self-consciousness or feeling*. Thus Christianity offers a comprehensive view of reality (internal theological perspective), while also being one historical religion amongst others (external empirical perspective). And every religion manifests a human capacity for religion (piety) grounded in a fundamental anthropological structure (feeling), a capacity to become aware of the ultimate givenness of all existence (philosophical perspective worked out in terms of a transcendental anthropology and ontology). 'Religion', then, describes contingent historical phenomena; 'piety' marks an essential capacity of human existence which all religions manifest; 'Christian faith' is a particular manifestation of this capacity under the impact of Jesus Christ. The capacity for religion is an essential anthropological feature because it is a specific determination of 'feeling' which together with 'knowing' and 'doing' forms the fundamental structure of human life. Feeling in this sense consists in a pre-reflective and pre-active awareness of our interdependence with the world to which we relate in knowing and doing. The particular determination of feeling *piety* is the 'feeling of utter dependence', i.e. the awareness that we exist in inter-dependence with the world only because we exist in dependence on God, the ground of our existence and of everything else, and that our dependence on him differs from all our worldly relations by constituting us rather than being constituted by us. This, in a nut-shell, is his argument. Let us look at it in more detail.

Theory of religion   In the external perspective the Christian faith is one religion amongst others. It is a living religion which may be described empirically in various ways. Sociologically it is a religious community which has characteristic institutions, ways of behaving and forms of believing, just as have other institutionalized forms of life, like the state or the scientific community. Historically it is a religious community or group of communities whose origins and developments can be traced in the wider historical context. In terms of comparative religion (or, as Schleiermacher uses the term, philosophy of religion) it is a particular type of faith, namely 'a monotheistic faith, belonging to the teleological type of religion' which 'is essentially distinguished from other such faiths by the fact that everything in it is related to the redemption accomplished by Jesus of Nazareth' (1830a, §11, p. 52).

This external empirical approach to the Christian faith, however, leaves two fundamental problems unsolved, viz. the problems of the *individuality* and of the *irreducibility* of faith.

Doctrinal exposition   Empirical description is unable to grasp the individuality of the Christian faith. It can only classify it as a particular example of a specific type of faith. But particularity is not individuality, and an individual person or community is more than one particular amongst others. Individuality - here Schleiermacher echoes a fundamental conviction of the Romantic movement - cannot be grasped by particularizing descriptions from the outside. It is the way persons or groups of persons continually constitute and reconstitute themselves through their actions, and conceive themselves in self-understanding and reflection. The individuality of the Christian faith goes beyond its being a particular religion: it depends also on its self-understanding and its internal perspective on itself and everything else.

Expounding this self-understanding is what Schleiermacher tries to do in his masterly work *The Christian Faith*, two aspects of which are especially worth noting. First, spelling out the dynamic individuality of the Christian faith means clearly distinguishing the living faith or piety of the Christian community from its doctrinal expressions. 'Doctrines are not propositions one has to believe on pain of eternal damnation; together with outward actions, they are ways in which the religious community externalizes the piety by which it lives. Hence there can be no final, permanently binding doctrinal formulas. On the contrary, it must always be the duty of the church to test the adequacy of its doctrines to its inner life' (Gerrish, 1984, p. 24). This is the task of theology, which unfolds the inner perspective of Faith by critical and persistent reflection upon piety as lived in a particular Christian community. The intuitive piety of a community of faith is the primary given; reflective belief secondary and dependent on it; and theology is a 'positive science' precisely because it starts from the living piety of a particular community of faith, upon which it reflects critically and systematically in order to enable this community or church to perfect its way of believing and way of behaving.

Second, then, theology is not faith but the secondary reflective elucidation of the primary expressions of faith from within. Now there 'is no other way of participating in the Christian community than through faith in Jesus as the Redeemer'. Hence everything in Christian theology and its doctrinal exposition of faith hinges upon a clear grasp of the redemption of mankind in Christ: christology is the centre of Christian theology; it is to be developed from the living experience of redemption as it originated with Jesus Christ and is mediated in the historical continuity of the Christian community; and it provides the key to a comprehensive Christian view of the whole of reality. Only a theology which is both centred on christology and all-comprehensive in scope will be true to the individuality of faith. Accordingly, Schleiermacher appropriates the Law-Gospel Model of Reformation theology by constructing his dogmatics around the antithesis of *sin* and *grace*, i.e. the human need for redemption and its actual achievement in Jesus Christ. No proposition about God, world or human existence in Christian dogmatics will be true to the living experience of faith in the Christian community unless it is grounded in christological reflection and qualified in the light of the fundamental antithesis of sin and grace.

Theory of piety   This systematic unfolding of the internal perspective of the Christian community may help to bring out the individuality of the Christian faith; but it does not thereby show that faith to be either irreducible or valid: Christian piety, belief and theological reflection may ultimately rest on confusion and illusion. Christianity would then still be an empirical phenomenon open to historical and sociological description; and it would still allow for an internal elucidation of its views. But these would fail to contribute to our knowledge of reality, and they would be barren with respect to truth.

Schleiermacher tries to exclude this possibility by arguing for the anthropological necessity of piety and its manifestation in religious communities. Particular faiths may be confused and particular communities misguided, but unless faith and the existence of religious communities as such are essential to human existence, we have no reason to prefer belief in God to atheism (1830b, §22). It is clear from the way the problem is posed that it must be solved both in the internal perspective of Faith and in the external perspective of Reason. For what is essential to human existence must somehow be present in Faith and in Reason. Hence the analysis may start from either perspective, for philosophical and theological reflection on its anthropological and ontological presuppositions must in the end yield the same result.

In theology - to take the approach which Schleiermacher has worked out in detail in *The Christian Faith* - everything is brought into relationship with the redemption accomplished by Jesus of Nazareth. But whereas there 'can be no relation to Christ in which there is not also a relation to God', the converse does not hold. Awareness of the relation to God is not restricted to the Christian faith but open in principle to all, simply in virtue of being human. For whatever exists is constituted by the relation to God, i.e. can relate to other beings in acting, interacting and being acted upon only because it is related to God. But we differ from other beings in that we can be aware that we are constituted by God or, as Schleiermacher puts it, absolutely depend on God. We not only exist in interdependence with other life; we are capable of becoming aware that this interdependence is not constituted by us or anything else with which we can interact but that we and everything else depend on something with which we cannot interact: God. For to exist is to be related to God and to interact with other beings which are related to God; the totality of reciprocal interaction, interdependence and mutual influencing and being influenced is the world; God differs from the world because whereas everything depends on him, he depends on nothing; so that we cannot interact with him, although we could not interact without him. He is the ground, not the totality, of reality; and we are those beings in reality who are capable of becoming aware of our being grounded in God.

It is the capacity for awareness of this foundational relation to God that Schleiermacher extrapolated from every Christian to every human consciousness. Not that we are all aware of God: to be aware of the relation to God is not to be aware of God but of our utter dependence on something which is in no way dependent on us or on anything with which we interact (the 'Whence' of our absolute dependence). Awareness of God is reflective awareness, the result of reflection on our feeling of absolute dependence; this feeling itself is a pre-reflective awareness which underlies all our knowing and doing, manifests itself in religious life and provides it with a basis that is irreducible to knowledge or morality. Thus although not everyone is reflectively aware of God, there is a pre-reflective awareness of being utterly dependent in all of us; and whereas reflective conceptions or symbolisations of God differ, this latter awareness fixes the common reference of all uses of 'God' because - as Schleiermacher claims - 'to be conscious of ourselves as utterly dependent' amounts to the same as 'to be conscious of ourselves in relation with God' (1830a, §4). According to him, therefore, the human consciousness necessarily involves the three irreducible factors, components or poles, 'world', 'self' and 'God', as can be shown by philosophical analysis. The main points are as follows:

1   Consciousness of the *world* results from our cognitive and non-cognitive interactions with our natural and social environments. *To live* is to interact with our environments in experience and action, to acquire, and to process, conscious and unconscious beliefs about our surroundings through intuition (*Anschauung*) and reflection (*Denken*), and to consider possible courses of action in the light of the beliefs we have acquired and the aims we want to achieve (*Wollen*). We cannot live without a *world-view* (*Weltanschauung*), a unifying and coherent bundle of perspectives on our natural environments (which form the basis of *physics* or the philosophy of nature) and on our social and historical environments (which form the basis of *ethics* or the philosophy of history). *Our world* is the totality of environments with which we interact, or can interact, from our particular place and perspective during the period of our life. And *the world* is the totality of reciprocal interaction from all places and at all times and as such the realm of all possible experience and action.

2   The *self* is (at the most general level) the necessary correlate of the world. Every world-consciousness is to be ascribed to a particular point of view which integrates a bundle of perspectives on its natural and social environments to a unifying and coherent view of the world (at a given time) or view of life (throughout a period of time). Thus every world-consciousness is relative to a particular self which interacts with the world from a certain place (the common anchorage of its perspectives) and during a given period of time (its life). As the totality of environments throughout the period of my life is my world, so the specific point of reference of all those environments throughout that period is my self: it is the centre of my cognitive and active orientation in the world throughout my life.

The self becomes self-conscious by reflecting on its particular place and perspectives, its cognitive and non-cognitive interactions with its environments, and its deliberations of possible courses of action. But this 'reflective self-consciousness' or 'I', as Schleiermacher puts it, which is characteristic of subjectivity is only a secondary and derived form of self-consciousness. It is itself grounded in something more fundamental: the 'immediate self-consciousness' (*unmittelbares Selbstbewußtsein*) or 'feeling' (*Gefühl*). This is the subjectivity-free and pre-reflective form of self-consciousness common to all of us in which the world is directly present to and accepted by the self. Whereas reflective self-consciousness emerges in the course of our interactions with others, immediate self-consciousness is not constituted, but presupposed by this process. It is the fundamental anthropological structure of contrast and correlation between self and world that underlies all knowing and doing and constitutes persons as centres of cognitive and active orientation in the world.

3 *God*-consciousness is a necessary ingredient of self-consciousness; not, however, of the reflective consciousness of the world or the self which differs from person to person and from one state of a person to another, but of the immediate self-consciousness which is common to every self in all its states in the world. Now the immediate self-consciousness is not given as such but only accessible in and through the concrete forms of self-consciousness and world-consciousness, and the same is true of the God-consciousness and its various manifestations in private and social forms of religion. But just as self-consciousness cannot be reduced to reflective self-consciousness, so God-consciousness is not a function of the various concrete forms in which it becomes accessible to us. It is a foundational structure of human existence that underlies all its concrete historical instantiations. But it is a real and not merely a transcendental structure in Kant's sense; it is real because it implies that its object, God, exists somehow and that we exist only because and insofar as we are related to God. God-consciousness is the pre-reflective awareness that it is impossible that we and our world exist and God does not exist, because to exist is to be related to God and to interact with the world.

More exactly, we have to distinguish two features in the term 'God-consciousness', a specifically determined *consciousness of God* and an underlying indeterminate structure of *god-consciousness* which is never without some particular concrete instantiation. The first requires a specific idea of *God* whose contingent content is a function of the material used to represent God symbolically and, accordingly, differs considerably between persons, groups and religions. For example, whereas in Judaism God is symbolized as commanding will which is recognized in the law (Schleiermacher, 1830a, §9.2), the Christian faith represents God as redemptive love which is recognized in Christ. But although they differ in their concrete representations of God, they agree in the common generic god-structure which they actualize differently. The second feature, therefore, is the non-contingent structure of *god-consciousness* which is the prereflective capacity, common to all rational beings, for awareness of an existential relation to that to which we owe our existence whereas it owes its existence neither to us nor to anything else. This, in its most elemental form, is the 'feeling of absolute dependence' which underlies and grounds our self-consciousness as well as our world-consciousness. Accordingly, in its most elemental sense the term 'god' is not a concept but 'signifies for us simply that which is the codeterminant in this feeling and that to which we refer our being in such a state' (1830a, §4.4). It is not something given directly in our experience of the world or of ourselves but only indirectly with our self-consciousness as the Whence of our utter dependence: it is that to which the totality of reciprocal interaction from all places and at all times is related. Independently of this relation it can neither be identified nor intuited nor conceptualized: it is not a possible object of knowledge but the ultimate presupposition of all knowing, being and acting. As such, it is not inferred from beliefs about the world or ourselves but immediately apprehended in the feeling of utter dependence; it can only be expressed in symbolic images and imaginative constructions which symbolize not merely God but the God-determination of our self-consciousness, i.e. our differing apprehensions of god and our interpretations of this apprehension; all attempts to conceptualize God must be relative to those first-order symbolic expressions; but both our God-symbols and our second-order God-concepts will only be adequate if they correspond to the fundamental structure of our common god-consciousness, i.e. if they construe God as the Whence of utter dependence.

It follows that whereas the various symbolic expressions of our consciousness of God are a function of our different states and stages of knowledge and belief and their corresponding symbolizations of God, our common god-consciousness can neither be derived from our knowledge or intellectual beliefs about the world (as the metaphysical tradition tried to do), nor from our knowledge of ourselves (as the idealist philosophy of subjectivity attempted to show), nor from our moral behaviour and its postulates (as Kant had argued). Rather it is an independent, irreducible and foundational element of human consciousness as such on which all piety and religion rests and which marks man as *homo religiosus*, as a being essentially open for religion because he alone amongst all beings can be aware of being constituted by God. That is to say, our god-consciousness is grounded neither in cognitive belief (*Wissen*) nor in moral behaviour (*Tun*) but in feeling (*Gefühl*), the feeling of utter dependence. And this feeling is neither a basic belief nor a practical postulate but something underlying both: the awareness of our ground of existence without which we would neither be, nor be able to know, nor be capable of acting.

Schleiermacher's account of feeling has been accused of being subjectivist either in the sense of reducing feeling to emotions or an emotive mode of consciousness or in the sense of the philosophy of subjectivity, its psychology of human faculties and transcendental ego. But for him feeling is neither a confused form of cognition (as Leibniz thought) nor a mere awareness of the structures of subjectivity (as Kant argued). It is a direct apprehension, different from both knowing and doing, of the fundamental structure of human existence: we, who have created neither ourselves nor our world, live, on the one hand, in reciprocal interdependence with the world and, on the other, in utter dependence on something which in no way is dependent on us or on our world. Schleiermacher describes this as an ultimate fact of existence of which we can become aware if we pay attention to the structure and determinations of our immediate self-consciousness. He does not offer discursive arguments for it in the sense of natural theology and its cosmological arguments for the existence of God. Reflective operations like this are necessarily secondary; they presuppose a concept of God which they attempt to show to be coherent and instantiated; and they are unable to ground religion. Therefore Schleiermacher rejects the approach of natural theology as irrelevant and beside the point. Not the reflective abstractions of natural theology but the concrete forms of positive religions are what count. They have to be analysed philosophically. For the empirical fact of religion points to the anthropological fact of piety and this to the ultimate ontological structure of our existence not only in relation with others but in relation with god, the Whence of all existence. Accordingly, empirical descriptions of religions can be grounded in a phenomenological description of religion which reveals the fundamental ontological structure of existence. The first present that which is contingent and specific in a given religion, the second that which is necessary and generic in all religions; and even if the modifications of the immediate self-consciousness which manifest themselves in a given historical religion should have to be explained as imaginative fictions and errors, as Schleiermacher points out, they would still manifest the fundamental human capacity and tendency to relate to the transcendent ground of existence (1942, p. 292). For whereas it is contingent fact how we conceive of the God to whom we are related, it is necessary fact that we are related to god at all.

It may be objected to this account of feeling that it is wrong to infer from the fact of our utter dependence that there is something on which we are all dependent or, if this is granted, that it is one and the same x on which we are dependent. This is true, and Feuerbach's critique of religion as the projection of the perfections of human nature into an imaginary being should not be dismissed out of hand. But Schleiermacher does not infer God from our utter dependence, and what may be true of a given concept of God need not to be true of god-consciousness as such. 'The feeling of utter dependence,' as Robert R. Williams has rightly remarked, 'is not an inference of the existence of something absent, but rather a discovery of a presence, a codetermination' (1978, p. 37). We discover that we coexist with one another only because we coexist with this Whence of our existence which is distinct both from us and from the world with which we interact; we do not infer its existence from any fact about the world or ourselves; rather we apprehend it as the necessary correlate of our own existence by becoming aware of our utter dependence.

Still, even if we take this apprehension to be a mode of discovery and not of inference, it is not obvious that we are all utterly dependent *on the same* source of dependence. The trouble with Schleiermacher's overall argument is not the existence of something on which we depend but that it is the same x on which each of us depends. Its existence is a self-evident implication of the discovery that we owe our existence in the world to something which owes its existence neither to us nor to the world. Therefore Schleiermacher is right in rejecting all inferential proofs of the existence of God because they present the self-evident correlate of our existence in the problematic form of reflective argument from premises to conclusions: awareness of the existence of the Whence of our utter dependence is prior to all argument; it is the presupposition, not the conclusion of discursive reflection. The problem with his approach is the *identity* of this Whence of our existence in different cases. For it is one thing not to be constituted by ourselves; another to be constituted by something else; yet another to be all constituted by the same x; and again something else to be constituted by God as understood in the Christian faith. Even if we grant that Schleiermacher has succeeded in showing the feeling of utter dependence on god and the pre-reflective awareness that we are constituted by something utterly different from us to be an essential element of human self-consciousness, it does not follow, at least not without further argument, that he has shown the necessity of God or of our common dependence on one and the same God. That we could not exist without god does not imply that the god without whom we cannot exist is God or that it is the same god for all of us.

For Schleiermacher it was obvious that if 'we are conscious of ourselves as utterly dependent . . . we are conscious of ourselves in relation with God'. For although symbols and concepts of God differ considerably in a religion and between religions, the relation with god, which is the organizing principle of all symbols and concepts of God, is the same in all cases. For the feeling of utter dependence is not a matter of human striving after God (as Schleiermacher is often erroneously interpreted) but of the divine constitution of human existence which precedes all human striving. However, the criterion of identity for 'god' which Schleiermacher offers is an abstract anthropological structure differently actualized from person to person. But even if we all exist in relation with some god, we need not for this reason exist in relation with the same god. Moreover, Schleiermacher not only concludes without warrant that the Whences of existential dependence in different cases are identical, he also identifies it with the God of the Christian faith. But this identification carries conviction only because Schleiermacher, even in his phenomenological theory of piety, argues as a theologian in the context of plausibility of the internal perspective of Faith. In this context, which presupposes the existence, oneness and creativity of God, it is a plausible move to identify the Whence of utter dependence with God the Creator, and to argue from the singularity of this God in the Christian God-consciousness to the identity of the Whence of the feeling of utter dependence in all of us. But this is much less plausible in the external perspective of Reason with its different contexts of plausibility and competing variety of concepts of deity. Here we need not only criteria which fix the reference of 'god' in terms of a fundamental anthropological structure but criteria which allow us to establish the identity of the ground of existence referred to in different instantiations of this structure. Without further argument we are not justified in claiming that the codeterminant of utter dependence is one and the same god in all cases. But what sort of argument would ground such a claim? This identity-claim is not an empirical hypothesis, so it cannot be established in terms of evidence and probability. But neither can it be established by a phenomenological analysis of feeling. Similarity in the structure of human self-consciousness is not enough to establish the identity of the codeterminant of this consciousness. Schleiermacher, therefore, posits the identity in terms of a rule of identification which states that awareness of utter dependence amounts to the same as awareness of God. However, if this is to be more than a mere (and problematic) piece of linguistic legislation, the rule needs to be justified. And this is possible only from *within* a given religion, because only here can it be established whether and in what way its use of 'God' matches the structure of god-consciousness and can be interpreted to be a concrete actualization and specific determination of the generic god-consciousness. Similarly, only within the perspective of Faith will it be possible to show whether and in what sense Schleiermacher's description of the Whence of utter dependence fixes the reference of the Christian use of 'God'. Thus in the end we are forced back from the phenomenological analysis of the general consciousness of utter dependence to the specific God-consciousness of a particular religion like Christianity which knows 'no general God-consciousness without a relation to Christ, and no relation to Christ without a copositing of the general God-consciousness' (1830a, §62.3). But then Schleiermacher's attempt to integrate the internal and external perspectives on the Christian faith in a uniform consciousness of truth carries conviction only to those sharing his standpoint within the Christian faith. The more his theory of piety became divorced from this point of view and its relation with a doctrinal exposition of the Christian faith and was understood to provide the foundation of an independent study of religions, the more his delicate balance of the two perspectives was destroyed.

Chapter 10

The Unity-in-Difference Model

The synthesis of internal and external perspectives, of the Christian view of the world and the world's view of Christianity and everything else which Schleiermacher had inaugurated, gave way to an antithesis when the eschatological nature of the original Christian faith was rediscovered. At the beginning of the nineteenth century Schleiermacher felt unable to assign to the doctrine of the Last Things the same significance as to the other doctrines of the Christian faith (1830a, §159). Towards the end of the century Overbeck pronounced a Christianity unable to make sense of 'the idea of the return of Christ' to be living 'with a corpse' (1963, p. 68). This sceptical patristic scholar acutely criticized modern Christianity and its attempts to harmonize Christian faith and modern culture as being totally incompatible with the original Christian faith. In the light of Christ's resurrection, which they regarded as the beginning and the promise of a general resurrection, the first Christians expected the present world-order to be doomed to imminent annihilation and sharply contrasted the old reality and the new, the coming kingdom of God. Overbeck saw no way of overcoming this incompatibility in that either we remain Christian and thus must shut ourselves off from the modern world, or on the other hand we live in this world and so cannot remain Christian. For him a synthesis between the internal perspective of Faith and the external perspective of Reason and culture was possible only at the price of a flat contradiction between the essentially eschatology-orientated faith of the first Christians and the emasculated and watered-down faith of the present-day church which, to his mind, had gone culturally native. Relentlessly he put his finger on the dilemma of modern theology: the eschatological nature of true Christian faith excludes any theological synthesis of faith and the world while the modern consciousness of truth excludes any fideist retreat to the safe shores of the internal perspective of Faith alone. Thus Christian theology is faced with an option between two unacceptable alternatives:

either it is true to the nature of the Christian faith, in which case it is incompatible with our modern understanding of reality and truth; or it insists on a synthesis of Christian faith and scientific truth, so that it is incompatible with the eschatological essence of the Christian faith.

Karl Barth agreed with Overbeck's diagnosis but not with the dilemma which he derived from it. He reacted to the breakdown of the neo-Protestant synthesis between the internal perspective of Faith and the external perspective of Reason by transforming Overbeck's external dilemma between 'Christianity and Culture' into an internal dilemma within theology itself by insisting that, as theologians, we have to speak of God, while as sinners we are unable to speak of him. Hence theology has to face a paradoxical situation of our having to do what we cannot do. Theology has to think this through if it wants to come to grips with the problem of perspectives. Barth's own solution was worked out in a *Unity-in-Difference Model* which, on the one hand, was developed from within the perspective of Faith and contrasted with the perspective of Reason but, on the other, reconstructed the difference between the internal and external perspectives as a theological difference within the internal perspective of Faith. In many respects this model is the theological counterpart to Hegel's Unity-in-Difference Model, which was developed from the external perspective of Reason and attempted to reconstruct the difference between the perspectives of Faith and Reason in terms of the dynamic difference between *Vorstellung* and *Begriff* within the external perspective of Reason (cf. Clark, 1971). But whereas Hegel sought to incorporate Faith into Reason, Barth sought to incorporate Reason into Faith. To understand his approach, therefore, we have first to consider his peculiar starting-point within the perspective of Faith before we analyse the structure of his Unity-in-Difference Model more closely.

I

That 'Christianity which is not entirely and completely eschatology ... is entirely and completely contrary to Christ' (1922, p. 298) Barth accepted from Overbeck (Jüngel, 1982, p. 71). But on the other hand he had learned from Kutter, Beck and - above all - from the two Blumhardts (Spiekermann, 1985, pp. 82-108), that it is possible to be true to the eschatological nature of the Christian faith without leaving or ignoring this world. 'Jesus is victor' - this motto of the Blumhardts he accepted to be the starting-point and guiding principle of all Christian existence and theology. Accordingly, the reality with which theology must deal is 'the reality of the risen and living Jesus himself, acting and speaking as a distinctive factor no less actual today than yesterday' (1979, p. 448). It is the reality of the resurrection in which the eschatological kingdom of God became manifest and which, in the proclamation of the Gospel, continually represents itself by the power of the Spirit. To state this clearly and to work out its implications was the main concern of Barth throughout his life, as is shown by a number of characteristic features of his theology. To mention but two:

1   It follows from this that theology refers not to a reality past but a reality present - present, however, neither in the sense of a historical past remembered by us nor in the sense of a permanent presence of timeless eternity. Rather it is the personal presence of the risen Christ, the revelation of God's love towards us; Christ freely makes himself present to us through the Spirit by interrupting the continuities of our life and calling us into community with the living God. It is a presence, as Barth put it in the *Commentary on Romans*, 'in which God encounters us not as something over against us but immediately and creatively, in which we not only see, but are seen, not only understand, but are understood, not only comprehend, but are comprehended' (1919, pp. 97-8). In short, it is the presence of Christ communicating with us in which we come to know God and not merely something about God.

2   The epistemological model of theological knowledge true to this personal co-presence of the risen Christ with us is not knowledge by description but knowledge by acquaintance, not propositional knowledge based on the authority of the church's teaching but personal participation in God's self-communication which precedes and grounds all human testimony and teaching. There is no knowledge of God worthy of the name that is not provoked by God making himself present to us. And the same is true of knowledge of Jesus Christ. Jesus was not an author of books. He communicated his message of the coming kingdom of God directly in situations of co-presence with his audiences, using parables 'to show the nearness of God and incite the hearer to decide for God' (Cupitt, 1979, p. 137). This communicative structure of his message is the clue to its proper understanding: God has come close, he is present and wants everyone to become aware of his presence. Precisely this situation of direct communication is continued by the Spirit after Jesus's death and resurrection when the medium itself became the message. Accordingly, true knowledge of God and Christ is rooted in the power of the resurrection and results from being drawn into the eschatological presence

of God by the power of the Spirit. This is the reality to which all theology refers.

Now it is far from self-evident that this is a reality at all. Viewed in the light of our common understanding of the world, the eschatological reality of the resurrection, on which Barth bases the whole of theology, is something 'positively not-given' (1929, p. 72) and cannot be inferred from anything given in our mundane experience. But precisely what appears to be most unlikely if not downright impossible according to our common understanding of reality is - as Barth puts it - the 'real reality' (1919, p. 59), i.e. the reality which determines what is to be counted as real and what is not. The eschatological reality of the resurrection which Christians confess in the Credo has ontological and criteriological priority over the experiential reality which we all share. The truth-claims of the Christian faith are the standards by which we are to judge what is real, not vice versa.

This is not quite the common-sense approach to the problem. In fact, it constitutes a massive and conscious contradiction to everything thought epistemologically acceptable in the light of the post-Enlightenment restriction of meaningful truth-claims to the formal truths of logic and mathematics and the empirical truths of science and history. In the critical post-Enlightenment atmosphere the long realist tradition in theology from Augustine to Hegel had foundered and came to be replaced by anti-realist theologies such as Schleiermacher's, especially - as was soon the case - where his 'feeling of utter dependence' was interpreted in a subjectivist sense which did not distinguish feeling from emotion and faith from belief. If, as Schleiermacher had argued, the Christian faith is to be understood as a specific determination of the feeling of absolute dependence and thus a particular historical type of the religious self-expression of pious self-consciousness, then in theology we do not talk about, say, God but about the Christian experience of God. Every theological statement has to be construed in terms of the self-expression of Christian consciousness, and whatever doctrine falls outside the range of possible Christian experience (such as the trinity) is to be rejected. This amounts to no less than saying that theological discourse fails to refer because all it does is to spell out in a systematic way the content of non-transparent or opaque expressions of the Christian consciousness. For example, it unfolds not the fact that Christ has risen, but that Christians *believe* Christ to have risen, and it explains this belief in terms of the particular religious experience of the Christian community. This momentous change of theological perspective from Christ to Christian faith in Christ is clearly signalled by the title of Schleiermacher's systematic theology, which is called not a dogmatics but an exposition of the *Christian Faith*. And the more this became understood in a subjectivist sense, the less theology was able to distinguish its internal approach from the external approach of the study or history of religions.

It is this whole approach which Barth uncompromisingly rejects. In theology we attempt to say something about God, not merely about human experiences of God. Therefore theology has to construe Christian discourse as being referentially transparent. That is, for Barth the that-clause in the sentence

Christians believe that Christ is risen from the dead

is to be interpreted extensionally, not intensionally. We may validly infer by existential generalization that someone has risen from the dead. And we may substitute other expressions for 'Christ' such as 'Son of God' or 'Lord' referring to the same person without changing the truth-value of this sentence. Of course, we may be wrong and this possibility of being in error is the risk the Christian realist takes. But if it is true at all, we cannot be mistaken about that to which we refer, although we may be mistaken in our articulations of it. Christian discourse is reality-depicting without claiming to be directly descriptive. Barth's theology reflects both sides of this.

To some this has looked like a return to a naive pre-Enlightenment orthodoxy. But it is not. In an important essay in 1929 Barth attempted to spell out the difference between his position and traditional versions not only of neo-Protestant idealism but also of old-Protestant realism. Like the latter he is a realist about the reference of Christian talk of God. But he differs from it in his account of the anchorage of this reference. In theology, according to Barth, we do not assume the 'subjective or objective reality' of God. We do not use the term 'God' to refer to something given in 'our outer or inner experience' (p. 63), an aspect or dimension of the objective empirical or historical reality over against us or the subjective reality of ourselves as cognitive, moral and religious subjects. Barth's position is more subtle and transcends the common alternatives of theological objectivism and theological subjectivism in which he believes theology has become trapped. When we talk of God, we refer not to a reality coextensive with nature, history or human experience, but to 'the truth in reality' (p. 72); not to what is given in or can be inferred from the given realities of our actual world, but to the true or real reality utterly beyond anything accessible to us by experience and reflection.

It is this combination of a strictly referential account of the language of faith with an explicit rejection of both realist (i.e. metaphysical or empirical) and idealist (i.e. empiricist or historicist) accounts of reality which is characteristic of Barth's theology. It not only marks it off from most other theologies of his time but also accounts for many of the peculiarities of his position. To mention just a few:

1   It explains the 'hermeneutics of contemporaneousness' (Jüngel, 1982, pp. 85ff) which he practised in his exegetical work to the dismay of professional biblical scholars because it allowed him to take his place alongside the biblical witnesses and not in the position of an onlooker.

2   It explains why he became so 'terribly indifferent' to 'historical questions' (Barth, 1973, p. 121) and refused to grant any specific theological significance to the historico-critical approach to scriptures. Instead he engaged in a realist reading of the biblical narratives and produced, especially in the later volumes of his *Church Dogmatics*, one of the most sustained narrative theologies that has appeared to this day.

3   It explains why Barth's theology is so ill-disposed towards the working out of a conceptually clear cut dogmatic system. He did not build layer upon layer but continually attempted 'to begin once more with the beginning' (Jüngel, 1982, p. 28). Thus his theology is full of revisions and discontinuities without, however, impairing the even greater continuity of its fundamental orientation.

4   It explains why Barth rejects every theology whose main concern is to answer problems posed by natural reality and our shared human experience instead of expounding the reality of God's revelation in the life, death and resurrection of Jesus Christ.

5   It explains the strong christocentric bias of Barth's theology. For a theology which is as strictly keyed to the eschatological reality of the risen Christ as is Barth's there are in principle two and only two closely related ways to proceed. Either it starts from the second article and is worked out in christological terms; or it starts from the third article and is worked out in terms of the doctrine of the Spirit. Barth took the first approach mainly for two reasons: on the one hand christology unlike the doctrine of the Holy Spirit has a highly developed doctrinal structure which provided him with conceptual models for the working out of his theology; on the other hand the doctrine of the Spirit had been compromised by idealist philosophers and theologians who, as Barth saw it, had turned it into a thinly disguised theological anthropology. However, as is shown by his permanent wrestling with Schleiermacher, he was never fully decided on the question whether taking the Holy Spirit as starting-point might not be the more effective way of working out a theology true to the

eschatological reality of the resurrection (1968, pp. 290-312).

The upshot of all this is that Barth claimed every time and every person to be immediate to the eschatological reality but unable to grasp it unless the Spirit opens his or her eyes to the final revelation of God in the life, death and resurrection of Christ. This basic conviction made him extraordinarily sensitive and critical of all other religious, ideological, or political claims to immediacy and revelation and explains the uncompromising clear-sightedness of his theology during the Nazi regime. It also allowed him, undisturbed by historical distance, to work out his dogmatics in direct dialogue with scripture and theologians of all times which resulted in a 'magnificent grasp and representation of materials drawn from the Christian tradition' (Roberts, 1979, p. 146) and which made his dogmatics one of the most significant ecumenical achievements of an individual theologian in our century.

In short, Barth starts from a realist position within the perspective of Faith. He construes theological discourse to refer not to what is given in, with and under our experiential reality, but to that which is not in our normal reality given, i.e. the eschatological reality of the risen Christ. But, so his critics asked, does this not amount to 'a total disjunction and alienation of his theology from natural reality' (Roberts, 1979, p. 145) and the wider fabric of religious, scientific, social, and economic relations? How is what he calls 'reality' related to 'the texture of reality as normally experienced' (p. 124)? These are the questions to which we have to turn next.

II

Barth calls the eschatological reality of God's saving action in his revelation the 'real reality', the Word of God the 'concrete reality' (*concretum*), and Jesus Christ, the incarnate Word of God, the 'most concrete reality' (*concretissimum*). This is to be taken literally. Compared to this most concrete reality everything else is at best abstract reality, that is, reality abstracted from this most concrete reality. It is held, as Barth put it, by God and 'only by him, over the abyss of non-existence ... It is real so far as He wills and posits it a real existence' (1936, p. 446). That is to say it would not even be abstract reality if it were not an abstractable dimension of the only concrete reality there is: the coming of God in the particular history of Jesus Christ in which, by the power of the Spirit, we are all integrated so that this particular history is the pre-history and post-history of all our individual lives. We exist abstractly if we ignore this concrete eschatological context to which our lives owe their reality. It is precisely by concentrating on this concrete reality of God's eschatological coming in Christ and by expounding it as the basis and frame of all reality that theology is realist.

Now this view of reality is quite a claim. It is - in Barth's own words - an 'attack' on our common understanding of reality (1934, p. 232). What we take to be concrete he calls abstract, and what to us looks at best highly improbable to him is the surest of realities. This - by common standards - blatant act of standing facts on their heads has been diagnosed as Barth's undigested Platonism or theological positivism (Lüthi, 1963, pp. 308ff; Pöhlmann, 1965, pp. 111-12). But this doesn't go to the heart of the matter. Barth 'takes up an exposed position minimally supported by the prevailing culture and maximally in agreement with mainstream Christianity' (Ford, 1979b, p. 198) by attempting a thoroughgoing reconstruction of the relation of God's eschatological self-presentation in Christ to our common reality in terms of the central doctrine of classical christology, the doctrine of the *hypostatic union*. The use of this christological model as an ontological paradigm is the clue to his conception of reality and marks it off from three common theological positions:

1 Contrary to all *theological separatism* he insists on the unity of reality and the unity of truth: theology differs from other disciplines in the sort of questions it asks about reality but not in the reality about which it asks questions.

2 Contrary to all *metaphysical constructivism* which attempts by way of abstraction to get beyond the contingencies of our world to a necessary structure behind it, Barth insists on the concrete self-representation of God's eschatological reality which is known not by inference but by perception and awareness of the way in which it makes itself present. The metaphysical approach grounds abstract reality in even more abstract reality. But the real is concrete, and the only fully concrete reality is God's self-concrescence with that which is different from himself in Christ.

3 Barth also rejects *theological immanentism* of a kenotic kind (Lüthi, 1963, p. 308). God has not entered our world by emptying himself into it. Rather our world enters God by being continually incorporated into him through judgement and grace, thus becoming real in the first place. Neither God's immanence in the world nor a deification of the world but the eschatological assumption of the world into God - that is Barth's answer to our question.

This, however, is to say that our world is permanently in the process of *becoming* real (or unreal, for that matter) by its eschatological *assumptio in Deum*. Taken by itself it is nothing but an abstraction of the only concrete reality there is: God's self-realization in the life, death and resurrection of Christ, the foundation of all this in the eternal will of God and its consequences in and for our world. It does not follow from this that what we experience as real is not real or only seems to be so. Rather it is a preliminary, penultimate, abstract reality which as such is in permanent danger of relapsing into non-existence. In short, our world of common experience is an *enhypostatic reality* which exists only in so far as it is incorporated into the concrete reality of God's saving self-realization in Christ. Taken by itself natural reality is an *anhypostatic abstraction*, unable to exist on its own and systematically at one remove from the texture of concrete reality (Roberts, 1979, p. 128; 1980, p. 166).

Now Barth was quite aware that this attempt to stand our common notion of reality on its head by reconstructing it in terms of classical christology rather than the other way round may look to some, if not to all of us, like 'a theological trick leading out of nothing into nothing' (1957, pp. 69-70). But before we turn away from him in dismay, or even disgust, we should note two things:

1   It is true that Barth does not offer any external arguments for the reality of the revelation, the resurrection or the eschatological presence of Christ. For him this is the shared faith of the Christian church which is induced not by argument or any other means accessible to us but by the free self-representation of the Spirit on the basis of the proclamation of the Gospel; and he understands his own task as a church theologian to consist not in the external justification of this faith (which he considers to be impossible anyhow) but in the critical exposition and conceptual clarification of it in order to safeguard the content and continuity of the proclamation.

2   However, it is this which requires the theologian to design models of thought which satisfy two criteria of adequacy. On the one hand they have to be true to the eschatological reality confessed and proclaimed by the church. On the other hand they have to preserve the unity of reality and the coherence of truth by enabling us to relate intelligibly the truth-claims of the Christian faith to what we know to be true by experience and reflection. This is precisely what Barth's theology has attempted to do. Thus if his theology is a trick it is one which neither ignores nor violates natural reality and our experience of the world. Barth does not exclude but includes the variety and plurality of our worldly experience within the theological perspective. He does not attempt, as his critics have complained, 'to preserve Christian theology from the indifference and hostility of a secular world' through 'a profound ontological exclusiveness' (Roberts, 1979, p. 145). Rather he unfolds in a painstaking and detailed way a theological

perspective of universal inclusiveness which incorporates and reconstructs the shared and public reality of our world within theology; and he achieves this by interpreting it theologically within the frame of reference provided by the christological exposition of the eschatological reality described. In this respect Barth's theology is not only an exemplary piece of constructive dogmatics but a sustained hermeneutical enterprise which does not deny the secularity of the world but reinterprets it theologically in the light of the presence of Christ and the world of meaning which it carries with it (Ford, 1979a, p. 84). Thus he starts from within the perspective of Faith; he rests his approach on a realist understanding of the eschatological reality of the risen Christ and the new life into which we are drawn by the Spirit; and he attempts to answer the problem of perspectives in terms of a christology-based model of Unity-in-Difference by which he hopes to overcome the difficulties which faced neo-Protestant theologies in the wake of Schleiermacher. Let us finally examine this model more closely.

III

The structure of Barth's Unity-in-Difference Model is best explained by reference to his theological interiorization of Overbeck's dilemma as described above. With this operation Barth does not fall back behind Overbeck to a neo-Protestant position with its mere co-ordination of the philosophical and theological perspectives. But neither does he fall back behind Schleiermacher to an old-Protestant position with its confinement to the internal perspective alone. He takes neither a simple theological nor a twofold theological and philosophical but a twofold *theological* approach to the problem of the external perspective of Reason. He interiorizes the whole problem and thus reproduces the discontinuity between the external and internal perspectives as a categorial distinction *within* the structure of the internal perspective of Faith.

Thus Barth repeats the same sort of theological operation with respect to the theologies in the tradition of Schleiermacher that Luther had performed with respect to the scholastic theologies of his time: he internalizes given external contrasts between theological and non-theological perspectives by reconstructing them in terms of internal distinctions within the theological perspective. But Barth performs this operation in a significantly changed situation. Luther had first shown the perspective of Faith to be a universal perspective by reconstructing the external co-ordination of Nature and Grace in terms of the internal distinctions between Law and Gospel and by using this as the basic guiding principle of theological thought. Barth, on the other hand, was faced with two distinct universal perspectives which he tried not only to co-ordinate but to integrate theologically. His theology, therefore, is not merely the unfolding of an internally differentiated universal perspective of Faith (as is Luther's) nor a co-ordination of a universal theological perspective with an equally universal philosophical perspective (as is Schleiermacher's) but the attempt to integrate this co-ordination itself once more *theologically*. It is precisely this which marks his difference to theologies of both the type of Luther and the type of Schleiermacher. To mention but two widely controversial examples: he brackets Luther's (and his followers') fundamental distinction between the Law and the Gospel once more theologically and interprets it as an internal distinction within the Gospel or grace of God, thus arriving at his much critizised formula of the Gospel and the Law as the guiding principle of theological thought; and in the same way he brackets Schleiermacher's (and his followers') view of religion and its (as he saw it) confusion of faith and piety once more theologically by interpreting religion and atheism to be nothing but two sides of the same sort of unbelief - our human rebellion against the grace of God.

The result of this interiorizing or integrating procedure is a more complex theology with a more sophisticated handling of the external perspectives. For whatever falls into the external perspective of the world turns up *twice* within Barths' theology. On the one hand it is reconstructed in strictly theological terms; and on the other hand it is present via a theological meta-perspective on its non-theological presentation. This combination of a direct theological perspective on everything and an indirect theological meta-perspective on non-theological perspectives on everything results in two distinct levels of argument in Barth's dogmatics. At a first level we find statements about theological topics such as Christ, faith, creation, or pre-history, at a second level theological statements about non-theological topics such as man, religion, the world or history. The statements at the two levels are related by what Barth calls the *analogy of faith*. Contrary to the traditional analogy of being, this principle functions within the sphere of faith alone. It is not a means of relating the perspective of Reason to the perspective of Faith but the interpretative principle by which we generate, *within* the perspective of Faith, indirect theological meta-statements on the basis of direct theological statements.

Put differently, Barth's dogmatics comprises two basic components: a constructive or dogmatic component which generates the basic theological categories, and an interpretative component which applies those categories to elucidate our experience of natural reality in the light of faith. The first component is the backbone of his dogmatics and unfolds the universal perspective of Faith in terms of a complete reconstruction of reality on christological foundations. The second component reproduces the reality normally external to theology within theology by interpreting it in the light of the perspective of Faith. This interpretation proceeds according to the principle of *analogia fidei*: it derives its interpretative categories from the dogmatic component and applies them to the pluriform materials of our normal perspectives on the world. Thus external reality is not denied but included in the perspective of Faith in order to bring out its theological significance.

The difference between these two components of Barth's dogmatics and their respective levels of argument is significant in a number of respects. I can only mention two:

1   Statements at the first level are all *singular statements*. They refer to individual topics like 'the faith', 'the person', 'the history', 'the time', 'the law' etc. which are directly derived from a systematic exposition of the eschatological *concretissimum* Jesus Christ. Statements at the second level, on the other hand, are *general statements*. They talk about classes of things like religions, human beings, social and political orders, religious communities and convictions, anthropological, psychological and sociological facts and theories of various sorts etc. Taken by themselves, these often differ quite widely from each other - Barth's treatment of 'natural theology' is a notorious case in point. But they are grouped together under certain theological headings which mark the theological point of view by which they are interpreted. Statements of this sort do not describe reality but articulate a theological meta-perspective on our private and inter-subjective experiences of the world. By concentrating on particular features at the expense of others they help to reduce their enormous variety and plurality in such a way that they become accessible to theological reflection and understanding in the first place. Thus they express what has come to be called the Christian 'experience with our experience' by placing everything which we experience in the specific interpretative frame of the Christian faith.

2   Although theology comprises these two distinct levels of dogmatic discourse and interpretative meta-discourse, it has but one grammar; and this is christology. It is the task of dogmatic discourse proper to work out the world of meaning that the presence of Christ carries with it; and because of the centrality of the resurrection everything it states is to be determined christologically. This amounts to nothing less than to a sustained hermeneutical process of

redefining virtually every dogmatic concept in christological terms: 'God', 'power', 'freedom', 'person', 'man and woman', 'predestination', 'history', 'time', 'law', 'being' and everything else is - in sometimes quite complicated and twisted ways - derived from the central eschatological reality of the risen Christ. But Barth does not content himself with the creation of a self-sustained realm of dogmatic discourse striving towards completeness. Separatist fideism of this sort is foreign to him. Rather he then re-applies these categories by the rule of analogy to interpret critically both traditional theological discourse and non-theological discourse alike. For example, what 'history' really means is shown by the one history of Jesus Christ which, when interpretatively applied to our common understanding of history, shows this to be at best a preliminary, abstract and inauthentic understanding of history. And the same is true of all other terms and concepts: for Barth it is the eschatological history of Jesus Christ which provides us with the prototypical understanding of the 'true God', the 'real man', the 'real reality', the 'real time', the 'true being', the 'true history' etc. To grasp this as clearly as possible by a sustained listening to the biblical testimony to the eschatological reality of the risen Christ is our first task as theologians. But then we have to go on and interpret our individual and social experience of our life and world in the light of what we have learned there: this is the second and no less important task of the theologian. Reading the Bible and reading the newspaper Barth considered to be the two pillars of theological existence. In short, Barth embarked not only on a christological redefinition of the whole of dogmatics but also on a hermeneutical reinterpretation of the language by which we describe and communicate our experience of the world. Small wonder that he died before he came to an end.

This is the structure of Barth's dogmatics and it allows for different ways of disagreeing with it: we can reject the way it develops its dogmatic component; we can disagree with the way it is used to interpret our reality of common experience generally or in particular cases where we find the principle of analogy ill applied. However, what we cannot do, I think, is to reject the two theological tasks with which Barth attempts to cope in the two components of his dogmatics: theology can dispense neither with a consistent doctrinal structure nor with an interpretation of reality in terms of it. Thus even if we reject the answers Barth gives we can hardly avoid the questions he asks.

But let me illustrate what I have described as Barth's method of interiorization and model of Unity-in-Difference. One could choose almost any topic but I shall take one that is especially controversial: his view of religion.

It is well known that Barth refused to interpret the Christian faith in terms of religion (as did neo-Protestant liberalism) or to identify Christianity with true religion (as did old-Protestant orthodoxy). For him these positions confused in their different ways the internal and the external perspectives on Faith and thus failed to distinguish clearly between *God's relation to man* (revelation), *man's relation to 'God'* (or what he takes to be God) (religion) and the *relation of man to God which corresponds to God's relation to man* (faith). However, by stressing the fundamental theological importance of distinguishing these relations Barth did not deny that religiosity is an 'essential structure of human consciousness', that 'religion is a general phenomenon of human existence' or that Christianity can be described and analysed as a religion (1927, pp. 399-400). This is not only possible but, given Christianity as it is, quite appropriate. What he denies is that external perspectives of this sort have any theological bearing before being internalized into and interpreted by the perspective of Faith. He offers just this sort of interpretation with his claim that 'religion is unbelief' (1956, pp. 299-300) - which, as should be remembered, is addressed primarily to Christianity and only secondarily to other religions.

To understand this much criticized claim one should note the level of argument at which it occurs. For Barth deals with both religion and faith in more than one way. Thus in the internal perspective of Faith religion is understood as unbelief; in the external perspective it is described as a general phenomenon of human existence; and in the theological meta-perspective on this external perspective it is seen as a human mode of existence which, because of God's eschatological co-presence with us, may *become* a more or less adequate expression of faith. And the same multiplicity of dogmatic approaches we find with respect to faith. Internally it is described as obedience, i.e. the human answer corresponding to God's revelation; externally it is described as religion; and in the theological meta-perspective on the external perspective on faith as religion it is interpreted as human unbelief. For no religious or non-religious way of life is by itself faith or an expression of faith. It can only become so by the grace of God.

The upshot of all this is that theology can in no way be built on the fact of religion. There may be religion without corresponding faith; and there may be Christian faith without there being religion. The Christian faith is not bound to exist in the form of religion, as both Barth and Bonhoeffer envisaged in their different ways. If faith is the eschatological human existence in the presence of Christ, then any mode of human existence may become or, for that matter, fail to become an expression of faith. Theology, therefore, cannot start from religious phenomena such as individual or communal beliefs, the church, or the history of Christianity. All these phenomena are ambiguous as to their faith-manifesting character. If there is to be an unambiguous starting-point at all theology has to take seriously that faith is essentially faith *in Christ*, i.e. a direct personal relation to the present Christ. But then, logically, for faith to exist Christ must be risen, alive and present. Accordingly the theological explication of faith is bound to become an explication of the eschatological reality of Christ: Barth's christocentric dogmatics is a clear consequence of his starting-point. The upshot of all this is that for theology to be possible Christ must have risen. Thus Barth quite appropriately summed up his position when he told the philosopher Heinrich Scholz 'that academic theology was based on the resurrection of Jesus Christ from the dead' (Busch, 1976, p. 207).

Barth's christology-based model of the Unity-in-Difference of internal and external perspectives corresponds exactly to his understanding of the eschatological assumption of our mundane reality into the reality of the risen Christ as suggested by the model of the hypostatic union of traditional christology. Small wonder that it is faced with the same sort of criticism: that it does not do full justice to the secularity ('humanity') of the world. Thus it is hardly surprising that critics of Barth from Pannenberg to Roberts have voiced the interests of the external perspectives; and this quite understandably so. However, the question is how to react to this theologically. Are we to wait for another Schleiermacher to co-ordinate Barth's complexly unfolded internal perspective of Faith with an equally complexly unfolded external perspective of Reason? And are we then to expect another Barth who once more interiorizes all this into the perspective of Faith - and so on? I do not think so. Of course, the dialectics of internal and external perspectives cannot be overcome and the formal operation of interiorization may be continued *ad infinitum*. But in a very important respect theological attempts to solve the problem of perspectives cannot go beyond Barth: there is no external perspective which in principle cannot be re-created and integrated internally by applying the conceptual machinery of his dogmatics. Of course, this may often lead to quite different results from the ones he himself has reached in his particular historical context. For, as I have pointed out, there are a number of ways of developing and using the two basic components of his dogmatics. But he has asked questions and worked out methods of answering them which, even if we depart from the particular answers he gives, will continue to engage theology for a long time to come.

Chapter 11

Harmony without Identity

There is no single solution to the problem of perspectives. But all solutions discussed are faced with a common problem: How can the internal perspective of Faith and the external perspective of Reason both have the same referent (or range of referents)? And how can we show what it is?

The first question might be answered by appealing to the *common world* of different perspectives. If a perspective is 'the view of the world from a given place' (Russell, 1971, p. 101), then perspectives have the same (range of) referents if they view the same world, or the same items in a common world, from different places; and they are different universal perspectives if their standpoints themselves belong to this common world. The second question might then be answered by saying what the perspectives refer to by finding either a *common range of reference* for them, or *common features of their standpoints*, or *common means of symbolic representation and communication* between them. The first produces *ontological conceptions of a common reality* (I); the second *transcendental conceptions of subjectivity* (II); the third *semiotic conceptions of language and the use of signs* (III).

I

Faith and Reason give us different perspectives on all referents because they are universal perspectives on everything that is. So they allow us to refer differently to anything. The argument underlying this widely held view can be summarized as follows: perspectives are views of the world from different places, partial perspectives views of some things, and universal perspectives views of everything, including themselves, from a given place. To every perspective there corresponds a perspectival world relative to the perspective's point of view. This world is real if what that perspective presents in one way is so independent of it that it can also belong to the worlds of other perspectives; but it is merely imaginary if it owes its existence solely to the perspective to which it corresponds. Different perspectives have a common world if their relative worlds can be integrated into a more comprehensive perspective. Because the relative worlds of universal perspectives include everything, they must have a common world and be perspective on the same reality. The perspectives of Faith and Reason are universal and therefore must have a common range of reference. And we refer to the same thing in the two perspectives if what we refer to can be identified unambiguously in terms that imply neither perspective.

This Common Reality Argument has several ontological and epistemological implications. Ontologically it implies a reality independent of our minds, and of our perspectives on (and social constructions of) the world. We may only access the world through our perspectives and their symbolic (and therefore socially determined) constructions; but there is more to the world than these perspectival ways of world-making. Reality allows many perspectives; and it is more complex than any of our symbolic reconstructions can represent it as being. Nonetheless, to 'grant that there is more than one true version of reality is not to deny that some versions are false' (Putnam, 1983, p. 19). Many things go, but not anything goes.

Epistemologically the argument assumes that the reality common to our perspectives may (at least approximately) be known as it truly is. All perspectives are selective, and not everything can be fully presented from any one point of view. Therefore we shall never completely know the world. But as reality is not constituted by but informs our perspectives, we can truly know it without having to be infallible. We can err, but only because reality is intelligible, that is, disclosed in our perspectives in a way that enables us to reconstruct it symbolically.

But before we can refer to the same (segment or aspect of) reality in different perspectives, that referent must exist, and be identified. It exists if it belongs to the perspective's common reality; and is identified by being located in that reality in a neutral way accessible from either perspective. Now this may have to be done differently for different kinds of referents: we may need more than one way to specify a common range of reference. And in fact, we do have to distinguish between approaches that base their account of a common reality on (1) god, (2) contingent facts taken to be essential to the internal perspective of Faith (Israel's escape from Egypt, the crucifixion of Jesus Christ), or (3) necessary ontological structures of reality. Let us look at them in turn.

1   The first approach argues that the internal and external perspectives focus on the same thing by focusing on god, whose existence and identity can be established beyond doubt in different perspectives. The argument for this can be summarized as follows: the reference of 'god' is neither ambiguous nor problematic, being fixed by the cosmological and the ontological arguments, the first showing that god exists if anything does; the second that if god is possible, he is necessary. But then there can only be one god to which therefore our different perspectives must all refer. God, as a necessary existent, belongs to reality without being identical with a part or the whole of the world or with one standpoint from which to view the world rather than another. The world is the totality of the relative worlds of all actual and possible standpoints, and every standpoint belongs to the relative world of some other standpoint. God, however, differs from the world by belonging to the relative world of every standpoint, and from every standpoint by belonging to all relative worlds. The first difference marks god's singularity, the second his universality. Combining the two differences (as Hartshorne does) gives us a notion of god as 'the most individual of universals' and 'the most universal of individuals' (1967, p. 36). God is the necessary correlate of every world viewed from whatever standpoint and, at the same time, the necessary correlate of every standpoint from which to view the world. Thus he is not one existent among others, nor the totality of what there is, but that without which nothing would be: the 'principle of existence' (p. 36). This principle does not differ between perspectives: it is the necessary correlate of every standpoint, as of every relative world. So necessarily we refer to one and the same when we refer to it, i.e. to god in either the internal or external perspective.

Some versions of this argument (e.g. Ward's) appeal primarily to the intelligible reality of the world; others (e.g. Schleiermacher's) to the reality and integrity of the standpoints from which we view it. Both make 'god' refer to the same thing in the two perspectives by exploiting a particular and irreducible *difference* without which the reality could not exist. The first version uses a difference between the world and god based on the contrast between the *totality of interacting entities* and the *universality of that which interacts with all of them*. The second version bases a difference between particulars and god on the contrast between the *particularity of all interaction between entities* and the *singularity of that which interacts with all of them*. However, both approaches have difficulty showing that anything *is* everywhere (i.e. interacts with everything else) and that whatever it is is identical with *God*, the object of worship. Even if *god* is constructed in both perspectives by combining the totality/

universality-contrast and the particularity/singularity-contrast, the problem is merely shifted to the internal perspective which has to show that *god* (in the sense explained) is that to which we refer when we use '*God*'.

2   The second way of specifying the reality common to our different perspectives is that of science and history. This has been the dominant approach since the Enlightenment. It tries to transform the problem of perspectives into a problem of different interpretations of common data ascertainable by science or history. Scientific (empirical or historical) *description* and *explanation*, which are taken to be objective and independent of perspectives, are distinguished from *interpretation* which is taken to be subjective and dependent on one's point of view. Scientific description provides indisputable data; religious, naturalist or other perspectives suggest equally admissable (even if mutually incompatible) interpretations of these data unwarranted by the empirical evidence.

Take for example the escape from Egypt under Moses. We can agree on all the knowable historical facts and still differ in our interpretation of them. For the naturalist the escape was due to a 'strong east wind' (Exodus 14:21), good leadership, good luck or Egyptian incompetence; for Israel, on the other hand, it was the paradigmatic act of God saving his people. The dispute is not about the facts but about their interpretation (or, if there are no uninterpreted facts, about different interpretations of the same facts). And whereas the scientific perspective, because of its canons of evidence, is supposed to describe the facts as they are, the religious perspective is supposed to be a questionable, at best admissible and in any case problematic interpretation of these facts.

But this distinction between facts and interpretations of them which 'if they have any sort of truth-value at all, have it as matter of convenience, taste, convention or something equally "subjective"' (Rorty, 1987, p. 283; 1979), is a myth as Davidson (1983; 1984), Rorty (1986) and others have shown. For Israel, in any case, it goes the other way round: the saving act of God is the undisputed primary reality of which the scientific perspective offers at best a faint abstraction unable to contain the real import of the events in question. In the religious perspective, therefore, the dispute is not about differing interpretations of the same facts but about what the facts are: is it 'the escape of Israel from Egypt' or is it 'the deliverance of Israel by God'? This not only poses the problem of whether there is, or can be, a privileged perspective from which we can evaluate all others. It also shows the irreducible difference between external and internal perspectives. Scientific descriptions and explanations concentrate on a few generalizable features of phenomena explainable by regularities and testable standards of experience. But science has difficulty coping with concrete, unique and 'rich' phenomena whose myriad of aspects resist scientific classification; and it cannot cope at all with cultural phenomena, whose internal perspectives of meaning can never be adequately matched by external descriptions. We cannot possibly see the difference between internal and external perspectives on Israel's escape from Egypt as a difference between historically ascertainable facts and their questionable religious interpretation. The external perspective does not simply present the facts 'as they are' without interpretation; and the internal perspective is not simply a subjective interpretation of those objective facts. The external perspective interprets certain empirically and/or historically accessible features of reality according to the canons of evidence of science and history. The internal perspective presents and interprets these and other features of reality according to a different canon which relates everything to God as the ultimate point of reference. The two perspectives do not provide different descriptions of the same event (e.g. Israel's escape from Egypt) but descriptions of different (though not incompatible or unrelated) events (Israel's escape from Egypt and God's deliverance of Israel at the Red Sea). They differ about what event it is that has happened and not merely about its proper interpretation. And although historical descriptions like 'Israel escaped from Egypt' are acceptable to both believer and unbeliever and to that extent independent of their different perspectives, they disagree not only on the (subjective) interpretation of the significance of this event, but on the status and role of this belief in their respective systems of beliefs, hopes and desires. For the believer the historical description describes only a partial and abstracted aspect of the real event, the saving act of God. That secures some co-reference across the two perspectives; but the historical description does not determine the identity of the event to which the believer refers or disclose the truth about what he believes has happened. It serves the purpose of historical inquiry, not of faith, and there is no reason why the former should be taken to provide a more privileged access to reality than the latter. Thus historical descriptions are not neutral in the sense of establishing the identity of that to which we refer in the internal and external perspectives. They provide a set of beliefs which have to be woven into both the internal and external systems of belief and made coherent and compatible with the other beliefs held. This establishes certain links between the two perspectives. But the historical descriptions do not state the objective facts whereas everything else remains a matter of subjective interpretation.

The model of description and interpretation, therefore, will not tell use how to say when two perspectives refer to the same thing. Facts are the results, not the data of interpretation: there are no uninterpreted facts, only different and differently related interpretations of things, states and events. Moreover, there exists no clear-cut distinction between description and interpretation: to subsume something under a general concept is a particular kind of interpreting something as something (cf. Dalferth, 1981, pp. 460ff). This is not to deny that interpreting is something we *do* and as such allows for more elaborate and conscious forms which involve entertaining a supposition, making a conjecture or expressing a hypothesis (cf. Wittgenstein, 1967, pp. 38-9; 1980, p. 8; Budd, 1987). But routine and unreflected perceiving and thinking, although more general, are not different in kind. They are just standard ways of interpreting something as something in the course of gathering and processing information about the world: ways which we owe to our linguistic environment. The fact is that 'interpretation' is the basis of all our (to use Schleiermacher's term) symbolizing relationships to our environments, and it underlies all our cognitive constructions of reality. Finally, the model of description and interpretation cannot account for the difference between internal and external perspectives. The believer and the non-believer may share descriptions (e.g. 'Israel escaped from Egypt') without therefore agreeing on the event and disagreeing on its significance, or agreeing on some of the facts and disagreeing on some others (e.g. God saved Israel), because they differ in that to which they refer. The empirical or historical descriptions shared do not show them to have the same referent but that they have different systems of belief to incorporate some common information. Whatever they believe about their referents must therefore be compatible with these descriptions. But it does not follow that their referents must be identical or their systems of belief consistent with each other. Empirical or historical descriptions do not provide criteria of identity for common referents but specify information common to both perspectives. Both believer and unbeliever must incorporate these pieces of information into coherent systems of beliefs. But internal coherence does not imply a common view of reality. And whereas methods of gathering and testing empirical or historical information do not differ between the internal and external perspectives so that we can at least come to agree about that which we must incorporate into our different systems of belief, it does not follow that what is thus accessible are the facts whereas everything else is interpretation. Science and history do not offer the only, or privileged, access to reality. They are one way to acquire true beliefs about (aspects of) reality, but not the only one.

3   The third way of trying to specify the reality common to different perspectives is to propose a system of ontological categories. For a long time Aristotle's metaphysics served this purpose; and in our century it has been vigorously renewed by A. N. Whitehead. 'Metaphysics,' he holds, 'is nothing but the description of the generalities which apply to all the details of practice' (1929, p. 19). Accordingly he thinks philosophy must frame a scheme of ideas for the interpretation of all experience which 'should be coherent, logical, and, in respect to its interpretation, applicable and adequate' (p. 4). This scheme is neutral as between perspectives because it comprises basic ideas and principles in terms of which all perspectives and their views of the world can be described and reconstructed.

This approach is obviously very abstract, concentrating on necessary structural aspects of reality, not on particular contingent features of it. But abstractions result from acts of abstracting. Abstracting is something we do, a kind of action; and actions could always have been otherwise. There is always more than one way to classify, compare and abstract the features of the world as conceived in our perspectives; more than one set of categories for describing reality's basic structures; and because ontologies are relative to our abstractive procedures, always more than one ontology.

These ontological approaches can be dogmatic (foundationalist) or heuristic (non-foundationalist). The dogmatic ones ignore alternatives and thereby appear to provide a definitive key to the ultimate structure of the universe. They fall foul of the relativity and plurality of ontologies, and mostly lead to reductive analyses of our perspectives which accept only what can be reformulated in their terms.

The heuristic approaches provide conceptual devices that may help to reveal links between perspectives; but they do not guarantee that we will actually find such links, or that those we do find will be adequate. They do not offer a definitive conception of reality, or a privileged neutral perspective to which all others have to conform. Rather they seek to secure *translatability* between perspectives by providing general categories to specify necessary aspects of reality applicable within all perspectives. It follows that the identity of referents across different perspectives is established not by their neutral ontological localization in reality but by rules translating identifications and descriptions of them from one perspective to another.

II

So much for attempts to specify what is common to internal and external perspectives as their common range of reference, or their common reality. A second major approach says rather that what lets us refer to the same thing in different perspectives is that certain basic conditions govern any viewing of the world, from any place. Not a common reality, but a common way of relating to it in cognition, is what enables co-reference across perspectives.

Since Kant, these common conditions of cognition have been expressed in conceptions of subjectivity or of the self. They distinguish a structure of transcendental categories (necessary *a priori* rules and operations for processing information and forming true beliefs) on the one hand from the contingent, empirical beliefs and desires which that structure constitutes and enables. This transcendental structure centres on an ineffable inner self (Kant's 'I think' or Fichte's noumenal agency), the ultimate subject of all these categories and beliefs. On this approach the internal and external perspectives can only differ in the contingent or empirical beliefs held by the believer and the philosopher, not in the transcendental operations by which both must form those beliefs. The latter are common to all perspectives: and whatever can be referred to by these fundamental operations alone must be the same in any perspective.

One recent and influential instance of this approach is the philosophical theology of Bernard Lonergan. He starts from the knowing subject; and he analyses its cognitional procedures at various levels of intentionality and consciousness, to extract the 'basic pattern of operations employed in every cognitional enterprise' (1971, p. 4). He does this by distinguishing 'categorial' and 'transcendental' modes of intending; those which 'vary with cultural variations' and those which are 'invariant over cultural change' (p. 11). His invariant transcendental modes are 'experiencing, understanding, judging, and deciding' (p. 14); and while he concedes that his account of them might be further clarified and extended, he thinks the pattern itself 'is not open to radical revision' because it 'is the condition of the possibility of any revision' (p. xii). Thus there is 'a rock on which one can build', namely 'the subject in his conscious, unobjectified attentiveness, intelligence, reasonableness, responsibility' (pp. 19-20).

One might ask whether this foundationalist and subject-centred approach does justice to the social, multiform and perspectival nature of our knowledge. Lonergan assumes a single, correct and complete understanding of the world and its history, at which we aim in our restricted acts of understanding, and which may be approached by their transcendental operations, their accumulation of 'correct' results and their elimination of subjective differences by 'conversion' (cf. Lash, 1975, p. 132). This complete understanding he takes to be not merely a goal but something we can strive for only because it exists *now* as the content of the one unrestricted act of understanding: God. Lonergan's ideal of a single and complete understanding of reality in God's understanding everything about everything is an essentially Platonic concept of divinity, as total truth and immutable knowledge of true reality, interpreted through the Aristotelian conception of God as the unrestricted act of *intelligentia intelligentiae*: transcendental subjectivity is being grounded in the transcendent creativity of God's *intuitus originarius*. The rock on which Lonergan builds turns out to be the reality not of the subject but of God.

But this begs the question. Lonergan's analysis of transcendental subjectivity presupposes the very reality of God which it is supposed to establish on the basis of transcendental subjectivity. It defines 'reality' in terms of the single, unchanging and perfect act of divine knowing: to be (real) is to be known by God. It derives reality's unity and unchanging character from a specific (Thomistic) and controversial understanding of God (1958, pp. 657ff). It thus begs the question with respect to the post-Enlightenment belief that reality is 'as Democritus conceived it rather than as Plato conceived it' (Rorty, 1987, p. 285). Now if this belief should be true (and it isn't incoherent and Lonergan doesn't refute it (Burns, 1987, pp. 140ff)), there can in principle be no single and complete view of reality: more than one view, equally correct, is always possible. Indeed it would be very hard to see what a 'complete understanding of reality' could *mean*. We can conceive reality as that which is known by God if we have reason to assume God to be; but it is not incoherent to conceive reality differently if we have reason to assume him not to be. The first is a plausible position in the internal perspective of Faith, the second a plausible position in the external perspective of Reason. Neither is incoherent or self-contradictory; and neither can show the other to be impossible. But then the decisive question is what makes us accept either 'It is possible that God exists' or 'It is possible that God does not exist'. Both are compatible with all our ordinary background knowledge and there are no *a priori* reasons for opting for either. Any answer to the question will involve a whole view of life and reality. In short, Lonergan's approach is based on ultimately theological assumptions which are in basic outlines those of the Thomistic tradition. It does not provide a neutral position for establishing the sameness of what we refer to in the internal and external perspectives. It merely underlines the fact that there is no such position, only participation in one perspective or the other.

But given its theological presuppositions, is Lonergan's approach internally coherent and convincing? Whatever is based solely on a transcendental pattern of operations must surely be one and the same from every standpoint and every perspective. But this, as Lonergan argues, is precisely the case with God. For the question of God rises out of our conscious intentionality and its *a priori* structured drive towards the intelligible and unconditioned. It is intrinsic to our transcendental subjectivity 'that our intending intends, not incomplete, but complete intelligibility' (1967b, p. 259). All our attempts to experience, understand, judge and decide anything assume that the universe is intelligible. But could 'the universe . . . be intelligible without having an intelligent ground' (1971, p. 101)? For in itself the universe is 'shot through with contingence' (1958, p. 656) and thus only incompletely intelligible. Hence our intention of complete intelligibility would be frustrated if we intended no more than the incompletely intelligible universe without going on to the completely intelligible intelligent intelligible that is God. Incomplete intelligibility implies intelligibility, which presupposes complete intelligibility. The ultimate condition of the possibility of intending the incompletely intelligible, contingent or, in Lonergan's phrase, the 'virtually unconditioned', i.e. that 'whose conditions are all fulfilled', is therefore said to be the existence of the 'strictly unconditioned', completely intelligible or necessary being God. As Lonergan summarizes his argument: 'If the real is completely intelligible, God exists. But the real is completely intelligible. Therefore God exists' (1958, p. 672).

This is the skeleton of all arguments for the existence of God in terms of the model of knowledge, explanation, justification and intelligibility which make God's existence the ultimate explanation of the existence and intelligibility of reality. However, unlike arguments developed by Meynell (1982) and Ward (1982), Lonergan's version argues not from the complete intelligibility of the universe to God but from requirements of transcendental subjectivity to a completely intelligible God who could account for the incomplete intelligibility of the contingent world. He does not simply equate the real with the world or universe. Rather the world is real only insofar as it is intelligible, and because it is only incompletely so, it is at best incompletely real.

What, then, is the real? Lonergan equates it with being, defining both relative to his transcendental operations: 'being' is 'the objective of the pure desire to know' (1958, p. 348), 'the real' 'the objective of an unrestricted desire to understand correctly' (p. 676). Being or the real are thus defined as the content of an unrestricted act of understanding, i.e. that which is known through the totality of correct judgements; and this, as we have seen, is said to be not only a human goal but a divine reality. But this extrapolation from restricted to unrestricted acts of understanding is not warranted (Burrell, 1967). We may be able to judge some things correctly without being able to judge everything correctly, and without the totality of correct judgements existing in any unrestricted act of divine understanding. Neither a contingent being's lack of *complete* intelligibility, nor its incomplete *intelligibility*, warrants postulating a primary completely intelligible being. Moreover, there is no *a priori* reason why the quest for intelligibility must be completely satisfiable. As R. M. Burns has pointed out: 'To assume that the natural desire for knowledge must in principle be fulfillable is . . . to rule out in advance the possibility that human nature could be absurd and the universe ultimately unintelligible' (1987, p. 76). But that possibility is not logically incoherent, and our acting on the contrary assumption is no proof of its truth. I conclude, therefore, that the minor premiss of Lonergan's argument is either true only by definition, or unfounded. It follows trivially from Lonergan's theological view of being as the content of the unrestricted act of divine understanding (cf. MacKinnon, 1964; Tyrell, 1974, pp. 168-9). But it cannot be adduced in support of this position.

Lonergan's argument fails for two further reasons. The idea of a self-explanatory God is vacuous, and the contingent cannot be made completely intelligible by the non-contingent (Burns, 1987, p. 139). As Swinburne has pointed out: 'never does anything explain itself'; nor 'can anything logically necessary provide any explanation of anything logically contingent' (1979, p. 76), since only what is necessary follows from the necessary; and whatever logically explains something contingent must itself be contingent. Similarly, to claim God to be self-explanatory is not to offer an explanation of his existence but to reject the application of the idea of explanation with its distinction between *explanandum* and *explanans* to him. If God exists, nothing could explain his existence; and for his inexplicable existence to explain what exists contingently, he cannot exist necessarily. Thus God's existence cannot be self-explanatory; cannot be necessary if it is to explain contingent reality at all; and cannot explain it completely if it is itself a contingent reality that could have been otherwise. Contingent reality implies neither the non-existence nor the existence of God. If God's existence explains contingent reality, it cannot fail to do so. But it does not follow from contingent reality that God exists or that if he exists he explains it or that it in fact has a complete explanation or that it could not be without God.

One can react to this situation in at least three ways. The first is to accept the problem of an explanatory relationship between contingent and necessary reality as stated and try to solve it (1); the second is to modify the problem by changing the underlying notion of God in a way that allows it to be solved (2); the third is to dissolve the problem by abandoning the model of explanation and justification in terms of which it has been set up (3).

1   Lonergan himself takes the first approach. He argues that a necessary ultimate ground of a contingent universe can ground it neither necessarily (for the reasons given) nor arbitrarily (for then it would be 'a mere matter of fact without any possible explanation'). Instead he thinks that it 'proceeds freely from the reasonable choice of a rational consciousness' (1958, p. 657), the immutable mind of God which 'in a single view grasps the totality of concrete patterns and in each pattern the totality of its relevant events' (p. 650). But this would still be a contingent act that might have been otherwise, and 'a contingent act remains contingent and therefore incompletely intelligible even if it is non-temporal and immutable' (Burns, 1987, p. 148).

2   Others like Ward have therefore tried another way. Since the necessary does not entail the contingent, God must be conceived differently if he is to explain the universe. He cannot be merely necessary; but neither can he be merely contingent if he is to be distinguished from the world. So God must be in some respects both necessary and contingent (Ward, 1982, p. 8). This requires a different account of his relation to the world which must, in some sense, be a relation of reciprocal interaction. And this poses a serious problem: how may necessity and contingency be combined in God in a coherent way? There have been at least three different attempts to do this in recent philosophical theology:

(a)   Whitehead and Hartshorne develop a dipolar conception of God. In his 'primordial nature' God is the necessary, changeless and eternal realm of potentiality, the totality of unrealized possibilities. In his 'consequent nature' he is the changing realm of actuality, the all-inclusive container of the real. The two natures are necessarily yet dynamically related. The possible cannot exist unless it is grounded in some actuality, and the actual cannot be the totality of the possible: it must be a sequence of compatible selections from the possibilities in the primordial nature. This is the process of the world, and its permanent creative advance into novelty. Hence God's two natures are related not directly but indirectly through the world-process. This, however, risks reducing God to an *aliquid mundi*, a mere abstract structure of a world-process that permanently provides the possibilities for the creative advance into novelty and permanently integrates what has become actual into the unity of his being.

(b) Ward therefore suggests a different solution. God is not a dipolar correlation of necessity and contingency but rather 'the one self-existent being in whom creation and necessity originate and in whom they are reconciled' (Wards, 1982, p. 3). God is not necessary in some respects and contingent in others: he is beyond this contrast, since he is the originator both of everything possible and of everything actual. He is not a mere abstract structure, nor a mere passive container, nor in the grip of some ultimate metaphysical ground, the creative advance into novelty. He is 'the absolutely originative creator of everything other than himself' who 'sets the final goal of the world' and 'plays a changing, modifying role within it' (p. 232). This is indeed a coherent notion of God, reminiscent of the Christian view of the trinity's involvement in creation as Father, Son, and Spirit. But the existence of this God cannot be asserted just because we want complete intelligibility and absolute explanation for the contingent world. We cannot prove that the world has such an explanation, for any proof would have to beg the question by assuming what it is trying to prove. If there is an explanation, it is because God exists, not because the world is completely or incompletely intelligible. It may be true that if God exists, there is an ultimate explanation of the world: it is not true that there is or must be such an explanation, or that because there is, God exists.

(c) Ward makes God the common originator of both necessity and contingency and argues *a priori* from this conception of God to the intelligibility of the world. Swinburne, on the other hand, starts *a posteriori* from the contingent world which requires, if anything, a contingent explanation. He therefore gives the contingent primacy over the necessary in God. 'God exists' is a contingent proposition: to 'say that "God exists" is necessary is . . . to say that the existence of God is a brute fact which is inexplicable' (1979, p. 92). For Swinburne God is the ultimate contingency even though his essence is an eternal essence so that 'if he exists at any time he exists at all times': what we may call a 'factually necessary existence' (p. 93). But then why not say that the world has a factually necessary existence or go beyond God to some further x which explains not only the world but also its theistic explanation? Swinburne answers the second question by pointing out that multiplying explanations without necessity gives no more explanatory power. The existence of God must be the *ultimate* 'brute fact' which explains everything but has itself no explanation. He answers the first by arguing that the ultimate explanation of the contingent universe has to be a personal one, which explains the phenomena by an action of a person, and the beliefs and intentions which govern it: so theism, but not the world, is a natural stopping-point for explanation.

But given all our ordinary information about the world, the idea of a personal explanation of it has little initial probability, as Mackie has pointed out (1982, pp. 100-1). And even if we accept it as the only possible ultimate explanation, why should we not then conceive the world itself in personal terms? To adapt one of Hume's arguments, if we can conceive the world after the model of a plant or an animal, we can also conceive it after the model of a person, or the body of a person. If by 'the world' we mean the totality of what there is, we blur the distinction between God and everything else; and if we mean by it 'all logically contingent things apart from God' - or, even more narrowly, 'all physical things spatially related to ourselves' (Swinburne, 1977, pp. 129f) - we exclude neither a Platonic under-standing of it as a visible body of an invisible *anima mundi*, nor a Spinozist monism which conceives God and the world to be one and the same reality, just as mind and body are different aspects of one and the same reality which in itself is neither. The issue turns on our model of the world, which is not something given in experience, but the idea of the totality of interacting realities that can be experienced. We can use a number of models, including that of a person, to con-ceptualize this idea. Not all such models are compatible with a Chris-tian understanding of creation, of course. But that counts decisively against a person-model only within the perspective of Faith, which argues not from the world to God as its ultimate explanation but from God to the world as his creation.

3   The third way of dealing with Lonergan's problem is not so much a solution as a dissolution of it. Rather than trying somehow to recon-cile the necessary existence of God to the contingent existence of the world, we stop trying to conceive the relationship between God and world in terms of explanation. There is no theological reason why it has to be conceived in terms of the model of knowledge, explanation, justification and intelligibility. On the contrary, to do so is character-istic of theoretical reason, with its preoccupation with epistemological problems, rather than of the practical reason of faith, with its trust in God as the ultimate guider of our life. Confidence in the intelligibility of reality may be a side-effect of faith in God, but it is not its primary

or central concern. Whereas the incompleteness of our explanations of reality neither establishes nor refutes the existence of a complete explanation, faith in God gives us good reason to orient ourselves in a reality conceived as his creation, even if that makes it only partially and incompletely intelligible to us. The prior conviction of the existence of God and of his salvific purpose for his creation is what, if anything, grounds our claim to a complete intelligibility of the real.

Thus it is with Lonergan's argument. Its theological assumptions, as we have seen, require it to be reformulated somewhat as follows: 'If God exists, the real is completely intelligible. But God exists. Therefore the real is completely intelligible.' This argument draws out the implications of a particular understanding of God's creative relationship to his creation. It does not establish the existence of God on independent grounds. If God's existence is inexplicable it cannot explain what is only incompletely explicable. This, as Kant has pointed out, would be to explain something which we do not understand sufficiently by something we do not understand at all. But to claim the inexplicable to be self-explanatory because even if we may not be able to understand the explanation God may still not be incomprehensible to himself (cf. Ward, 1982, p. 8), is to deprive the notion of 'explanation' of all content and explain something which we do not understand at all by something which in principle is beyond our understanding.

III

Perspectives have ranges and standpoints, but they also have contents. The possibility of referring to the same thing in the different perspectives of Faith and Reason can be explained not only in terms of ontological and transcendental considerations but also by reference to common means of symbolic construction and communication in and between perspectives. Not only a common reality and common transcendental structures of our standpoints ground the possibility of co-referentiality across perspectives, but above all the common semiotic means of gathering, constituting and transmitting information through selection, symbolization, interpretation and communication.

We have met this linguistic approach in Luther's insistence that theological and philosophical discourses are mutually intelligible because the same language is used in both of them. We can find out whether and how we speak of the same thing in their different realms if we know the *language* used (Hebrew, Greek, Latin, German, English etc.) *and* the *grammar* which governs their discourse. The grammar constitutes the difference between the two realms, the language what they have in common. More generally, our linguistic competence is what enables us to understand theological and philosophical discourse, while our philosophical competence (our knowledge of the principles of philosophy, science, morality, politics) and our theological competence (the ability to differentiate between law and gospel) is what enables us to participate in those discourses.

The linguistic medium common to different perspectives can be looked at in two different ways. We can look at it as a *cultural* phenomenon: the patterns of discourse and systems of language, with all their theoretical (competence), empirical (performance) and historical (diachronic) aspects as studied by linguistics, history, sociology, psychology, biology and ethnology. That is the *empirico-hermeneutical approach*. It investigates our actual conceptual equipment and the factual structures of our systems of concepts, language, beliefs, norms and actions, which characterize particular forms of life in our cultural matrix. It is descriptive, and is sensitive to the contingent particularities of our manifold forms of life; and it has dominated much recent analytic, pragmatist and hermeneutical philosophy. But we can also view languages as *anthropological* phenomena, i.e. instances of our distinctive human capacity to constitute, use and communicate through verbal and non-verbal signs. This is the *semiotico-transcendental approach*. It seeks the principles of the constitution of signs, meaning and information, and the general rules which govern verbal and non-verbal communication in all possible cultural contexts and ways of life. This has been the dominant approach of linguistic, semiotic and pragmatist transcendentalism and of the foundationalist versions of analytic and hermeneutical philosophy.

These two approaches are not mutually exclusive, but they do mark two distinctive strands in contemporary philosophy and theology. One concentrates on the contingent normative features of a given way of life, system of beliefs or cultural perspective, and seeks to elucidate 'the intratextual descriptive intelligibility' (Lindbeck, 1985, pp. 113ff) of these cultural patterns by saying what they mean to their adherents. The second elaborates what is common to all their uses of signs. It looks for the 'deep grammar' of our cultural forms of life: the principles of communication and semiotic activity on which they are based. These principles are also contingent, of course, but their contingency is categorial. They state the transcendental conditions of the possibility of all intratextual intelligibility: our cultural forms of life must all actualize them somehow.

The neo-Wittgensteinian position of D. Z. Phillips is a paradigm of the first descriptive approach. For him (as for Wittgenstein) religion is a practical, not a theoretical matter. To be religious is to follow a picture (or set of pictures) or story which regulates one's life. The picture of a particular religion is governed by a particular 'grammar' which provides internal criteria for justifying the beliefs and actions of its adherents. But the picture admits of no external support: the *whole* way of life of a religion cannot be justified, in particular not by reference to what there is and how things are. Religion differs fundamentally from science in that religious beliefs do not function as hypotheses which empirical evidence may verify or falsify.

But science no more provides a privileged access to reality than religion does or any other way of life. For, as Wittgenstein pointed out, the 'connection between "language and reality" is made by definitions of words, and these belong to grammar, so that language remains self-contained and autonomous' (1969, p. 97). There are many ways of describing reality, but no way of using language to get outside itself. 'Any kind of explanation of a language presupposes a language already' (1964, p. 54). All we can do is study the grammar of the various 'language-games' in which we are involved. We can find out what their rules allow, and can trace the 'natural history' of these cultural forms and their grammars. There is such a history because we are all born into a contingent set of linguistic forms of life which we interiorize through the normal processes of socialization. But ultimately the adoption of a language-game (or network of games) rests on convention, and is in this sense arbitrary. 'A *reason* can only be given *within* a game. The links of the chain of reasons come to an end, at the boundary of the game' (1969, p. 97). The final appeal in any chain of reasoning is thus to the contingent fact that the language-game is played. Even universal norms of reasonableness will have to be found *within* our actual language-games, and not in some neutral, framework-independent or game-transcending language. We all exist in networks of natural and cultural contingencies which we cannot radically transcend. We can understand and learn to control them to some extent, and we can change from one cultural context to another. But we cannot step outside them altogether, ground them in something less contingent or show them to be intelligible in a more than merely contingent way. All we can hope for is to learn how to live with these networks of contingencies. And religion plays a vital part in this as one of our fundamental ways of coping with contingency.

However, the descriptive approach does not commit us to arbitrariness or irrationalism. We may agree with Wittgenstein and Lindbeck that 'the norms of reasonableness are too rich and subtle to be adequately specified in any general theory of reason or knowledge' (Lindbeck, 1985, p. 130) and still insist that internal rationality (the only kind we have) manifests basic rules of semiotic deep grammar. Our forms of life and language-games, being a contingent part of our cultural matrix, may only admit of contingent explanation: we can still ask how these and other such forms can exist at all. This is the question which the second approach seeks to answer. We can play language-games and have cultural forms of life, because we use and constitute signs. We exist in sign-worlds which we have constituted. Culture is part of our nature, and the basis of culture is our capacity to constitute and use signs.

This has been said to have religious implications. Eilert Herms has argued that it shows that we exist in 'dependence on transcendence' (1978; 1982). His argument is a critical reconstruction of C. W. Morris's theory of signs, and can be summarized as follows. Signs are not things but relations. They are constituted in a process of semiosis or signification S in which an interpreter A uses something B (a physical medium like sounds or marks on paper) as a sign C to refer to a referent D. This process involves two interconnected relationships. The first is the contingent relation of A constituting C by using B to refer to D. This entails the independent spatio-temporal existence A and B: B is not constituted by A, but used to refer to D by C, a process which does not constitute A but is just one of its activities. The second relation is the self-reflexivity of this whole process S which constitutes its spatio-temporal identity and without which it would not be the semiotic process that it is. The self-reflexivity of S means that none of its terms (A, B, C, D) are what they are independently of it. In particular, this relation is not just an activity of A, but something 'in which A participates in utter passivity' (1982, p. 185): a necessary feature of A's spatio-temporal existence and identity, presupposed by everything else ascribed to A. But if A must participate in (some) S, the self-reflexivity of all processes of semiosis in A is the necessary 'ground of existence' of all contingent acts of semiosis by A. Hence, Herms concludes, 'the semiotic self exists in dependence on transcendence' (pp. 187f).

This argument is a semiotic reworking of transcendental versions of the cosmological argument that attempt to ground the contingent in the necessary; and it fails for similar reasons. First, of course all our semiotic activities depend on our existence and identity - and these are not among our activities. But it does not follow that they are the activity of someone else, or the activity of one and the same for all of us: they are not activities at all. Second, the necessary structural aspects of the process of semiosis may differ from the contingent performance of semiotic acts; but this does not make the former the 'ground of the existence and possibility' of the latter. The impossibility of engaging in semiotic acts that are not self-reflexive processes does not point beyond itself to a transcendent reality in which it is grounded. It is a modal fallacy to conclude from 'S (the process of semiosis) is necessarily self-reflexive' that 'S is necessary'; a transcendental fallacy to conclude from 'Every S is necessarily constituted by something else' that 'Every S is constituted by something necessary'; and a logical fallacy to conclude from 'No S is completely self-generating' that 'There is something which generates all S'. Third, of course we cannot produce anything (things or signs) unless other things exist (including us) which we have not produced. But this mundane fact does not demand a transcendent reality to produce all those things. Semiotic processes may necessarily depend on something else: it does not follow that they depend on something transcendent.

More promising is the following analysis of sign-processes. Every process of signification requires some interpreter A and some physical medium B to be involved in three types of relation: the pragmatic relations between A and the sign C (constituting, using, understanding, interpreting); the semantic relations between C and the referent or designation D (meaning relations such as Fregean sense and reference); and the syntactic relations between C and other signs (both within and without the system of signs to which C belongs). So every semiotic act involves four types of selection:

1   a selection of signs out of a system of signs (syntactics);
2   a selection of meanings out of a system of meanings (semantics);
3   a selection of sign-users out of a totality of sign-users (pragmatics);
4   a selection of physical means (matter) in terms of which signs are constituted and communicated by us.

These four types of selection relate our semiotic acts to *four fundamental dimensions of possibility*. Every semiotic act is syntactically related to the totality of our possible repertoires of signs and rules (the *cultural* dimension of our reality). Semantically it is related to the totality of our possible meanings or (if it complies with the law of non-contradiction) of our possible worlds (the *ontological* dimension of our reality). Pragmatically it is related to the totality of possible communities of sign-users (the *personal* dimension of our reality). And physically it is related to the totality of our experienceable reality - to all means of transmitting energy that can be used and experienced by us (the *natural* dimension of our reality).

But these four dimensions of possibility entail *three dimensions of actuality*. They presuppose an actual community of sign-users (some actual *persons*), an actual repertoire of signs (some actual *culture*), and the existence of physical media for the constitution of signs, and the communication of meaning through them (*nature*).

The natural phenomena which we use as media in acts of signification and communication owe their function to us, but not their existence. They belong to *nature*, exemplify causal processes and obey laws which we have not created but can only discover. On the other hand, the cultural phenomena we use (our repertoire of signs and rules) owe both their function and their existence to us. They belong to *culture*, follow rules created by ourselves, and are as such something we have decreed and not merely discovered. Nature exists independently of our actions, while culture exists only because of our actions. Signs in use necessarily involve both nature and culture, and our acts of signification and communication can be studied in both their natural and their cultural dimensions. Thus phonetics and phonology are different studies of the sounds of a given language. The former treats them as natural phenomena following scientific laws, the latter as cultural phenomena governed by linguistic rules. As a cultural system of meaning the latter have an organization different from that imposed by laws on natural phenomena. Of course, in actual use the cultural phenomena necessarily involve natural phenomena: but neither of them can be reduced to or replaced by the other.

Since all our sign processes must combine culture and nature in this way, they have an essentially dual character. This duality reflects their function: to help us by natural means (but cultural meanings) to develop out of the actualities and determinations of nature the possibilities and freedom of culture. We are free but finite agents because we are by nature cultural beings who exist and act both in nature (as *bodily* agents) and in culture (as bodily *agents*). But although we depend on both nature and culture, we depend on it in different ways. As we must act, we must always be transforming nature into culture and thus enlarging our fields of action. This lessens our dependence on our natural environment at the price of an ever greater complexity of the self-created moral and social problems which our freedom presents.

We can never completely overcome this fundamental duality in our life, of dependence and creativity: the law-governed realities of our natural existence and environment, and the rule-governed creation of new cultural realities by our individual and common actions. We are free and creative beings, yet permanently tied to what has not been created by us. This fundamental duality shows up most clearly in that of our acts of signification and communication, whose dual structure reflects the dual structure of our existence as human persons in nature and culture. Persons exist in communities, not in isolation. But communities are not just collections of persons. They are processes and institutions of communication involving (in rudimentary or elaborate form) the use of signs, of interpretative and communicative symbols and patterns of action, and the sharing of a common culture, language and history. Our semiotic repertoires, in particular the languages we share with others, enable us to extract meaning from the universe in similar ways and thereby communicate across our various perspectives with each other. Because we all share to a greater or lesser extent semiotic means and rules of meaning for the cognitive construction of views of the world, we can successfully communicate between our different perspectives on it.

Yet although our common codes of verbal and non-verbal signs, symbols and actions enable us to share our views, they do not guarantee that our use of them actually refers to the same reality in our different perspectives. Signs do not as such unambiguously fix or rigidly name their referent. They become referring and identifying expressions by the way they are used. But not even similarity of use will guarantee identity of reference. There is always a difference between what a sign may mean and what it does mean: between its potential meaning (system) and its actual meaning (text); and between what its producer means it to mean and what its receiver takes it to mean. This difference is the creative source of individual and context-sensitive articulations of meaning and of understanding (and misunderstanding) these in more than one way. Communication through signs allows alternative interpretations and different grades of understanding. For we can use signs significantly without being able to define their meaning, or to be clear what exactly we mean by them. 'I certainly could not define either "oak-tree" or "elephant"; but this does not destroy my right to assert that no oak-tree is an elephant' (Geach, 1976, p. 39). So there may always be more to an act of signification and communication than we intend or could pin down. In this sense the use and understanding of signs is always a creative activity. It is not just a matter of transmitting identical meanings or information from speaker to hearer. It is a creative process of interpretation, which involves a grasp of similarities and differences at all levels of understanding. This is the source of all culture which is based on rule-governed yet free processes of signification and communication. For to use signs is to engage in a hermeneutical process of communication and interpretation with no internal limit and no definite end. That is why we must combine the empirico-hermeneutical and the semiotico-transcendental approaches into what might be called a *semiotico-hermeneutical* approach if we want to be true to the two poles of human cultural activity - creativity and control.

This approach does not claim to fix the identity of referents from different perspectives. It secures translatability between perspectives in terms of a common semiotic repertoire. But it does not offer neutral criteria for identifying what they refer to. For it understands translatability as a cultural process in which we are continuously engaged, trying to find out whether or not we refer to the same God, world or humanity in the perspective of Faith and the perspective of Reason. We combine the perspectives semiotically in a permanent process of 'assimilation by interpretation' (Lindbeck, 1985, p. 138). But during the process, we cannot permanently establish the identity of our perspectives' referents. We can only secure our perspectives' harmony by continuous communication between them. This requires translatability of our referring expressions, but not identity of our referents. For translatability is all we need for mutual understanding; and securing it is not a matter of discovering the true nature of reality. It is a matter of creatively designing semiotic means to be used and interpreted in either perspective. In short, semiotic creativity, not the discovery of truth, is the key to translatability; and translatability, not identity, is what we need to harmonize our perspectives.

PART III

REVELATION AND REFLECTION

Chapter 12

Reflection and the Quest for Clarity

Christian theology is the intellectual quest for clarity about faith in Christ and its view of reality in the internal perspective of Faith. It is a permanent process of 'faith seeking understanding' faced with two major hermeneutical problems. First, it has to understand the Christian faith and its manifestations in the Christian community which logically, factually and historically precede theological reflection: this is the *reconstructive task* of theology. Second, it has to understand the whole of reality in the light of (its reconstruction of) faith: this is the *constructive task* of theology. Accordingly, the interpretative process of theology involves both *explication* and *elucidation*. It seeks to understand faith through the reflective explication and conceptual reconstruction of its data in systems of Christian doctrine; and it seeks to understand reality through its reflective elucidation and conceptual construction in the light of faith and its doctrinal reconstructions.

Both interpretative tasks are intrinsically related and have found different and sometimes sharply controversial solutions. There exists not only a variety of doctrinal explications of the Christian faith in the different ecclesial and theological traditions of the Christian churches, but also an even greater variety of theological interpretations of reality in each of these various traditions. Different theologies compete in their explications of faith as well as in their elucidations of reality. The first set of differences is due to different developments of the internal perspective of Faith; the second also involves differences about the proper way of relating the internal perspective of Faith to the external perspective of Reason. However, all the problems thus raised underline that although both interpretative tasks are central to theology, the first is the more fundamental one: the explication of faith is a necessary condition for the elucidation of reality in the light of faith. On this fundamental task of theology I shall concentrate in that which follows.

The process of explication differentiates between theological reflection (reflective or doctrinal beliefs) and that upon which it reflects (the intuitive piety of faith and its verbal, non-verbal and trans-verbal manifestations). This difference is the second major source of problems in the relationship between theology and philosophy. For theological reflection uses philosophy (in the widest possible sense) in a variety of ways in its attempts to clarify, understand and conceptually reconstruct the Christian faith. Now faith is not directly accessible to theology (or other kinds of reflection) but only indirectly through its manifestations in the life of faith, i.e. in the beliefs, discourses, actions and institutions of Christian believers. Thus there are three levels of problems to be distinguished in theological reflection:

1 There is the ontological or existential level of *God's activity* in revelation and faith (as well as in everything else, including theological reflection) which is presupposed in everything theology says, thinks or does. To understand this divine activity and its implications for ourselves and the whole of reality is the main aim of theological reflection.
2 There is the ontic or experiential level of human manifestations of faith in verbal (*figurative discourse of faith* in prayer, proclamation and confession), non-verbal (*beliefs and actions of faith* in the individual and common life of Christians), and trans-verbal forms (*symbolic actions of faith* in private and public worship). These are the (empirical) data of faith which (in principle at least) are accessible to theology and from which it seeks to reconstruct the faith which they manifest.
3 Finally, there is the theoretical or conceptual level of *theological reflection and discourse* about faith on the basis of its various manifestations in the life and history of the Christian community. Theological reflection differs from other reflective activities by its subject-matter (faith and reality in the light of faith) and from other (non-theological) reflections of the same subject-matter by its standpoint and perspective (faith as manifest in Christian beliefs and actions). But the reflective elaboration of the perspective of Faith is a cognitive and conceptual task, and it is here that philosophy is used in a variety of ways.

The two main ways of using philosophy in theological reflection are *method* and *metaphysics*. The first or *instrumental* use assigns a merely ancillary function to philosophical thought in theology. The second or *foundational* use conceives it to lay the foundations of the theological superstructure. Let me briefly characterize both types of approaches.

Instrumental use

The *instrumental use* employs philosophy not as a system of categories which specify the basic structure and character of reality but as a set of conceptual devices for analysis, reflection, and argument. This can involve a variety of things, but the following are the standard ways of employment:

1   The *formal use*: Philosophical disciplines like logic, theory of argumentation and methodology provide canons of rational argument which apply to all areas of thought including theology. For although faith involves mysteries, these do not resist reason but invite rational exploration; and although reflection cannot penetrate the depths of revelation, it is self-defeating if it revels in paradox and contradiction instead of operating according to the formal principles of thought and communication which are valid in every area of human inquiry.

2   The *hermeneutical use*: Philosophical principles and methods of interpretation are used to understand the true meaning of scripture and of other verbal and non-verbal, written and unwritten expressions of faith. For although the Christian message will not be accepted as true without the testimony of the Spirit, the exegetical, historical and interpretative tasks of theology are not different in kind from those of other disciplines which involve the interpretion of documents and monuments of the past and present.

3   The *constructive use*: Philosophical patterns of argument and reflection are used to elucidate, clarify, reconstruct and systematize the beliefs invoked and expressed by faith. In this constructive use theology ncessarily goes beyond faith in at least three respects. First, it not only conceptualizes what is already expressed in the figurative, symbolical, metaphorical and narrative discourse of faith but also explicates what is only implied or presupposed by it. Thus whereas faith talks *to* God in prayer, theology talks *about* God to whom Christians pray and even reflects on his existence which is not a topic of Christian prayer or confession but the unquestioned presupposition of everything faith says and does. Second, theology conceptualizes not only *what* faith confesses (semantic content) but also *that* it confesses (pragmatic situation), and therefore investigates the implications and presuppositions not merely of the content but also of the act

of faith. Thus it elucidates not only the belief-content of faith as it is summarized, roughly speaking, in the theological and christological doctrines of the first and second article of the Apostles' creed. It also explicates the act, character and life of faith in the Christian community *in via* and *in patria* which, again roughly speaking, pertains to the pneumatological doctrines of the third article of the creed. Finally, theology goes beyond faith in that the process of theological reflection, especially in a scholastic environment, is bound to become *self-reflective*. It then reflects not only on (the content and act of) faith but also on its own theological reflections of faith. This accounts for the prominence of methodological considerations in modern theology. For constructive theological thought moved naturally from the content-orientated   christological   and   theological   (trinitarian) reflections of the first centuries through the act-orientated anthropological and pneumatological reflections of medieval and Reformation theology to the reflection-orientated methodological considerations of post-Enlightenment theology.

4   The *critical use*: There is no constructive use of philosophy which does not also involve its critical use as a set of criteria for determining what is adequate or inadequate, possible or impossible in theological reconstructions of faith. In content- and act-orientated types of theological reflection this takes primarily the positive form of a critical determination of the essence of the content and/or act of faith in terms of criteria which are derived from normative statements of the Christian faith; and in this case theology functions as arbiter of what is truly Christian in the pluriform cultural manifestations of faith. In reflection-orientated types of theology, on the other hand, it takes the negative form of a critical determination of the limits of our human capacities to reflect on matters of faith and theology in terms of criteria which are derived from critical inquiries into human understanding; and here philosophy functions as arbiter of what is epistemologically possible and rationally acceptable in faith and theology.

5   The *apologetic use*: The constructive and critical uses of philosophy in theology are, as a rule, explicitly or implicitly combined with its apologetical use. This may take the weak and defensive form of refuting, by means of philosophical reflection and argument, philosophical and other external objections to faith and theology by showing them to be ill-founded, incoherent or inconclusive. But this can establish no more than that, as far as these objections go, the truths of faith are not impossible, its concepts of God not incoherent, and its claims not unintelligible. Or it takes the stronger and justificatory form of proof of and rational support to Christian beliefs;

and this transforms the apologetic use of philosophy in theology into its foundational use of theology.

Foundational use

The *foundational use* assigns the role of final arbiter in theological matters to philosophy. Theological reflection, it is argued, is not autonomous but depends on presuppositions which are far from self-evident. Materially it presupposes the facts of faith which it seeks to understand by way of critical and systematic conceptual reconstruction; and methodologically it depends on certain implicit assumptions about the working of language, the nature of our conceptual equipment and the character of reality. It is these assumptions and presuppositions which philosophy seeks to justify by meta-physical and meta-theological argument; and different philosophies have offered different types of justifications ranging - to mention but two recent examples - from Swinburne's neo-Cleanthean probabilistic arguments for the existence of the god of theism (cf. Phillips, 1985, pp. 91ff) to Wagner's neo-Hegelian theory of the absolute subject as the absolutely self-determining self-determination (Wagner, 1986, esp. pp. 572ff).

Understood in this broad sense the foundational use of philosophy is the more comprehensive or generic version of the foundationalist position and its quest for evidental ultimates of knowledge in the wake of Descartes and Locke. This foundationalist version of the foundational programme comprises three components: the laying of foundations by reference to certain egological (Cartesianist) or empirical (Logical Positivist) experiences and the cognitive claims based on them; the testing of foundations by exposing these claims to the process of radical doubt; and the certifying of foundations by showing them to survive the process of doubt unassailed (cf. Surin, 1986, p. 236). But the experiential (empirical or egological) starting-point is not essential to the foundational programme as is shown by Platonist and Hegelian attempts to secure the rational basis of theology by justifying its presuppositions. The common characteristic of all of them is rather that they, in their different ways, attempt to provide non-theological foundations for theology. But this is either trivial or confused. It is trivial if we conceive theology as a human activity which rests on the same biological, psychological, sociological etc. foundations as all our other activities. However, it is confused if we conceive the content of theological reflection, i.e. the acts and claims of the intuitive piety of the Christian faith and its manifestations to be in need of non-theological justification. They can either be justified theologically or not at all. But there is no way to derive theological conclusions from non-theological premisses: the attempt to explain Christian beliefs and actions in terms of psychological, psychoanalytic or sociological theories is not only for anthropologists like E. E. Evans-Pritchard 'dead as mutton' (1965, p. 100; cf. Phillips 1983). It is basically confused because it involves a mixing of external and internal perspectives on faith and the misleading attempt to ground the internal perspective of Faith in the external perspective of Reason. (However, to reject foundationalism for this reason is not necessarily to opt for an autonomist position in Phillip's sense. Revelational theology, as we shall see shortly, offers a non-relativistic solution to the problem of foundationalism in theology.)

It may be objected that this account is much too crude. Faith and theology are not monolithic, and it would be more appropriate to distinguish, with Thomas Aquinas, between the 'preambles' and the 'articles of faith'. The former comprise truths like the existence and metaphysical attributes of God which, because they are accessible to reason, can be demonstrated. The latter include truths like the trinity and the incarnation which cannot be demonstrated but only rationally defended because they are above reason though not contrary to reason. However, it is precisely this distinction between (non-theological) preambles and (theological) articles of faith which is problematic. For either it is a non-theological distinction which amounts to saying that 'the conditions of the truths of faith are established by philosophy' (Charlesworth, 1972, p. 74) and that faith is not autonomous but depends on reason and philosophy. Or it is a theological distinction which is then to be justified on theological grounds; and we have seen that the Nature-Grace Model which underlies Thomas's account rests on precisely such theological convictions. But then preambles of faith are not non-theological presuppositions of theology, for the distinction between preambles and articles of faith is one drawn *within* theology and its system of reflective beliefs. It refers to different kinds of belief and different types of theological reasons for these beliefs. For in the theological system of beliefs we can justify beliefs by reference to other beliefs, infer new beliefs from old ones, prove certain beliefs on the basis of others and offer good reasons for less obvious beliefs in terms of more obvious ones. But all these are rational moves within the circle of theology, and while we have to safeguard the coherence of our system of beliefs and its consistency with beliefs about other matters which we have reasons to believe to be true, we cannot derive theological beliefs from non-theological ones or offer non-theological justifications for theological beliefs or vice versa. In short, philosophy can and must be used within theology, but it cannot be used to ground theology: the rationality of theology does not depend on non-theological rationality of whatever sort.

However, although the rationality of theology is not derived from philosophy, it is different from, and yet related to, the rationality of faith. This is the source of the problem of reflection. Faith is grounded in revelation and the passive constitution of persons in the self-communicating presence of God. Theology, on the other hand, is a human cognitive activity which differs from other intellectual endeavours by its specific standpoint (faith), subject-matter (God's activity in revelation and faith as they become accessible through Christian discourse, beliefs, actions and institutions), and objective (the attempt to understand what faith claims to have received through revelation). It aims at intellectual clarity about faith; it seeks to achieve this by a conceptual reconstruction of the existential structure of faith on the basis of its manifestations in the experiential structures of Christian life; and it thus involves the cognitive transformation of faith from its imaginative manifestations in the beliefs expressed in first-order discourse of faith to its conceptual explication in the reflective beliefs expressed in second-order theological discourse.

It is the task of Christian dogmatics to perform this transformation as clearly as possible and as comprehensively as necessary, and it is beyond the scope of this study even to begin with it. All I can do here is to exemplify the kind of problem it raises with respect to a central issue in the relationship between theology and philosophy: the Christian conception of God. The conceptual reconstruction of the idea and knowledge of God which Christians use and articulate in prayer, proclamation and confession in answer to the revelation purportedly received in Jesus Christ through the Spirit is central to the theological process. It must answer at least the following questions: What sort of knowledge is conveyed in and through revelation? What kind of conception of God results from it? And how does it relate to conceptions of divinity in philosophy and other kinds of theology? These are the questions on which I shall concentrate in the remainder of this part.

Chapter 13

The Content of Revelation and the Knowledge of God

What is revealed in revelation? It is sometimes claimed that God does not reveal propositions but himself. This is a misleading way (cf. Penelhum, 1971, pp. 91ff; Helm, 1982, pp. 25ff) of making an important point. Revelation is not the divine promulgation of propositions about things which we do not (yet) know through means beyond the ordinary course of nature. It is an act of direct, yet mediated, communication between God and us which opens our eyes to the ultimate reality of our existence *coram deo* - not through propositional information from (or about) God but through personal confrontation with God. He discloses himself as loving will and creative love by acting for us in Jesus Christ, and interpreting his actions to us through his Spirit, in a way which enables us to understand ourselves, God and the world in ways otherwise not possible for us. This, of course, involves acquiring new beliefs which we did not have before and which can be spelled out in propositional form (cf. Swinburne, 1981, p. 124). But the 'propositions formulated on the basis of revelation have a secondary status. They do not constitute the content of God's self-revelation but are human and therefore fallible verbalizations, constructed to aid both the integration of our religious experience into our own minds and the communication of religious experience to others' (Hick, 1974, p. 29). Moreover, God's self-revelation does not enlarge our first-order knowledge of natural reality by first-order information about supranatural realities such as the trinity or the incarnation which 'could not at all appearances be obtained by mere reflection on the natural world' (1974, p. 178). Rather it presents something like second-order information about the proper frame for interpreting, understanding and evaluating all our knowledge by disclosing the self-communicating love of God to be the ultimate structure, ground and goal of all there is. That is to say, the *content* of revelation is precisely what *constitutes* revelation: the self-communicating love of God; and the *form* of revelation is the *self-*

identification of this divine love to us in Christ and through the Spirit as the creative ground and goal of everything.

This self-disclosure of God's creative love (as I shall show in more detail in Chapter 18) provokes a complete re-organization of our view of reality and our place in it. It ruptures the given structures of our experience and orientation and provides the point of reference for the working out of a new frame of orientation by directing our minds and lives to what is of ultimate existential significance for us. Of *ultimate* existential import, however, is not information *about* anything, not even about God, nor information purportedly *from* God, but only *God himself*; and of ultimate *existential* import is not knowledge, not even knowledge about God as love, but our total conformity to the divine love in all dimensions of our individual and social existence. We are to trust, to love and to worship God with all our heart, and this involves, but goes beyond, believing information from or about him to be true: it requires building up and sustaining a personal relationship with him. This is impossible without knowing him (rather than merely about him), and it requires him somehow to be present, accessible and identifiable for us. Precisely this, Christians claim, he has made himself in Jesus Christ and continues to make himself through the Spirit; and it is this which they mean by 'revelation'.

The central idea of the Christian concept of revelation is therefore that *in Christ and through the Spirit God identifies himself as Creative Love to the receiver* by establishing an existential relationship with him or her. In this we become aware of our factual situation before God (*homo reus ac perditus*) and he becomes accessible to us as the saving lord of all life (*deus iustificans vel salvator*). Accordingly, a 'doctrine of revelation is an account of God's identifiability' on the basis of God's self-identification to us in Christ (Thiemann, 1985, p. 153). This divine *self-identification* is the salvific content of revelation; it is *salvific* because it is an act of divine self-communication (and not merely something divinely communicated) in which God presents himself to us as the love whose free and creative union with us not only constitutes our existence and deserves our loving response but which continues to do so in spite of our ignoring and not responding to it; and this essentially pragmatic and not merely semantic content of revelation accounts for both the unity and the diversity of Christian beliefs about God, the world and ourselves.

Revelation, then, is primarily an existential event in which we become aware of being constituted as persons *coram deo* by God's self-communicating love to us. This is not to deny that revelation is cognitive, but it is so in a very peculiar and distinctive way. It establishes a strict correlation between our knowledge of God and of ourselves and our world (*cognitio dei et hominis*). To know God on the basis of his self-identification to us as Creative Love is to know ourselves as existing before God who has constituted us and wants us to live in communication and communion with him. This involves knowing (as is made explicit by theological reflection) that God exists; that we owe our existence to God's creative love towards us through which we are constituted and maintained (creation); that God's creative agency is intentional and guided by a purposeful will for his creation; that as God's creatures we owe it to him to live in conformity to his will; that we in fact ignore or wilfully deny the obedience and honour we owe him (sin); that through his revelation in Jesus Christ God has reconciled us with him and given us the chance of living a life of responsive love (grace); and that in his mercy - in the words of Luke (Acts 17:30) - 'the times of ignorance God overlooked, but now he commands all men everywhere to repent' (redemption). The world comes thus to be seen as the field of creaturely activity constituted by the free love of God in which we can lead, or fail to lead, a life that corresponds to the will of God and the ultimate purpose of our existence.

It is the task of Christian dogmatics to elaborate all this. But it is clear that the knowledge disclosed in revelation is peculiar in that it is knowledge of something which exists not independently of being known but is constituted in and through its being known (Fischer, 1983, pp. 13ff). We owe our existence to God even if we do not know and acknowledge that fact; and God remains our creator even where we ignore or deny it. But we are not saved unless we know and acknowledge it; and to come to know it is not to acquire a justified true belief about something which is the case whether we know it or not. On the contrary: to be saved is to know that one is saved. As I cannot be John's friend unless I know myself to be his friend so I cannot be saved by God unless I know myself to be saved by him; and as I cannot know myself to be John's friend without knowing that certain sorts of behaviour towards him are appropriate while others are not, so I cannot know myself to be saved by God without knowing (at least in a rudimentary way) about the practical implications of this for my behaviour towards God and my fellow-creatures. That is to say, revelational knowledge is not factual but *orientational*, and it is not theoretical but *practical*. It is practical because by its very nature it has normative implications: love expects to be returned freely, and the creative love of God expects to be returned freely and completely by the creature. And it is orientational because it involves the reciprocal location of knowing subject and object known in a common frame of reference which is constituted by the relationships of creative love and provides a comprehensive ordering perspective on the whole of reality: there is no knowledge of God on the basis of revelation without corresponding self-knowledge, and conversely (Dalferth, 1981, pp. 47ff); and all revelation-based knowledge of God, the world and ourselves is knowledge of the workings, forms, failures, and achievements of love. That is not to deny that revelation-based knowledge involves various sorts of factual and theoretical knowledge about God, ourselves and the world. But these are embedded in our orientational knowledge and available only as abstractable aspects of our knowledge about our place and tasks *coram deo* and *coram mundo*.

But, then, what sort of theological conception of God can be derived from revelation-based knowledge in the sense outlined? To answer this let us look at the use of 'God' in Christian discourse of faith.

Consider the referential use of 'God' in expressions like 'God has forgiven you all your sins'. In order to understand this we must have, amongst other things, some discriminating knowledge about God which allows us to distinguish him from everything else. Without it we can neither identify and clearly think or speak about him nor love and worship him. Now we are able to discriminate something from (all) other things if we can locate it in our vicinity, recognize it when we encounter it, know some distinguishing facts about it or know that it is none of the things which we can identify in any of these ways (Strawson, 1971, p. 77; Evans, 1982, pp. 89ff). That is to say, we must have a capacity to identify it positively (ostension, recognition, description) or negatively (exclusion).

All these strategies lead into difficulties in the case of God (Dalferth, 1981, pp. 583-606). Discriminating knowledge about God cannot be purely negative, i.e. comprise information only about what God is *not*. For if 'God' is merely a word for what we know when we know nothing, we cannot be sure that it is used to refer to anything at all. All our positive knowledge, however, is derived from either *perception* (the gathering of information in situations of co-presence of perceiver and object perceived), or from *memory* (from perceptions which we have received in the past and can remember), or from *testimony* (the information gathered by others and communicated to us, perhaps through a long chain), or from *reflection* (the conceptual processing of information which we have derived in either of the ways mentioned), or from *self-reflection* (the thinking about oneself as *inter alia* perceiving, remembering, communicating, reflecting). Accordingly, whatever we know is acquired in terms of one or more of three basic epistemolgical paradigms: the *demonstrative paradigm* (perception), the *descriptive paradigm* (memory and testimony) and the *reflective paradigm* (reflection and self-reflection). (These are not unrelated. Descriptive knowledge, for example, may be based on my own past demonstrative knowledge or on the testimony of others about their demonstrative and/or reflective knowledge. To spell out these relations in detail raises many complicated philosophical problems. But the distinctions are clear enough for our purposes to get along with.)

Most of what we actually know (or claim to know) about God falls either into the category of descriptive knowledge because it is information about God communicated to us from others or, less often, into the category of reflective knowledge because it arises from our thinking about the information which we have received. It is that sort of knowledge which is propagated in Christian catechetical teaching and critically reflected, elucidated and elaborated in standard Christian theology. But descriptive knowledge is a hybrid. It is either remembered first-hand or acquired second-hand knowledge because it is derived from our own past demonstrative knowledge or from the testimony of others about their demonstrative and/or reflective knowledge. Yet we may err in what we remember, and be deceived in what is communicated to us; therefore we need strategies to evaluate, test and justify the truth of what we (think we) remember and what is communicated to us. We commonly define knowledge not simply as true belief but as justified true belief; and we accept a belief as justified if it can be shown (or made plausible) to be true in terms of demonstrative and/or reflective knowledge. The decisive question, therefore, is *whether there is any demonstrative and/or reflective knowledge about God* in terms of which we may be able to justify our common descriptive knowledge about him.

Agnostics (for a variety of reasons) refrain from answering this question or reject it, while atheists answer it in the negative. But even those who attempt to offer positive answers do so in quite different ways. At least three cases can be distinguished. *Mythical theology* typically conceives knowledge of gods in terms of the *demonstrative paradigm*: it results from the perception of gods and from interpreting experiential phenomena in terms of divine activities. *Metaphysical theology*, on the other hand, argues that knowledge about God cannot be demonstrative but only *reflective*: God cannot be perceived and theistic interpretations of experiential phenomena are arbitrary unless grounded in reflective knowledge about God. *Revelational theology*, finally, agrees with metaphysical theology that God cannot be perceived but insists nonetheless that there is *demonstrative* knowledge of God albeit not in the way conceived by mythical theology: it involves not merely our interpretation of experiental phenomena in terms of divine activities but, above all, God's self-interpretation to us in and through experiental phenomena. Both the metaphysical and revelational approach have been combined in a variety of ways in the history of Christian theology. But they offer characteristically different answers to the question before us because they favour fundamentally different epistemological paradigms for knowledge about God; and whereas metaphysical theology has always had a natural affinity to philosophy due to its reflective paradigm, it is the demonstrative paradigm of revelational theology which has always kept it at a natural distance from philosophy. To assess their strengths and weaknesses we have to examine their different answers and the main arguments for them.

Chapter 14

Types of Reflective Knowledge about God

One of the convictions shared by both theology and philosophy is that God is not one of the phenomena of our experiential world: only myths present gods as phenomena, but God is not one of the gods and theology not mythology. If, therefore, knowledge about him cannot be acquired in perceptual situations, it seems that it cannot be demonstrative but has to be reflective.

Now reflective knowledge is (justified) true belief derived, on the one hand, from our (individual and communication-based common) perceptual gathering and conceptual processing of generally accessible information about the world and ourselves and, on the other, from our reflection on such processes, their structures, presuppositions and the resultant conceptual schemes. Beliefs arrived at in these ways are conceptual, take the form of propositions and pertain to the possible. They cannot be knowledge unless they are internally coherent and externally consistent with other true beliefs. But coherence and consistency is only necessary, not sufficient for beliefs of this sort to qualify as knowledge. Not everything possible is also compossible; the totality of what is possible vastly exceeds the totality of what is actual; and the totality of our conceptual beliefs includes not only propositions about what is actual in our spatio-temporal world in which time passes and events unfold but also propositions about what is possible in our actual world or in some other world. That is to say, although reflective knowledge may involve true belief about some actual existent (something phenomenally given: a *datum*) or some possible existent (something that might be phenomenally given: a *dabile*), it most characteristically is true belief about:

something that although it could not be phenomenally given allows us to explain otherwise puzzling facts about phenomena or about those who experience phenomena (*theoretical constructs* like electrons or the Ego); or

something that could not be otherwise given the structure of our
actual world (something necessary in our actual world: a *contingent (structural) necessity* or ultimate brute fact like the nature of
our spatio-temporal manifold); or
given the structure of our actual experience of our world (something
necessary in our experiencing our actual world: a *transcendental
necessity* or ultimate reflective fact like the categorial schemes in
terms of which we experience); or
given the structure of our acting in our actual world (something necessary for us as agents: a *practical necessity* like freedom); or
something that could not fail to be as it is (something necessary in all
possible worlds: an *absolute (structural, transcendental, or practical) necessity*).

Reflective knowledge about God without a coherent concept of God
is impossible, but conceptual coherence is not sufficient for knowledge about him: he must also exist. Yet if God cannot be perceived in
fact, he is no *datum* (actual existent), and if he cannot be perceived in
principle, he is no *dabile* (possible existent). Consequently knowledge
about him cannot be inferred from what we know in experience
because - as Hume and Kant have shown - we can argue from things
experienced to things that might be experienced, but not to something beyond experience altogether. But then, if God is no *dabile*, he
can only be a *cogitabile* (Wagner, 1986, pp. 575ff), i.e. a theoretical
construct, or a contingent, transcendental, practical or absolute
necessity; and if reflection is to lead to knowledge about God we have
to be able to decide whether our conceptions of God are mere constructions of something possible (fiction), or theoretical constructs
(useful fictions), or reconstructions of a contingent, transcendental,
practical or absolute necessity. So what kind of *cogitabile* is God? Let
us briefly look at the five possibilities mentioned:

1   God cannot be a theoretical construct because the term 'God'
does not (any longer) function in scientific theories which aim at
explaining facts about the world or ourselves. Electrons have a place
in physical theory because they throw light on a particular area of
reality, suggest new lines of inquiry and allow for experimental
testing; and the Ego is used in (some) psychological theories because
it helps to explain a number of puzzling facts about our acting,
believing and knowing. But this is not so in the case of God. This term
functions in metaphysical theories which are not tied to particular
areas but seek to provide an overall understanding of reality; and
'God' is used in order to throw a particular light on the whole of reality
and to suggest a certain attitude to all experience. But then this case

cannot be strictly parallel to that of theoretical or practical constructs but must be understood differently.

2   Some, like J. Hick or R. Swinburne, have taken God to be a contingent necessity or ultimate brute fact. Thus for Hick 'the existence of purposive intelligence' is 'an ultimate fact' which explains everything but is 'not a candidate for explanation' itself (1979, p. 50). Similarly, Swinburne has argued that God is the ultimate brute fact that explains the universe better and with a higher probability than any rival hypothesis. But he does not hold that God is a logically necessary being, not only because he believes this to be an incoherent idea but because 'the non-existence of God is logically compatible with the existence of the universe' (1979, p. 120).

3   Many philosophers have rejected this, but for different reasons. Some follow Kant in taking the idea of God to be a transcendental necessity demanded by the general conditions of possibility of human knowledge. Understood in this way 'God' is not a concept applicable to reality but an indispensable regulative idea of our knowledge of reality: we require it in order to give completeness and unity to our theoretical knowledge of what is true about the world of our experience. 'God is not,' as Kant put it, 'a Being outside of me, but merely a thought within me' (1936, p. 145). Yet it is not an arbitrary thought because the tendency of our mind to see the world of experience as a unified and connected whole naturally leads us to explain it in terms of 'an all-sufficient necessary cause' or God. We only have to be careful not to reify this regulative principle and mistake it for an actual entity. For although the ideal of a unity in the explanation of the world is necessary, it 'is not an assertion of an existence necessary in itself' (1787, B 647). More recently, Alvin Plantinga has offered a relativistic version of this type of argument by describing belief in God as a properly basic belief which may be part of the foundation of a person's noetic structure (1979, pp. 12-13; 1981). According to him, a belief is rational if it is evident with respect to the beliefs that form the basis of our noetic structure; this may be the case either by being supported by some foundational beliefs or by being itself part of the foundational set of beliefs on which we rely as evidence for non-basic beliefs; and belief in God is rational in the latter sense. But whereas for Kant God is a regulative idea of human knowledge as such irrespective of the concrete form it takes in a given person, belief in God understood in Plantinga's sense may be basic to some persons but not to others so that - as J. Kellenberger has pointed out - it will be rational for one to believe in God and for another not to believe in God (1985, pp. 102-3).

4   Similarly, some have followed Kant in taking God to be a practical necessity, i.e. a necessary postulate of practical reason. The highest good which is the object and final end of pure practical reason can only be attained if morality (the fulfilment of our moral obligations) and happiness coincide; but this is obviously not the case in this life; therefore we have to postulate both our immortality and the existence of God or otherwise 'would have to regard the moral laws as empty figments of the brain, since without this postulate the necessary consequence which is itself connected with these laws could not follow' (Kant, 1787, B 839). God, then, is necessary not for morality as such but for the bringing about of the highest good. This, however, leaves us without any (theoretical) knowledge about God because we cannot make any truth-claims about him.

5   This Kantian attempt to reconcile freedom and reason by distinguishing sharply between knowing and acting, theoretical and practical reason and, accordingly, the impossibility of theoretical knowledge of God and the necessity of postulating God as a regulative idea of morality and the unity of knowledge has met with little approval. Philosophers in the onto-theological tradition like Hegel, Hartshorne or Ward have argued in different ways that God cannot be practically necessary but theoretically unintelligible. If he is possible at all, he is necessarily actual because he cannot fail to exist. The concept of God differs from all other concepts in that we cannot accept it as coherent and remain agnostic about whether it is actually instantiated or not: God is either impossible or a logically necessary being. Thus if there is to be any reflective knowledge about God at all, it must be knowledge not about whether the concept of God is actually instantiated but rather whether this concept is meaningful and coherent; and being coherent is enough for it to be instantiated because it 'is a conceptual truth that any possibly necessary being is actual' (Ward, 1982, p. 26). However, the cogency of this argument depends on the interpretation of the notion of the possibility of God as 'It is possible that God exists' and not 'It is possible that God does not exist'. In the latter case the same type of ontological argument would establish not the necessary existence but the necessary non-existence of God. But we have seen that there are no theoretical *a priori* reasons for choosing one of the two interpretations rather than the other.

These are the main types of reflective knowledge claimed about God. To discuss them it may be useful to place them in a historical and systematic perspective. Metaphysical theology has always insisted that true knowledge of God (as opposed to religious imaginations and mythical pseudo-knowledge) can only be acquired via the reflective route; and, corresponding to its differentiation into reflection and self-reflection, it has developed two characteristically different types of approaches in the history of Western philosophy in terms either of the *paradigm of reflection* or the *paradigm of self-reflection.* The first derives the notion and knowledge of God from a critical reflection of information about the *world* and/or the *self*, and has characteristically taken the form of *cosmological, ideological* and *rational* metaphysics. The second derives it from a critical reflection of our *ways of acquiring information* about the world through perception and reflection and/or our *ways of arriving at knowledge* of our subjective and intersubjective selves as free agents through self-reflection, and has been developed above all in terms of *transcendental, absolutist* or *interpretative* metaphysics. In chapters 15 and 16 I briefly characterize these different approaches.

Chapter 15

Metaphysical Theology in the Paradigm of Reflection

Cosmological metaphysics

Following the lead of Greek philosophical theology the *cosmo-theological tradition* of Western metaphysics (Rowe, 1975; Craig, 1979; 1980) has argued that God, although he is not one of the experiential phenomena of our world, can somehow be inferred from them - by way of the principle of causality or, since Leibniz, by way of the principle of sufficient reason. Demonstrative and reflective knowledge about the world (including ourselves as part of the world) provide the data which, because their full intelligibility requires complete explanation in terms of their ultimate cause or ground, lead to knowledge about God. Thus classical metaphysics (Platonism, Aristotelianism), neoclassical metaphysics (Process Philosophy) and modern scientific metaphysics (Shepherd, 1975; Schlesinger, 1977; Swinburne, 1979) start, in different ways, from information about the world and conceive God in terms of ontological, cosmological, psychological, biological or personal models as the ultimate and self-explanatory ground of the being of and order in the world.

However, although they all agree that the actual existence and character of the world is ultimately unintelligible without the actual existence of God, they differ considerably in the details of their conceptions of God and their account of the kind of knowledge arrived at in cosmological inference. The differences are due not only to changes in scientific theory and logical method but above all to two basic metaphysical contrasts. The first is that between *immanent* and *transcendent* metaphysics (cf. Walsh, 1970, pp. 84ff; Körner, 1984, pp. 53-161), i.e. those who, like Aristotle and Whitehead, conceive the opposition between appearance and reality to be a difference between more or less adequate kinds of experience and more or less perfect kinds of existents within one and the same reality, and those who, like Plato and Plotinus, conceive it to be a difference between different kinds of reality and between experience and the possibility of transcending experience altogether. The second is that between *a priori* and *a posteriori* metaphysics, i.e. those who, like Farrer or Ward, claim the status of necessary truths for their metaphysical explanations, and those who, like Schlesinger and Swinburne, claim a higher probability for them than rival explanations. Thus Aristotelianism has conceived the divine as *a* being rather than being itself: God is the most eminent and perfect being in the universe. But this presupposes that he can be compared to other beings, which is only possible if he is somehow related to the less perfect beings and participates in the same order of reality; thus although he exists in the most exalted and excellent way, his existence is analoguous to that of beings of lesser order. Others have argued, in particular in the neo-Platonist tradition, that God is not a being, not even the most exalted one, but the ineffable ground of being which utterly transcends everything we can experience, know or express; accordingly, negative theology, not analogy, has been central to its doctrine of God. Both types of approach have been decisively criticized by Hume and Kant, who had shown that what cannot be experienced in principle cannot be a cause or ground of what falls within experience. Thus either God is inferred cosmologically from what we know in experience, then he cannot be utterly beyond experience but must be a being which is in, or a part of, the world of experience; or he is truly God and as such utterly beyond anything we can experience, then he cannot be known by cosmological inference.

Ideological metaphysics

If God cannot be inferred from reality as experienced by us he might be inferred from the reality of our ideas. This is the *mentalist approach* which, following the Augustinian tradition, Descartes has taken. Augustine had argued under the impact of neo-Platonist ideas that the human mind, if purified from the distortions of sense-experience by the action of the will, can arrive at knowledge of God's existence although it cannot comprehend him. Reason, the supreme element in the human mind, is capable of apprehending eternal and unchangeable truth; if, therefore, there is anything more excellent than eternal truth, it is God; if not, truth itself is God. In either case, although God is greater than we can conceive, we at least cannot deny that he exists (*De libero arbitrio* II. xv).

Descartes accepted the conclusion but not the argument for it. For him the question was not whether our knowledge about God is true but whether we can be certain that it is true. Certainty, however, is not a matter of will but of reason; reason has its standards set by the clarity and certainty which are achieved in mathematics; and for metaphysical knowledge to be certain it must not fall below but surpass these standards. Now mathematical knowledge is certain because it is demonstrative and follows from precisely defined terms and self-evident axioms. But how can evidence of this sort be achieved in philosophy and its search for first principles? Not by demonstration, but by doubt. For knowledge to be certain it must be shown clearly and distinctly that what is known is so and cannot be otherwise; but everything that can be doubted could be otherwise. Therefore, as Descartes argues in his *Meditations on First Philosophy*, doubt is the method to achieve certainty in philosophical matters because it helps to exclude what cannot be certain. The point of his method of doubt is not a psychological but a logical one: If X, a mental content of our consciousness, can be doubted, then being conscious of X does not entail the existence of X because it is not incompatible with there being no Xs; if, however, it cannot be doubted without self-contradiction, then we can be certain that what we are conscious of is true. So doubt is not purely negative, i.e. uncovering what is not certain. Rather turning doubt on itself allows Descartes to refute the supposition that mental contents can always be contemplated without existential commitment. For whereas I can doubt all knowledge derived from sense perception and even the truths of mathematics, I cannot doubt that in doubting I exist. Descartes thus arrives at the indubitably certain idea of himself and, by further analysis of this idea, at the idea of God, the most perfect and powerful being which cannot not exist. This idea must be innate because it is so basic that it could not have been derived from sense experience, and so simple that it cannot be a product of our imagination. If, therefore, the indubitably certain idea of ourselves is necessarily linked with the indubitably certain idea of God, we have certain knowledge about God: as thinking logically entails existence, so thinking God logically entails his necessary existence.

However, the analogy is mistaken. Even if we grant Descartes that 'I doubt, therefore I exist' is certain because 'I doubt' is incompatible with 'I do not exist', this is not so in the case of God. Whereas the certainty about my existence arises not from *what* I doubt but from the fact *that* I doubt, the certainty about God's necessary existence arises from *what* I think, not from the fact *that* I think. But the semantic inconsistency of the latter case has not the force of the pragmatic inconsistency of the former. My doubting entails that I exist, and God's thinking entails that he exists. Yet my thinking God does not entail that God exists but that if God exists, he exists necessarily. Thus even if we accept Descartes's arguments for the certainty of 'I doubt, therefore I exist' and of 'I think God, therefore God exists necessarily', it does not follow that 'God exists' is certain. For this to be certain we need to establish the certainty not only of 'I doubt, therefore I exist' but also of 'I exist, therefore God exists'; and this cannot be done after the pattern of the *dubito* argument because 'I exist' is not (at least not without further arguments) incompatible with 'God does not exist'. So the mentalist case for reflective knowledge about God seems to rest entirely on the problematic empirical hypothesis of the innateness of the idea of God which cannot be sustained in the light of empiricist, critical and evolutionary epistemologies of Locke, Hume, Kant, Piaget and others.

Rational metaphysics

In contrast to inferential metaphysics of the cosmological and ideological type, philosophers in the *onto-theological tradition* like Leibniz, Hartshorne or Plantinga try to base their reflective knowledge about God not on *a posteriori* considerations about facts and actualities but on *a priori* considerations about possibilities and compossibilities. They start neither from the self and its factual ideas nor from the world and its factual structures but from more formal and more general considerations about categorical and metaphysical truths which exclude no positive possibility and apply positively to any actuality (Hartshorne, 1955). Thus they rest knowledge about God not on the proposition 'I exist' but on the more general 'Something exists'; and they claim a necessary relationship not between God and this actual world but between God and one world or another. Not the existence of this world but 'the existence of any world at all is what proves God' (Hartshorne, 1967, p. 83); God is not inferred from but implied by everything that is because 'To be is to be known by God' (Hartshorne, 1955, p. 296); and if it is possible that God exists, then he exists necessarily.

The force of this kind of argument depends on our accepting that God's existence is possible. For if God's existence is either impossible or necessary, the possibility of his existence is all we need for concluding that he exists necessarily; and for this it seems to be enough that the notion of 'God' understood in terms of perfection, unsurpassability or maximal greatness is internally consistent. But this is not so. Consistency is necessary but not sufficient for the rationalist's argument to get off the ground. For the notion of the possibility of God's existence is ambiguous: it may mean either (1) 'It is possible that God exists' or (2) 'It is possible that God does not exist'. Either case presupposes the internal consistency of the notion of God, but the former entails his necessary existence, the latter his necessary non-existence. So we require arguments beyond the mere consistency of the notion of God for choosing between (1) and (2). These arguments cannot be purely conceptual but must be based on experience; and they will appeal either to the experience of God's reality (or actuality) or of his non-reality (or non-actuality). For whereas those who believe (for whatever reasons) in the reality or presence of God will opt for (1), those who believe (for whatever reasons) in the non-reality or absence of God will opt for (2). Now experience cannot guarantee its own validity, and the credibility of experience-based claims depends on the evidence adduced. But whereas the claim of God's absence or non-reality seems to be well-supported by our post-Enlightenment experience of reality, the appeal to his presence and reality in and with our everyday experience, in special 'religious experiences', or in his revelation will not convince the sceptic as long as there are no intersubjective testing procedures for this claim. In short, without being antecedently persuaded of the existence of God in one way or another rational metaphysics does not get off the ground (Dalferth, 1986).

Chapter 16

Metaphysical Theology in the Paradigm of Self-Reflection

Cosmological, ideological and rational metaphysics follow the route of reflection to arrive at reflective knowledge about God. Another group of approaches takes the route of self-reflection. They aim at knowledge about God not by reflecting on the world or the self or the nature of possibility but by reflecting on *our reflecting on* the world, the self and possibility. One of the first to suggest this line of approach was Nicholas of Cusa (1401-64). In his dialogue *Idiota de Sapientia* he asked: How is it possible to conceive and conceptualize God if God is greater than can be conceived? And he answers: Not directly by trying to comprehend the incomprehensible but indirectly by forming a concept of our forming concepts, by conceptualizing our conceptualizing. Thus to conceive God we have to conceive our conceiving, i.e. not only *what* we conceive but *what it is to conceive*; and because conceiving (like experiencing, understanding, reflecting) is an activity of a conceiving (experiencing, understanding, reflecting) subject, knowledge of God must be based on self-knowledge of the subject. This was the line of approach that culminated in the idealist systems of the nineteenth century which conceived God in terms of egological, social, historical or interactionist models as the ultimate ground of subjectivity and intersubjectivity, the absolute identity of necessity and freedom or the ultimate unity of the totality of being and the universality of knowledge. Once again there are at least three different types of approaches to be distinguished.

Transcendental metaphysics

Kant's critical philosophy is the paradigm for this approach. God is not a reality over against us which could in any way be known by theoretical reason. Rather the notion of God is to be construed relative to the conditions of the possibility of experience, knowledge and moral fulfilment: God is not an objective reality but an 'Ideal of Reason', a regulative principle necessary for the systematic unity of our knowledge about the world of experience; and he is - in the realm of practical reason - a postulate of practical reason necessary for the achievement of the highest good. But this amounts to saying that there is no knowledge about God that could be true or false: all theoretical knowledge is limited to what can be experienced, yet God is not a *dabile*; and conceptual analysis on its own yields knowledge only of conceptual structures: 'Through concepts alone, it is quite impossible to advance to the discovery of new objects and supernatural beings; and it is useless to appeal to experience, which in all cases yields only appearances' (Kant, 1787, B 667). But although we cannot know about God in any real sense, the idea of God is necessary for us. Not, indeed, to be able to know at all, but to achieve unity and coherence in our knowledge of the world; and not to be able to be moral and act responsibly as free agents, but to achieve the object of pure morality, the highest good. In this peculiar sense, then, God is necessary: not because *he* is a necessary being which exists in every possible world so that if anything is possible, he is actual; but because *we* cannot know coherently and achieve our moral objective without postulating him. God is not necessary, but, for us, it is necessary to postulate him.

Kant's critical philosophy and agnostic philosophical theology is not the only version of transcendental metaphysics. Following the scholastic tradition Bernard Lonergan has offered a much more positive account of it. Like Nicholas of Cusa and Kant he insists that in order to understand God we have 'thoroughly to understand what it is to understand', for then we not only will 'understand the broad lines of all there is to be understood' but also 'will possess a fixed base, an invariant pattern, opening upon all further developments of understanding' (1958, p. xxviii). Hence he claims that 'it is one and the same thing to understand what being is and to understand what God is' (p. 658). Now the idea of being 'is the content of an unrestricted act of understanding' (p. 644), and God, accordingly, is 'the most meaningful of all possible objects of our thought' (p. 669). This object is not merely an object of thought because - as Lonergan argues - 'If the real is completely intelligible, God exists. But the real is completely intelligible. Therefore, God exists' (p. 672). This is not an ontological argument. It agrees that we have to go beyond mere conception in order to conclude God's existence. But it remains firmly within the tradition of reflective knowledge about God because it insists that 'what has to be

added to mere conception is not an experience of God but a grasp of
the unconditioned' from premises that are true (p. 672). These
premises are developed in a transcendental analysis of the act of
unrestricted understanding and can be summarized as (1) 'The real is
completely intelligible' and (2) 'If the real is completely intelligible,
God exists'.

However, although the argument is developed not in terms of the
structure of reality but of our understanding reality, it is a transcendental version of the cosmological argument and shares all its
deficiencies (cf. Mackie, 1982, ch. 5). (1) Even if we agree that some of
what we can know is completely intelligible it does not follow that all
is or that everything there is can be known and explained. For to be
intelligible is to be intelligible *for us*, and something is intelligible for
us if we can answer why it is and why it is in the way it is. But this, as
Swinburne has shown, is possible if we can produce an explanation *F*
of the *explanandum E* in question which 'includes both a cause, *C*, and
a reason, *R*, which together necessitated the occurrence of *E*'; and it
is 'the completist fallacy' to assume that nothing could be fully
explained in this way unless everything is or can be explained (1979,
p. 73). Thus not everything has to be completely intelligible for something to be completely intelligible; conversely we have no reason to
assume the complete intelligibility of all reality from the complete
intelligibility of some reality. (2) Even if we grant that not only something but everything real is completely intelligible, it does not follow
that God exists. For if everything is completely intelligible then there
is nothing of which we cannot answer why it is and why it is in the way
it is. But it is one thing to claim everything *within the universe* to be
completely intelligible because every part of the universe can be
explained in terms of some other part of the universe, quite another
to claim the *universe as a whole* to be completely intelligible. We do
not have to assume the latter for the former to be true, so that there is
no reason to assume a being distinct from (part of) the universe which
explains why it is and why it is as it is. Even if everything within the
universe can be explained in terms of something else it does not follow
that there exists a being in terms of which everything else can be
explained and which itself is self-explanatory; and even if there were
something self-explanatory because its very description provides the
reason why it is and why it is as it is, this, as Spinoza has shown, may
well be the universe itself. In short, the cosmological argument, in
either its traditional or transcendental form, does not establish
knowledge about God. God's existence may be sufficient to infer the
complete intelligibility of reality, but not vice versa.

Absolutist metaphysics

It is the fundamental insight of Hegel's philosophy that the complete intelligibility of reality is not the basis but the consequence of our knowledge about God. We have to begin with it if we want to arrive at it; we could not arrive at it if we started from something completely different from it; and we could not begin with it if all knowledge did not somehow already involve knowledge about God. Thus, for Hegel, the question is not how to arrive at knowledge about God from some other knowledge but how to develop the knowledge of God which we already possess from its rudimentary forms towards completion. For him, there is no way into knowledge about God from outside but only its elaboration to ever greater completion from within: the beginning and end of our knowledge of God are indeed different, but it is a difference-in-unity because we are always, in all areas and at every level of our knowledge, already involved in the process of knowing God.

This is the fundamental conviction which permeates the whole of Hegel's philosophy: knowledge about God is not something to be inferred from other knowledge but that which includes all other knowledge. It is not more abstract and obscure than other knowledge but more concrete and certain because all other knowledge is only partial, incomplete and abstracted from it. It does indeed know progress and improvement like all other knowledge, but improvement in our knowledge of God is not independent of improvement in other areas of knowing. In short, if philosophy wants to be more than 'sounding brass, or a tinkling cymbal' (1822, p. 243), it must systematically begin with, rely on and aim at knowledge about God. Thus for Hegel to *begin* with the knowledge of God is to presuppose that rationality rules reality in a process of active self-realization; that this can be shown because it is one and the same rationality, i.e. the rationality of the divine Spirit, which is ontologically at work in reality and epistemologically in and through us; and that the structure of this dynamic rationality can be described and reproduced as a system of categories of pure thought which are, in the famous phrase of Hegel's *Logic*, 'the presentation of God ... *before* the creation' (1831, p. 44). Yet Hegel not only claims this but actively *relies* on it in the working out of his philosophy. Thus he attempts to justify his assumption of the rationality of reality by showing in detail that the categories of his *Logic* capture the rationality revealed in nature, history and the variety of our cultural forms, and that they allow the representation of the evolving rationality of the whole of reality in

the form of a scientific system of all truth on its way towards completion. It is precisely this process by which we *arrive* at full knowledge
about God, although we shall not finally possess it before the point of
completion of the system of truth is obtained. For 'the true is the
whole'; 'the whole completes itself through its development'; and 'the
Absolute . . . is essentially *result*', because 'only at the end is it that
which it is in truth' (1807, p. 24).

It was the failure of Kant's transcendental metaphysics, and its
underlying philosophy of subjectivity, to establish knowledge about
God which led Hegel to his complete reversal of approach: he
describes the possibility and growth of knowledge about God not in
terms of the knowing subject and its attempts to grasp, understand,
know and explain reality but in terms of the dialectical self-realization
of the Absolute Spirit on its way to Absolute Knowledge in both the
history of reality and our growing knowledge of it. For him God is not
merely a transcendental Ideal of Reason but Absolute Spirit, i.e.
Spirit knowing itself as Spirit; and the process of its coming to know
itself is the twofold process of the history of the world and of the
growth of our knowledge of the world. Now knowledge is analysed by
Hegel not in terms of a subject and its cognitive activities *vis-à-vis*
objective reality (as *naive realism* does) nor as the synthesizing activity of a self which subsumes particular contents received through
intuition under the general concepts of the understanding (as *critical
realism* does) but - and this is Hegel's *absolute or idealist realism* -
as a productive process of consciousness with two interrelated components or poles, i.e. the consciousness of what is known (object of
knowledge) and the self-consciousness of the knower (subject of
knowledge), which become successively integrated in a dialectical
process of self-determination which actually generates truth. Knowledge, in short, is the self-creating synthesis of object-consciousness
and self-consciousness; and self-knowledge, accordingly, the self-
creating synthesis of self-consciousness and the consciousness of the
self as being self-conscious: it is not immediate knowledge of oneself
but the process and result of the productive overcoming of the
bifurcation or difference between the self as knowing and the self as
known. If this analysis is applied to the problem before us, then the
self of which the Spirit is conscious is not the immediate consciousness of its being conscious but - in Hegel's realist version of
Aristotle's *noesis noeseos* - that in and through which the Spirit
becomes self-conscious, i.e. the whole process of the history of the
world with its emergence of finite consciousness, self-consciousness
and God-consciousness in and through which the Spirit achieves its
Absolute Knowledge.

The same approach can be described from the perspective of the human knower and the reality known in this process in the following way: reality is not made up of unrelated discrete particulars but a continuum, both spatially, temporally and ontologically; the knowing human subject stands not *vis-à-vis* reality but is part of the very reality which it attempts to understand; and it comes to know reality precisely insofar as in and through its knowing, reality itself comes to know itself. Now reality can only come to know itself because it is essentially (albeit externalized) Spirit, and it can come to know itself completely only because it is Infinite Spirit. Knowledge, however, essentially involves a difference between the subject and object of knowledge. Self-knowledge, on the other hand, requires the identity of the subject and object of knowledge. Hence self-knowledge, because it involves both identity (*qua self*-knowledge) and difference (*qua knowledge*), essentially manifests the structure of identity-in-difference; and this, according to Hegel, is borne out by the social genesis of self-knowledge: we come to know ourselves not immediately but in and through our relationships with others who are different from us. But we can acquire self-knowledge in this way only because these others are not totally different in kind from us: we can recognize them, and they can recognize us, as spirits. This enables us, in a process of reciprocal assimilation and accommodation, to acquire knowledge of ourselves by critically appropriating their knowledge of us. This, according to Hegel, is true of the self-knowledge of both finite and Infinite Spirit. They can come to know themselves not immediately but only mediated through something different from themselves; but whereas for finite spirit these are other finite spirits, for Infinite Spirit it is the whole process of the emergence of finite spirit and its attempts to understand itself, the world and God.

There are many aspects of Hegel's philosophy with which one might quarrel. For our purposes, however, the basic problems are not the details of his system but its basic presuppositions: his conviction that rationality rules reality, and that the rationality of reality is identical with the divine Spirit externalized into the world. Let us briefly look at these in turn.

First, it is by no means obvious that reality is rational, and Hegel's notorious dictum 'The rational is real, and the real is rational' has been attacked and criticized for a variety of reasons. However, Hegel does not plead for an uncritical justification of what is the case. On the contrary. The rational is the criterion of what is to count as real; we know this criterion if we grasp the rationality of the Spirit; and we can grasp it precisely insofar as the Spirit manifests itself in our minds. Hence we can grasp reality as rational by perceiving the manifestation of the infinite rationality of the Spirit in it. But not everything that is is real in this sense: the irrational is part of the history of the world, but it is doomed to be overcome by the rational in the ongoing process of the self-realization of the Spirit. In short, Hegel is affirmative not of that which is the case but of the Infinite Spirit and its dynamic presence in everything that is the case. Finite and infinite reality are dynamically related; we cannot really know the finite unless we grasp the infinite in it; this is impossible unless we have already some idea and identifying knowledge of it; and this we have precisely insofar as the Spirit manifests itself creatively in our minds and pure thoughts.

Everything, therefore, hinges on the basic claim that what is rational in reality is the rationality of the divine Spirit which progressively manifests itself in it. Obviously, this could not be true if either the ideas of the Spirit and its self-realizing rationality were self-contradictory or reality were unintelligible, not dynamic and would manifest no, or no significant, rationality. But although Hegel invests immense energy to exhibit the fact and character of rationality in all areas of reality from logic and pure thought through nature and all the specialized disciplines that investigate nature to history, society, the state and the cultural achievements of finite spirits in art, religion, and philosophy, this is not enough to bear out his claim. The intelligibility of reality in all its facets is a necessary but not sufficient condition for the truth of it. On its own it is compatible not only with Hegel's dialectical idealism but also with, for example, Marx's dialectical materialism. There is nothing impossible in agreeing with Hegel on the intelligibility and dynamic character of reality and yet explaining it not as the manifestation of the Spirit but in terms of mundane natural and economic forces. Furthermore, neither side in this dispute is in a position to disprove the other merely by reference to the facts. For both are meant to be *universal*, i.e. reflexively applicable to themselves and capable of explaining themselves in the same terms as everything else, and *comprehensive*, i.e. compatible with all the facts including their own existence. This may be wrong. But the question at stake between them is not primarily one of facts but of the frames in which facts are to be placed, interpreted and explained; and frames, especially if they are meant to be all-comprehensive and universally valid, can only be made plausible in terms of their formal coherence, consistency, general applicability, adequacy and power to produce fruitful insights into the structure and character of reality. Thus that all events in reality, including our experiences, explanations and theories, are moments in the divine life of God and that the rationality which we can discover in the world is the rationality of the divine Spirit cannot in principle be 'read off' from finite reality as such: it necessarily transcends every particular insight because it is the frame and presupposition of all insights. But what reasons are there to believe this basic presupposition to be true given that it is neither impossible nor incompatible with what we know about reality?

For Hegel it is the fundamental speculative insight which, as such, cannot be justified in terms of something more fundamental but only confirmed in the working out of the philosophical system. Yet precisely this pragmatic confirmation proves it to be more plausible and convincing than any alternative for at least two reasons. The first and *philosophical reason* is its unrivalled integrating power and superiority as a principle of epistemic coherence and unity of knowledge. It allows understanding of other positions and insights as partial truths of a complex and internally differentiated process of truth which includes both world and God and ensures that everything that can be known is a component of a coherent system of knowledge. The problem here is not only the pervasive optimism according to which even the false, the negative and the irrational can be reintegrated as moments of the true and rational; the problem is above all that it seems to be difficult if not impossible rationally to criticize this position from any point other than the point of completion of that system (cf. Rosen, 1982). But whereas Popper and others have concluded from this that Hegel's philosophy is to be rejected because it is immune to criticism, others have claimed that he and Popper 'represent the only fallibilist traditions in modern philosophy' (Lakatos, 1976, p. 139). His coherentist approach is diametrically opposed to the foundationalist quest for the evidential ultimates of our knowledge from Descartes through Kant to the Logical Positivists: all our beliefs are potentially vulnerable and have to be tested against other beliefs. There is no absolute primacy of the self; but neither is knowledge merely a social product. For Hegel it is rather - and this is the ultimate *religious* reason for his optimistic trust in truth and reason - a product of interaction between divine (infinite) and human (finite) spirit. In short, Hegel replaces the self-centred approach of modern philosophy since Descartes not simply by a pluri-centric and other-involving one (cf. Rescher, 1973, pp. 332-3) as pragmatists have done since the days of Charles S. Peirce but by a rigorously God-centred approach: to be is to be known by God, and to know is to know that one is known by God.

Thus Hegel's philosophy ultimately rests on deep-seated religious convictions; and it comes as no surprise that his second and even more important *religious reason* for his basic claim is its, as he sees it, conformity with the Christian revelation. He understood his God-centred approach to be not only grounded in the Christian faith but to

consummate philosophically what Luther had inaugurated theologically: God, who became incarnate in Jesus Christ and is present in his
Spirit, is not merely the transcendent beginning and end of everything but the immanent, active and universal mediation and reconciliation of all separations both within finite reality and between finite
and infinite reality: he is the absolute reality than which nothing more
real can be conceived and without which nothing is, or could be, real.
Everything that is somehow participates in the dynamic life of God: it
is a moment in the process of the divine Spirit on its way to Absolute
Knowledge.

The problems which this raises have been pointed out most
emphatically by Kierkegaard. The Christian faith, he argued, which
for Hegel supports if not justifies his fundamental speculative
insight, is completely misrepresented and resists all philosophical
efforts to capture and rationally universalize it. Its particularity cannot be overcome philosophically by integrating it into an all-
encompassing system. It does not seek rational grounds to vindicate
itself. It has nothing to do with speculative truth. It 'belongs to and
has its home in the existential, and in all eternity it has nothing to do
with knowledge' (Kierkegaard, 1965, p. 110). In short, it is 'a relation
from personality to personality' (p. 110) and the believer not only
'believes against the understanding' but 'also uses understanding to
make sure that he believes against the understanding' (p. 504). So the
issue turns on the correct interpretation of the Christian faith and its
alleged or denied cognitivity - a topic which has been at the centre of
debate in recent philosophy of religion. Hegel, at any rate, was an
unashamed cognitivist, and his whole system bears witness to it. However, he was not a reductionist as sometimes claimed (Charlesworth,
1972, p. 177) who reduced faith to speculative knowledge. Rather he
was an all-inclusive cognitivist who not so much redescribed the
Christian faith as a species of metaphysics as developed his metaphysics as a redescription of the whole of reality in the light of what
he took to be the basic insight of faith. Faith, as it were, was the context of discovery of his basic insight; the whole of reality its field of
application; and philosophy the mode of its detailed working out and
speculative confirmation. Thus Hegel's absolutist metaphysics
presupposed what others first tried to establish: that knowledge
about God is not only the end but in fact the beginning of all sound
philosophy.

Interpretative metaphysics

It was the interpretative aspect of Hegel's approach that survived even when his metaphysics ceased to catch the imagination because its basic convictions were no longer shared. Metaphysics took a hermeneutic turn; philosophical speculation was replaced by interpretative views of the world, philosophies of life, or scientific worldviews; interpretation became 'the peculiar philosophical activity of thought' (Barnes, 1950, p. 169) and the analysis and elucidation of the interpretative principles and frameworks which govern our views of the world and our various forms of life and ways of living in the world the primary philosophical task. For all experience, belief and action involves interpretation but some interpretations are more illuminating and adequate than others. Therefore it is the task of philosophical reflection to elucidate as clearly as possible and in as much detail as necessary the interpretative principles that inform our prephilosophical experience in all areas of life, thought and action.

This can be done in more than one way, as philosophers as widely different as Heidegger, Gadamer, Collingwood, Wittgenstein, Quine or Ricoeur have shown. But they all manifest the characteristic feature of the interpretative metaphysics approach: the distinction between a (pre-philosophical) *interpretandum* (a specific area of life, experience and action, or the structure of life, experience and action as such) and a (philosophical) *interpretans* (a philosophical theory or system of categories for reconstructing the *interpretandum* in question). Foundationalist versions of this approach like nineteenth-century historicism or twentieth-century (logical) positivism take the *interpretandum* ultimately to consist in facts or data which can be distinguished from their interpretations, to which they are only externally related. More radical (and more adequate) versions insist that there is no *interpretandum*, in any case not in the realm of culture and cultural artefacts, which is not itself constituted by and therefore analysable as a relationship between *interpretandum* and *interpretans*. For example, to interpret a historical event like the French revolution or the crucifixion of Jesus is to elucidate the internal relationship between certain natural events, human actions and their specific meanings against a wider context of meaning. The event is our *interpretandum*; but it is itself structured as a relation between *interpretandum* and *interpretans* which we try to elucidate in our interpretation by reconstructing (amongst other things) how the agents involved understood their actions and how their contemporaries and later generations interpreted and reinterpreted them. There is no way to step outside the circle of interpretation or to arrive at a definitive philosophical reconstruction of this event, only a piecemeal process of elucidating the interpretative relationship which constitutes the *interpretandum* in question against the complex background of meaning implied and presupposed by it.

Interpretative metaphysics thus conceived can be *revisionary* or *descriptive*. It can suggest and specify principles and frameworks in the light of which we *should* conceive and interpret reality; or it can describe and clarify the pre-philosophical convictions which in fact govern our experience of and thought about the world and ourselves. Most types of interpretative metaphysics in our century from Heidegger and Collingwood to Wittgenstein and Ricoeur have taken this latter approach.

Collingwood, to discuss only him, conceived the task of metaphysics to be the study of 'absolute presuppositions'. All our knowledge is relative to questions which we ask. But every question and answer proceeds on assumptions which are presupposed to be true. If I ask how your father is I imply that you have a father. This presupposition may itself be understood as an answer to a further question, e.g. whether or not your father is still alive, and when this is possible Collingwood speaks of a 'relative presupposition'. But it may also be understood to mean that all human beings have parents or, even more generally, that *ex nihilo nihil fit*, which cannot (or until very recently could not) sensibly be made the subject of further questioning or be established by consulting the facts. Presuppositions of this sort are 'absolute presuppositions'. Absolute presuppositions cannot be said to be true or false. They cannot be justified by deducing them from more basic principles, and they are not empirical generalizations which we would be prepared to give up in the face of adverse evidence (or if they are they are thereby shown to be not, or no longer, absolute presuppositions). Principles of this sort are not 'read off' but 'read into' experience; they constitute our (individual or common) framework for a coherent view of the diverse types of our experience; and whereas they can be modified under the pressure of experience or replaced by alternative presuppositions, they cannot be proved or disproved.

The absoluteness of such presuppositions is not a property of the views in question but of the way they are held: they are treated as absolute, i.e. as the organizing principles of our orientational knowledge or large-scale cognitive map by which we integrate and unify the many different types of experience into a coherent and consistent system of beliefs. But they are not to be confused with ultimate presuppositions in transcendental metaphysics (cf. Nygren, 1972, chs. 7 and 8). Ultimate presuppositions are epistemologically necessary in the sense of underlying all our experiencing, reasoning and argumentation. They are part of our categorial structure analysed by transcendental reflection. But (*pace* Walsh, 1970, pp. 159ff) these categorial principles are not what Collingwood has in mind. His absolute presuppositions are contingent and relative to a given person, group of persons, age or culture; and the absolute presuppositions of one person, group, age or culture are not necessarily identical with those of another. Absolute presuppositions may and do change; and precisely this is impossible for ultimate presuppositions. Ultimate presuppositions, we might say, are part of the categorial structure of our *knowledge*, absolute presuppositions of the cognitive structure of our *orientational* knowledge. But even if we all experience and interpret the world according to a common set of categorial principles, it does not follow that we all arrive at the same cognitive map of reality or the same orientation in the world. Thus Collingwood's interpretative metaphysics goes beyond transcendental metaphysics precisely in that it concentrates on the structure and principles not of our knowledge as such but of our historically contingent *orientational* knowledge.

In this type of approach claims to knowledge about God can be based on either the *interpretandum* or the *interpretans*. In the latter case 'god' is introduced as an interpretative category used to illuminate (aspects of) our experience of reality. 'The concept of God,' as John Macquarrie (1984, p. 29) argues, 'is an interpretative concept, meant to give us a way of understanding and relating to reality as a whole.' But then the 'god'-category has to be defined as clearly as possible in contrast to the other categories of our frame of interpretation, and its introduction has ultimately to be justified by reference to the *interpretandum*. Yet as God is neither an experiential *datum* nor a *dabile* we have to show what is our experience of the world that requires that we use it. Four types of answers are usually given.

1 The structure of *experience as such* and of our ways of acquiring beliefs and knowledge about the world require the use of the 'god'-category. Thus it has been argued by Barnes that 'only by positing God can *all* the different spheres of experience be synthesized'. To achieve this is epistemologically necessary, and it makes God 'a rationally compelling hypothesis'. For 'any entity which performed it would be God' and 'different hypotheses would be simply differing conceptions of God' (1950, p. 177). But it is not enough to posit god as the ground of all contingent (knowledge of) reality. For unless this being which we are rationally obliged to posit exists

independently of our positing, it cannot serve its purpose. Hence we are faced with the dilemma of choosing between foundationalism or fideism: either we argue for its independent existence along the lines of cosmological, ideological or rational metaphysics (which is not convincing) or we presuppose it without argument in our analyses (which is not compelling). To take either kind of approach presupposes some prior theistic convictions grounded in some specific experience. Thus 'an essential prerequisite for the construction of a theistic metaphysics' along these lines is some specific experience which not only requires us to posit such a being but in which 'the nature of this Being is disclosed to a limited extent' (p. 178).

2   Not the structure of experience as such but *specific kinds of experiences* require the introduction of the interpretative category 'god'. T. W. Jennings has described and analysed such experiences in (what he calls) the 'ontological', 'aesthetic', and 'historical region', i.e. experiences like peace, despair, awe, wonder, joy, terror, dread, hope, grief, love etc. (1985, chs. 6-9). These are not specifically religious or crypto-religious experiences in that they need not necessarily be interpreted in religious terms. But they all lend themselves to religious interpretations and form the experiential basis of god-talk. For they are all areas in which creative events occur which rupture or interrupt the given experiential structure of our life, and which require us to re-organize and re-arrange our system of beliefs accordingly. The fundamental tension between creativity and control in our existence is particularly obvious here. It gives rise to god-talk when something occurs which resists assimilation to the structure of our language and experience so that we can only attempt to schematize it in terms of criteria like importance, transcendence and 'the generically human' (1985, pp. 63ff). If this kind of experience is the *interpretandum* of the category 'god', its use involves reference to the special character of the experiences in question which stand outside the ordinary ways of structuring our experience and, on the other, to the new 'integration of all our experience on the basis of these events' (pp. 129-30). There can be no doubt that this captures some central features of interpretative talk of god. But it does not explain why we should use 'god' rather than some other category to mark both the point of rupture of our former orientation and the point of reference of our new orientation; why this should lead to monotheistic talk of god rather than polytheistic talk of gods; and how all this links up with traditional Christian ways of talking about God.

3   Somewhat different is an approach that concentrates on specifically *religious experiences* like mystical experiences (cf. Louth, 1981) or the experience of the 'holy' and other religious phenomena

described by R. Otto, W. James, N. Smart and others. They are the source of religion because they rupture the (linguistic) structures of our individual and common experience in a sometimes shattering and always irresistible way. And they pose the task of re-orientating our lives ('conversion') by requiring us to reinterpret the whole of our experience and our place in it from their point of view. These experiences (or at least some of them), are said to require theistic interpretations. Yet it is notoriously difficult to mark off specifically religious phenomena from their non-religious functional equivalents; and even if there are intrinsically religious phenomena in the sense outlined, it is by no means obvious that they necessarily give rise to god-language or need to be interpreted theistically. The criteria by which we mark off religious from non-religious phenomena are culturally conditioned and derived from some prior understanding of religion; and whenever we interpret religious phenomena theistically we do so either because they occur in a theistic context (external perspective) or because they themselves manifest a theistic meaning and self-understanding (internal perspective). In either case it is a specific (self-)interpretation which marks them off as religious or theistic; and as religious phenomena are cultural and social phenomena which are not adequately described unless it is taken into account how the persons involved would have described them, the justification of introducing the category 'god' in interpreting the phenomena in question has in the last resort to rely on phenomena which disclose themselves as religious and self-interpretatively theistic to us.

4   This approach concentrates on such self-interpretatively theistic phenomena or *revelatory experiences*. These manifest the features of religious phenomena (rupture and re-orientation) but are marked off from other such experiences by their self-interpretative character, which suggests a specific new orientation in the world: we have to use the 'god'-category for interpreting them because they interpret themselves to us in terms of this category. Revelatory experiences are always specific and manifest a particular understanding of god or God which can only by abstraction be related and compared to others. Interpretative metaphysics based on such experiences, therefore, is the metaphysics of a particular religion or religious tradition: it is the (self-)reflective working out of the knowledge about god/God and reality implied in a particular religion and its foundational experiences. But in this kind of approach interpretative reflective knowledge about God becomes virtually indistinguishable from interpretative revelational knowledge of God worked out reflectively. And to this we have to turn next.

Chapter 17

Revelational Theology

I

Demonstrative knowledge about God appears to be impossible because God is not a *datum* or a *dabile*. Reflective knowledge, on the other hand, presents God as a *cogitabile*, but fails to show that this is more than a mere *Gedankending* (mere thought) - and this is not enough for theological reflection which seeks to conceptualize something that is, and should be, worshipped. The metaphysical approach may enable us somehow to identify something as god, but whether what we identify as god is really God rather than an idol is not clear. Moreover, identification is an attention-directing device (Rescher, 1973, p. 106) and descriptive identification, even where it specifies a unique individual, may always miss its target and the specific referent at which it is aimed (Millar, 1975). Even if we agree with the metaphysical approach that the intelligibility of the universe requires us to postulate a self-explanatory being and that there cannot be more than one such being, we may still ask whether this contributes towards identifying the God of the Christian faith. The idea of a self-explanatory being is of little or no help for identifying God in the cross and resurrection of Jesus Christ. It may be a fully coherent idea, yet nothing may be identified by it; and even if there is someting identified by it, it need not be the God to whom Christians refer. In short, all out attempts at identifying God are precarious unless our identification of God corresponds to God's self-identification to us in Jesus Christ. Hence the idea of *self-identification*, not of self-explanation, is central to theological reconstructions of the Christian knowledge of God.

It is not enough for this idea to be coherent, or instantiated in principle, for others, or for God himself. If it is to serve its purpose it must be the idea of God's self-identification *to us*, i.e. to us *personally*. Divine self-identification is not the same as human reports about it.

Others can inform us only by description about God's alleged self-identification to them. But descriptive identifications are problematic communicative devices for fixing the reference of 'God' because they can be fully coherent even if nothing is identified by them. The principle of charity notwithstanding (cf. Swinburne, 1981, pp. 13-4), identifications of this sort inform us not so much about God as about how others think (or want us to think) about God. They may seek to convey true information by what they say; but they may be wrong. Thus the self-identification of God differs from descriptive identifications of this sort in at least three respects:

1 Self-identifications are communicative acts between different, yet co-present participants in which one (the identifier) discloses his or her identity to the other(s). They are acts, not merely reports about an act of identification. As a communicative act the divine self-identification constitutes a situation of co-presence between identifier (God), identified (God) and the human addressee of the identification in which we communicate not with others about God but with God about himself: he is both subject (identifier) and object (identified) of this act.

2 As a communicative act between co-present participants God's self-identification involves an informational link between God and the addressee of the identification. For to identify God on the basis of his self-identification to us is to take him to be the source of the information on which our identification of him rests. This presupposes (a) the existence of an information channel between God and us (for otherwise we cannot communicate *with each other*); (b) the participation in a common system of communication (for otherwise we cannot *communicate information through signs* to each other); and (c) the possibility of (symbolic) interaction (for otherwise we do not communicate in a *situation of co-presence*). Now the only channels through which we can communicate are physical channels, and the totality of what is or can be used as a physical channel in processes of communication is *nature*. Similarly our only systems of communication are systems of (conventional) verbal and non-verbal signs, and the totality of such systems is *culture*. Hence all our interactions are performed through natural and/or cultural means. This is also true of the communicative interactions between God and us, as Christians confess: God identifies himself to us in Jesus Christ (nature/culture) and through the Spirit (interaction). He communicates to us who he is and what he is through the mediation of Jesus Christ, a specific human person (nature) in a specific historical context (culture). We know about this divine self-identification through the Gospel communicated to us by others (nature/culture); and we know this message to be

true by communicating with God, who makes himself present and accessible to us in his Spirit. What is communicated about him is thus confirmed in communicating with him (interaction). For while Jesus Christ *is* co-present with us eschatologically as the risen Lord, he becomes *known* to be co-present with us *in a salvific way* through the Gospel (culture) and its reception in faith through the Spirit (interaction). Just as God's self-identification in Jesus Christ constitutes the content of the Gospel message, so his self-presentation as Spirit confirms this message to be true and makes us accept its identification of Jesus Christ as the human mediation of God's self-identification by placing us in the presence of God and vice versa. In short, an essential part of the *content* of the Gospel is precisely its *mode of reception in faith*: there is no way of presenting God's self-identification as salvific love apart from his self-presentation of it. Unless God identifies himself to us as love through the Spirit by confirming the Gospel message to be true, we cannot receive this message as God's self-identification to us but only as his purported self-identification to others.

3   God's self-identification helps us to locate God relative to us, and us relative to God. Locating something or someone is an epistemic activity which issues in *orientational knowledge*, i.e. the 'capacity to find one's way about, and so discover, or to understand how to discover, where in the world one is' (Evans, 1982, p. 162). This involves the capacity to locate oneself relative to others (and vice versa) in a physical or spatio-temporal sense (Where am I? Where is x?), a social sense (What am I relative to x and x relative to me - brother or master, friend or foe?), and an existential sense (Who am I? Who is x?). And this requires us to perceive *order* in the various dimensions of our life, i.e. to discriminate and 'give attention to similar differences and different similarities' in all areas of life and experience (cf. Bohm, 1972, p. 254). We cannot locate ourselves and others physically, socially and existentially without organizing our world cognitively in terms of basic structures and relationships which obtain in its various realms and must not be ignored if we want to act adequately, successfully and in a way that is true to our actual situation. Thus the capacity to locate ourselves physically depends on our *theoretical knowledge* about things and events and their relations in our environment. The capacity to locate ourselves socially depends on our *practical knowledge* about how others view themselves and others, including ourselves, with respect to them. That is, we have to know how they conceive and understand themselves and others; and if we want to act adequately in the social sphere we have to proportion our actions not only to what we believe about them but also to what we believe they believe about us: we act and behave differently if we believe them to

regard us as friends rather than foes. Finally, the capacity to locate ourselves existentially depends on our *knowledge of ourselves* relative to how others identify and know us; and as not all of this is compatible with what we believe ourselves to be, our self-knowledge and own identity depends crucially on our capacity of critically evaluating our identifications by others.

All this is also true with respect to God. But whereas we can infer what others believe about us from what they do and say, there is not inferential knowledge of this sort in the case of God. Even if his existence could be established inferentially, this would not tell us what he thinks of us and how, therefore, we should behave towards him, others and ourselves. Orientational knowledge of this sort is only available through his self-identification and self-communication to us. For in disclosing who he is and what he is for us, he at the same time discloses that he is and what he expects of us. He may introduce himself as our God without reference to any previous knowledge of or about him on our part ('I am that I am, thy God') or by identifying himself with someone about whom we already know something ('I am the God of thy father, the God of Abraham, the God of Isaac, and the God of Jacob'). In either case it is assumed that we have some understanding of the term 'God'; and in either case God cannot identify himself to us unless he is somehow co-present and co-localized with us although not in a spatio-temporal sense. Revelation-based knowledge of God is demonstrative in character without being knowledge of a phenomenal *datum* or *dabile*. For central to the Christian idea if revelation is the idea of God's co-present self-identification in and through something that is different from him: Jesus Christ. Accordingly, all Christian knowledge of God is direct though mediated knowledge not merely *about* but *of* God, who identifies himself to us as creative love in Jesus Christ and through the Spirit. It reflects the (hermeneutical) differences and relations between who and what is known in and through Jesus Christ (God as love), how it is known in and through him (Jesus's life, death and ressurrection), and that it is known in this way (Spirit). It is thus irreducibly dialectical in structure although - and this is what trinitarian reconstructions seek to safeguard - (christological) comprehensibility prevails over (theological) incomprehensibility in its content, whereas (pneumatological) incomprehensibility prevails over (epistemological) comprehensibility in its form.

Christian theology advocates revelation-based identifications of God because it seeks to be true to God's self-identification in Christ. This is the point from which it starts and that it presupposes. Hence its insistence on the idea of divine self-identification: not that we identify (and intepret) something as God but that God identifies (and interprets) himself to us in such a way that we can form (more or less adequate) information-based conceptions of him which control our believing, experiencing and acting in all areas of life and thought.

II

If this is what is meant by divine self-identification, how is it possible? God is not a phenomenon of our experiential world and cannot identify himself to us demonstratively. Could he do so semiotically, i.e. through the use of (conventional) signs? Not without somehow getting involved in the realms of nature and culture. 'I am the God of thy father, the God of Abraham, the God of Isaac, and the God of Jacob' only works as a self-identification of God (ignoring for the moment the problems of such a literalistic reading of Exod. 3:6) because it uses signs which belong to one of our systems of communication (culture). And as we can communicate only through physical channels, we cannot receive and interpret signs independently of some natural phenomena which we use as signs (nature): information-based identification of God necessarily involves the interpretation of natural phenomena as revelatory of God.

It may be objected that it is not incoherent to suppose that God could communicate truths about himself to us immediately, i.e. without the use of signs. This is true, but only for context-free truths. He could simply illuminate our minds to grasp the truth of the proposition 'God is the God of Abraham'. But we cannot, not even by divine illumination, become immediately aware of the truth of 'I am the God of Abraham'. For this requires us to desambiguate the idexical 'I' in this proposition by reference to its pragmatic setting; and as this, in the case of God, is not given phenomenally it must be specified propositionally. But while it is possible to incorporate pragmatic settings into propositions, desambiguate indexicals by dates and names, and thus transform indexical propositions into propositions that we may come to know by divine illumination, no set of identity propositions about God can replace the proposition 'I am this God'. The pragmatic context of identification necessary for understanding this proposition must in the last resort be specified by reference to some phenomena in our vicinity which are interpreted as revelatory and as fixing the reference of 'God'.

Similarly, it is not incoherent to suppose that God could identify himself to us by using phenomena, e.g. clouds in the sky, immediately as signs; this would be miraculous but the idea is not incoherent. Yet even then he would have to use them according to one of our systems of communication if they are to convey information. Actually, however, God's self-revelation is *mediated* in that God participates in our systems of communication through Jesus Christ, who identifies and interprets God to us as unbounded love. More specifically, Jesus Christ identifies God to us in his message and life; God acknowledges this identification as true by identifying himself with Christ in his death and resurrection; and the Spirit enables us to acknowledge what we hear from Christ and about Christ in the Gospel to be true and an adequate identification of God. Hence without Christ no identification of God; without identification of God no revelation; without revelation no identification of Christ as the one who truly identifies God. But then God's revelation in Christ requires the co-presence not only of God and Jesus Christ but also of the human receiver and Christ; and because the dead and risen Christ is co-present with us not in body but in Spirit, there is no revelation without the co-presence of God, Christ and Spirit with us.

This situation of co-presence is the revelation which is, or should be, the normative point of reference of all Christian theology. It is a complex situation which involves three irreducible, mutually dependent and cumulatively operative processes of identification:

1 At the historical level *Jesus* identified God as fatherly love to us in his teaching, life and death (the identification of the God of Israel as the father of Jesus).
2 At the ontological level *God* identifies himself to us in the life, death and resurrection of Jesus Christ (the self-identification of God with the God identified as father by Jesus).
3 At the epistemological level the *Spirit* identifies Jesus's identification of God as God's self-identification in Jesus Christ to us (the identification of Jesus's identification of God as the true and faithful historical manifestation of the ontological self-identification of God).

The first process establishes the historical anchorage of the Christian identification of God in the life of Jesus; the second the ontological foundation of its claim to truth in the life of God; the third the epistemological certainty about its truth in our life. The second is the basic process: without it the first and third could not lead to knowledge; the first is necessary for the second to become epistemologically accessible to us; the third for the first to be accepted as knowledge. All three processes are necessary for the identification of the referent of Christian talk of God. For only together do they fix this referent unequivocally. We do not know *God* (but only something claimed about God) if we know that Jesus identified God as father and that Christians identify Jesus as Christ because they believe him to be the authoritative and ultimate communication of God's self-identification. To know him (and not merely about him) God has to identify himself to us so that we can base our identifications of him on information received from him and thus locate him relative to us and vice versa. This is the case when through the power of the Spirit we come to accept the Gospel message about Jesus Christ as the true account of our situation before God and of God's attitude towards us. In short, the situation of co-presence is revelatory if it establishes *orientational knowledge of God* which allows us to identify him on the basis of information received from him, enables us to locate God and ourselves relative to each other, and thus provides the basis for developing a coherent conception of God and a comprehensive view of reality.

It is important to see that by its very nature God's self-identification is not tied to a particular situation in the past but is continually reconstituted by the proclamation of the Gospel and its reception in faith. For the content of the Gospel message comprises Jesus's descriptive identification of God; the descriptive identification of Jesus Christ as the authoritative and ultimate self-identification of God by the Christian community; and the self-presentation of the Spirit who makes us accept this message as true in faith. Only together do they fix the reference of Christian talk of God (Dalferth, 1984, pp. 188-9). At the same time they delineate major aspects of the Christian knowledge of God both with respect to the situation of revelation (the rupture of our structures of experience) and the orientational re-working of our knowledge of reality in the light of it. For in his revelation God identifies himself and what he does to us; and by thus disclosing why he does it, he reveals the ultimate ground and goal of all there is to us. Theological reflection can accordingly specify who God is (trinity); what God is (divine love); where God has made himself accessible (Jesus Christ); what God does (revelation or reconciliation through Christ; inspiration or redemption through the Spirit); and what therefore (ultimately) is and shall be (creation and eschatology).

III

It follows that concepts of God in theological reflection are characterized by three significant features: they are derived from the explication of the divine self-identification and therefore essentially centred on Jesus Christ (*christological character*); they are based on the figurative expressions of faith in Jesus Christ which use available means of communicating meaning to articulate what ruptured all available structures of meaning (*(meta)-symbolic status*); and they play a specific role in the elucidation of reality by marking the ultimate point of reference of an all-inclusive view of reality (*orientational function*). For the task of theology is not only to *explicate* the divine self-identification and its reception in faith as clearly as possible (primary task) but also to *elucidate* the whole of reality in the light of it in as detailed a manner as is necessary (secondary task).

In this sense all Christian knowledge of God is grounded in his self-revelation to us in Christ through the Spirit as received in faith and expressed in the basic Christian confessions of faith. To explicate this revelatory event on the basis of these expressions is a necessary ingredient of all theological reflection about God. But to be adequate it must take into account both the (semantic) content and (pragmatic) occurrence of the divine self-identification. The first results in the christological and soteriological content of the Christian concept of God (God is redeeming love, God for us, creator and sustainer of new life, saviour, *deus iustificans vel salvator*), the second in its eschatological character and (contingent) hermeneutical form (God is *id quo maius cogitari nequit* and yet to be addressed in words of our ordinary language; he is totally different from anything given in worldly experience and yet to be thought of in terms of concepts and ideas derived from worldly experience). For wherever the divine self-identification occurs (comprehensibility) it ruptures the experiential and linguistic structures of our previous orientation in the world, disrupts our ways of perceiving and participating in reality, and establishes a fundamental difference between the old life and the new (incomprehensibility). Reference to this radical eschatological rupture which resists assimilation to given structures of experience and language is an essential ingredient of the meaning of 'God'. It is encapsulated in the notions of divine creativity and transcendence and constitutes the irreducible dialectics of comprehensibility and incomprehensibility in Christian concepts of God.

On the other hand, the continuing exigencies of life after the occurrence of this event of divine self-identification force us to re-orientate ourselves and our whole view of reality in the light of this rupture-experience. Disorientation gives way to new orientation both in the individual life of faith and the life of the Christian community. This is reflected in the concept of God. The term 'God' now comes to mark not only the creative eschatological rupture of all previous experience but also the normative point of reference for our re-ordering of and re-orientation in reality. It names that which in Jesus Christ and through the Spirit creatively ruptures our life and transforms it into a new life in which we consciously begin to live as creatures in community with our creator. Incomprehensible *creativity* and comprehensible *order* thus form the two irreducible poles of the Christian concept of God. But they also constitute the permanent tension within it. For if we stress the first pole at the expense of the second, God comes to be conceived as the Wholly Other who is understood in radical contrast to all our worldly experience. If, on the other hand, we stress the second pole at the expense of the first, God comes to be conceived as the Ultimate Structure of Reality which is implicit in all our experience of the world and ourselves. Between the two extremes there are a variety of ways of combining the aspects of creativity, disruption and dislocation, and of order, control and reliability in concepts of God. They all attempt to relate incomprehensibility (the rupture-aspects) and comprehensibility (the order-aspects) in God, but they differ in either placing divine incomprehensibility over comprehensibility, or vice versa. In the former case the concepts of God follow the (Augustinian) paradigm of 'silence qualified by parables' (Miles, 1959, p. 165), in the latter case the (Thomist) paradigm of appropriately qualified models as proposed by I. T. Ramsey (1957). But as God resists assimilation to our human perspectives, he can never be conceptualized in a fully adequate way: he is *greater* than anything that can be thought. On the other hand, as he is the creative centre of orientation for the Christian view of reality, he must be conceptualized somehow: although greater than anything that can be thought he must be *thought* in a way that allows us, individually and together, to orient ourselves reliably in reality. And as every concept of God has to safeguard the identity of the God whom it seeks to conceptualize on the basis of the Christian faith, God will only be thought adequately in Christian theology if he is conceptualized christologically.

Thus the first essential feature of a Christian concept of God is its *christologico-eschatological character*, i.e. its intrinsic relation to the radical rupture-experience of God's self-revelation in Jesus Christ through the Spirit to us. Its second feature is its *(meta-)symbolic status*, i.e. its conceptual derivation from the figurative, metaphorical and narrative expressions of faith in Jesus Christ. Its third feature is its *orientational function*, i.e. its view of God as the ground and foundation of absolute location in and ultimate order of reality. The first feature summarizes what theology assumes to be given in the Christian faith which it seeks to explicate; the second marks the basic hermeneutical difficulty for this explication; and the third the permanent task of both the life of faith and theological reflection. However, contrary to the metaphysical approach, revelation-based theological reflection starts from the first and not from the third feature in construing its concept of God; and because it starts from the eschatological rupture-experience of Jesus Christ it is not the existence of God but the structure of life and reality in the light of God which is the main problem of theology. It presupposes the radically contingent event of divine self-identification (revelation) and faith which it seeks to explicate and on the basis of which it attempts to elucidate the whole of reality. Thus its approach to the problem of conceptualizing God starts from the contingent and particular (revelation) and explicates its universal significance without generalizing it by pursuing it through a number of methodologically distinct levels of reflection. This can be briefly outlined as follows.

IV

Revelation, I have argued, conveys orientational knowledge. Orientation involves reciprocal location in a common frame of reference and the selection and organization of relevant information in individual and common systems of belief. Accordingly, concepts of God based on revelation are attempts to integrate conceptually

that which ruptures the experiential, linguistic and social structures of our lives in the occurrence of faith in Jesus Christ as God's self-identification to us;

that which is thereby disclosed as the ultimate, and ultimately incomprehensible, creative ground of our own existence and of the existence and order of reality;

and that which, for this reason, functions as the focal point of reference for the Christian (re-)orientation in reality.

The diversity of these elements explains the specific structure of Christian concepts of God. It accounts for their christological character as well as for the irreducible dialectical tension between their strands of incomprehensibility (creativity, disruption and dislocation) and comprehensibility (order, re-location and reliability). Through their reference to faith in Jesus Christ they are rooted in the specific occurrence of God's self-identification within the structures of history, life and experience. This involves reference to the objective pole of these occurrences which is common to all of them

(Jesus Christ) as well as to their subjective pole, which varies with different persons and times (faith). The contingent nature of the latter is manifest in the context-dependent figurative expressions of faith and in the rich imagery in which Christians speak to and about God. For all expressions of faith in prayer, confession, narrative and proclamation are conditioned in a threefold way:

1   They are *culturally conditioned* in that they use the symbolic (verbal and non-verbal) means available to the believer in his or her specific socio-historical context.

2   They are *experientially conditioned* in that they use those symbolic means which bear a specific semantic relation to the regions of life in which the rupture-experience has occurred or which seem particularly apt to serve as *models* for expressing this experience. Thus biblical talk of God characteristically uses socio-morphic models taken from family relationships (father, son, love, punishment, reward) or social and political relationships (ruler, king, law-giver, lord, saviour, liberator, covenant), all of which exemplify the model of *personal agency* as the dominant biblical model of God (cf. Ramsey, 1973; King, 1974). Christians have continued and at the same time enriched this tradition by combining it with models of God taken from ontological, aesthetic and historical regions (cf. Jennings, 1985, chs 6-8). But they all serve as models *of God* only insofar as they mark the rupture of the experiential context under consideration which resists assimilation to the available symbolic structures. They achieve this at the symbolic level by means of negation ('God is *not* . . .') and qualification ('God is *like* . . . *but* . . .'), i.e. by qualifying the chosen model (father, lord) in such a way that the irreducible difference between God and world (the region of experience from which the model is taken) is safeguarded (eternal father, almighty lord). By thus pointing to the incomprehensible in and through the comprehensible, the models become (dynamic) models of transcendence (cf. King, 1974, ch. 2). However, they are *Christian* models of God only if they determine this transcendence christologically and qualify the model of God by reference to Jesus Christ.

3   They are *christologically conditioned* in that the meaning of 'father', 'love', 'almighty lord' etc. is determined by the story of Jesus Christ (and, in and through this, by the story of Israel): God is 'father' in that he suffers with his son; God is 'love' in that he seeks the community of the despised and of those who ignore him; God is 'almighty lord' in that he is capable of self-limitation and of making himself accessible to us in creation and history. The models are taken from the world of experience of those who use them; they are qualified, to mark that in their application to God they are not to be

understood literally; and the qualification is specified by reference to Jesus Christ, whose story provides us with the criteria for selecting the appropriate aspects of meaning of the models used for God.

The hermeneutical process underlying this approach is clearly exemplified by the New Testament attempts to understand Jesus Christ and his message of the kingdom of God. In Matt. 12, for example, we find models from the Jewish tradition (temple, son of David, Solomon, prophets like Jonah) used to explain who Jesus is. However, in order to convey the incomparable status of Jesus, they are qualified by stating Jesus to be 'more' or 'greater' than the temple, Solomon, Jonah etc. The some hermeneutical dialectics of comparability and incomparability is characteristic of the use of the titles applied to Jesus. Thus Mark 8 shows that Christians could apply the title 'Messiah' or 'Christ' to Jesus only after it had been purged of its misleading political overtones and redefined in the light of his suffering, cross and resurrection. More generally, it was the story of Jesus Christ which modified or redefined the meaning of the terms, titles predicates, and models used to elucidate and communicate the mystery of his life. The variety and difference of these terms manifests the different and manifold contexts in which Jesus Christ was experienced in faith as God's salvific self-identification. Many of these terms, titles, predicates and models were originally unrelated and brought into a semantic relationship only by their common reference or application to Jesus Christ. Gradually, however, through liturgical practice and theological reflection, they were brought into a closer semantic relationship and integrated into a common field of meaning. And this in turn required theological reflection to state explicit rules (dogmas) of how these terms have to be used and understood if the process of semantic integration is not to transform and distort the Christian faith which they were used to express. In short, we have to use terms taken from familiar areas of life if we want to understand and talk about Jesus and his relation to God and to us. We take those terms which have an intrinsic relation to the region of life in which the rupture-experience of revelation and faith has occurred for us. But all terms used have to be qualified if they are not to be misunderstood: they serve only as approximate pointers to the mystery of the divine self-identification to us which we attempt to convey with their help.

What is true of Jesus Christ is also true of God. Discourse of faith in prayer, confession and proclamation uses a variety of models to talk to and about God. At the beginning these have primarily been taken from the Old Testament and Jewish background; but soon ideas from Hellenistic and other religious traditions came also to be used. Some such models like Father, Almighty, Creator, Saviour, King, Lord or Judge figure prominently in the biblical texts and have become widely accepted in the Christian community. Some of them already formed clusters in the tradition from which they were taken. Others became semantically related to these and among themselves by their common use in liturgical contexts and, increasingly, through theological reflection. Biblical models like Father or Love served as crystallizing centres for the integration of other models either (through liturgical usage) into networks of models like those used in the Apostles' creed or (through theological reflection) into super-models like Agent-in-Action which is taken to be the depth structure of the various agent-models of God used in biblical and ecclesial discourse. This gradually led to the formation of a tradition of Christian thinking and speaking to and about God. But the development has not been homogeneous, and in the various Christian churches, traditions and theologies there has always been an important fringe which was not, or not (yet) sufficiently, integrated into what came to be regarded as the mainstream tradition. Thus whereas some have taken the idea of divine impassibility to be essential to the Christian understanding of God, others have insisted that only the idea of a suffering and compassionate God is at harmony with the biblical witness and the story of Jesus Christ (cf. Creel, 1986).

These and other reasons soon showed the need for explicit regulations in the Christian community about how the models of God used in the figurative discourse of faith are to be understood and conceptually developed and what kind of models are appropriate to the Christian faith. Theological doctrines of God thus began to explicate the grammar of the models used in biblical and ecclesial discourse; and the trinitarian and christological dogmas set out what came to be widely accepted as the minimal set of meta-rules about the rules which are to be followed in Christian talk of God. This in turn provoked theological reflection to offer interpretations and explications not only of the models of God used in the discourse of faith but also of the doctrines of God worked out in theological and dogmatic discourse. This led to the adoption of second-order theological models of God like the model of *causality* in scholastic theology, the model of *life within* in Schleiermacher, or the model of *being in becoming* in Barth, which not only imply widely differing or even incompatible ontologies but serve to elucidate talk of God both in (figurative) discourse of faith and in (conceptual) theological discourse because they are applicable in all areas of life and thought. They all state different though positive theological meta-rules about how to interpret Christian talk of God in order to understand it to be ultimately intelligible. Anselm, on the other hand, formulated the corresponding negative meta-rule that whatever (first- or second-order) model we use in talking of and thinking about God, what we say and think will ultimately be beyond intelligibility because God is greater than anything that can be thought, said or conceptualized. For if 'God is finally a mystery, our conceptual grasp of him will take us only part of the way' (Macquarrie, 1984, pp. 25-6). Thus when we reconstruct Christian talk of God in terms of the model of causality, or of life within, or any other model we have to qualify it in such a way that the irreducible difference between our conceptualizations of God and the God whom we attempt to conceptualize is marked according to the rule of analogy that 'no likeness can be discerned without a greater unlikeness having to be discerned as well'.

This, at least, is how a major theological tradition has sought to come to grips with the problem of God in theological reflection. But it involves a basic difficulty. Together the two kinds of theological meta-rules just mentioned indeed capture the dialectics between comprehensibility and incomprehensibility which are characteristic of all Christian concepts of God. But they do so in an abstract way which disregards the contingent origin of these dialectics in Christian thinking about God: they are due to the eschatological rupture-experience in Jesus Christ on which all Christian talk and thought of God ultimately rests. But then not any kind of comprehensibility will do for the concept of God but only one which accords with the christological conditioning of Christian talk of God: what is comprehensible of God is due to his self-identification to us in Jesus Christ through the Spirit. Accordingly, if we want to insist on the rule of analogy in our reflections about God, we have to modify it in accordance with this basic fact and reformulate it christologically (cf. Jüngel, 1983, pp. 261-98): 'no unlikeliness can be discerned without a greater likeness having to be discerned as well' - between God and Jesus Christ as well as between Jesus Christ and us.

This is more than a mere verbal modification. It has material and methodological consequences for theological reflection. In explicating faith it will not try to understand the manifold models of God used in the discourse of faith and the various doctrines of God worked out in theological discourse in terms of a second-order theological model of God like *'causa sui'*, *'spiritus infinitus independens,'* or 'all-determining reality' etc. which is unspecific and abstract enough to make sense of Christian and non-Christians uses of 'God' alike. Rather it will attempt to specify rules which show how talk of God at the conceptual level of theological discourse is related to, and must be re-translated into, the discourse of faith from which it is ultimately derived. Only in this way will it be able to ensure that incomprehensibility will not prevail over comprehensibility in theological reflection. It is not the abstractive generalization of a God-structure and its respecification in terms of a doctrine of analogical predication that is the way to make sense of theological concepts and doctrines of God but their interpretative re-translation into the story of Jesus Christ and the discourse of faith of the Christian community (Dalferth, 1981, pp. 648-78).

Similarly when we turn to the task of elucidation and the problem of the orientational function of the concept of God (cf. Kaufman, 1981, pp. 32ff). Theological reflection which follows the traditional metaphysical route of analogy in its attempt to conceptualize God must unfold its interpretation of reality from a point of view which it cannot definitely fix because in its conceptualization of God incomprehensibility always prevails over comprehensibility. But then what is gained by the wider applicability of the concept of God is lost in informational content and orientational power: if God's reality can only be grasped so vaguely that it is consistent with any natural view of the world and explanation of why the world is as it is, it is defective with respect to its selective powers and therefore unable to perform its orientational function both cognitively (knowledge) and normatively (action).

Not so when theological reflection follows the revelational and christological route. It then insists on the Gospel of Jesus Christ as the normative human witness to the specific rupture-experience which fixes the reference of all Christian uses of 'God' and, on the other, on the working of the Spirit as God's self-communicating presence without which no one is able to accept the Gospel message as true. Concepts of God based on this approach will still exhibit the dialectics of comprehensibility and incomprehensibility. But the former will dominate the latter, and God's saving activity manifest in the story of Jesus Christ and made evident to us through the working of the Spirit will provide a definite orientation for the Christian life in the world. The outlines of this orientation are most concisely summarized in the creed and in the rule of love (Matt. 22:37-9). The former outlines the cognitive pattern of Christian beliefs (knowledge), the latter the normative pattern of Christian life (action). In Jesus Christ and through the Spirit God has revealed his love for us, and we exist in conformity to the divine love if in faith we exist in conformity to the living Christ who inspires us to mature reflection and responsible action. This is selective enough to exclude many possible views of reality and courses of action in the world; but at the same time it does not compel adoption of a single version of Christian life but allows for a great variety of Christian existence in the world.

To sum up; according to the Christian grammar of 'God' this notion is misused if used apart from its orientational function. To know *God* is to acknowledge him as *my God*, and this relational and pragmatically localizing aspect of 'God' is essential for any understanding of it: 'God' ceases to function adequately in theological reflection where it is reduced to the status of a principle of theoretical knowledge or a regulative ideal of practical knowledge. For if knowledge of God is intrinsically orientational knowledge, then theological concepts of God are inadequate in form if they do not conceptualize the orientational function of God (*God for us*), and they are inadequate in content if they fail to conceptualize the specific Christian orientation (*God is love*). Theological reflection therefore insists on the insoluble relationship between God and orientation. To show why and in which sense requires me finally to return to a closer examination of the notion of orientational knowledge of God.

Chapter 18

Revelation and Orientation

We not only exist in the world but live in it, and we cannot live in it without interpreting it in order to orient ourselves and thus become capable of acting in it. For acting presupposes knowledge of what is the case as well as what might be the case, and in particular the knowledge of how under identical circumstances we could have acted otherwise. We therefore cognitively reconstruct our manifold natural and cultural environments on the basis of our unceasing organic interrelation with them as a common field of action or world in which the actual is placed against a permanent background of the possible. The complexity of our world is thus reduced by selecting some of the available information and ignoring others, and the resulting *orientational knowledge* helps to guide our actions by allowing us to *locate* ourselves in our world and to *order* the world with respect to us. Only knowledge with these *localizing* and *organizing functions* is orientational knowledge. This is also true of revelation-based knowledge of God. So let us look at these two functions more closely.

I

The localizing function of revelation

Localizing something is identifying, not merely describing it. Identification, however, is reciprocal. It is a cognitive process in which something is identified to someone in such a way that the addressee of the identification and the object of identification are localized relative to one another in a common frame of reference. This may be done either demonstratively in situations of co-presence, or descriptively through the use of signs. If I ask you to meet me at the Eagle, a pub which you do not (yet) know, I may either point it out to you or describe it to you in a way that will enable you to find it. In the latter case to give you a description which is true of this pub is not enough: it must be a description which will enable you to find out how to get there, and this requires it to be such that you can locate yourself relative to the place it describes. This can be done in a variety of ways, and in everyday life we all employ various systems of identification for things in our natural and cultural environments: names, dates, spatial locations, family relations, social functions etc. They all have in common that they cannot be used to locate something for us unless we are capable of locating ourselves relative to the thing located in this way; and this presupposes not only some (rudimentary) knowledge of the thing in question but also some (rudimentary) self-knowledge without which we are unable cognitively to relate ourselves to other things and persons. In short, without self-knowledge there is not orientational knowledge.

'Self-knowledge' is an ambiguous notion. At least the following dimensions of meaning must be distinguished: first, the knowledge of *who* I am (identifying self-knowledge); second, the successively acquired and continuously changing knowledge of *what*, *where* and *how* I am (characterizing self-knowledge); finally, and implied by the others, the knowledge *that* I am (existential self-knowledge). The three understandings are related in such a way that without characterizing self-knowledge there can be no existential self-knowledge, and without identifying self-knowledge there can be no characterizing self-knowledge. But then the knowledge of who I am is the focus and foundation of all our self-knowledge: without identifying self-knowledge no self-knowledge.

Knowledge of who I am is not merely a bit of true information about me but a capacity - the capacity for identifying myself. This characteristically involves owning and using a name: to know who I am is to know myself as the one who is called (named) such-and-such. Yet we only have names because we are given names by others who identify and distinguish us from others by that name. Hence to be addressed and named by others is necessary for knowing who we are and what name we own; without having been addressed we can have no identifying self-knowledge.

Addressing others is a basic form of human cummunication. In addressing someone I identify him as someone whom I know or perceive in a specific way, and by the way I address him and the things I tell him I communicate to him how I know or perceive him. If he identifies himself in the way I have addressed him, he knows himself as I know him and as I have communicated that to him. Self-knowledge of this sort is knowing myself as I am known by others. But all self-knowledge originates in this way and is basically of this sort, with the result that I cannot know myself unless someone else knows me, and cannot come to know myself unless others communicate to me 'that' and 'how' they know me. Since I cannot identify (or localize) others without being capable of identifying myself, I cannot identify myself without being identified by others.

It follows that identifying self-knowledge can originate only in and through personal communication and linguistic interaction with others who reflect my identity back to me. Linguistic intersubjectivity is a necessary condition of objective knowledge as well as of personal self-knowledge. For the capacity to locate myself and others develops only if others talk *to*, not merely *about* me. And our identifying self-knowledge always reflects how those know us who actually communicate with us: it locates us relative to the way others locate us in actual communication.

The communication which generates self-knowledge involves neither only two nor all persons and potential communicators in a given life. Self-knowledge is a product of social intercourse that can occur only in a society of at least tripersonal structure. The person whose address enables me to locate myself relative to his knowledge of me cannot derive his own self-knowledge (wholly and exclusively) from my knowledge of him: he must have derived it from someone else's knowledge of him. But whereas tripersonal communication is necessary for identifying self-knowledge, total communication is impossible. We cannot communicate with all others although we must communicate with some others; and whereas there are for each of us some persons with whom it is more likely that we communicate than with others, it is always a matter of selection and contingency with whom we actually communicate. Thus the development of our self-knowledge is intrinsically linked with the development of our personal identity. For to exist in a plurality of communicative relationships confronting us with different and often conflicting views about us forces us to sift and sort out what we accept as adequate identifications of us from the inadequate ones. As being identified by others in communicative processes is essential for the constitution of our self, so the critical evaluation and appropriation of these identifications in reflective processes is essential for the development of our personal identity on the way from the public to the private self.

We all use a variety of strategies for critically appropriating how others identify and locate us. But this process of critical appropriation is coextensive with our life: we are continuously on the way to our personal identity. Thus the strategies for building up our personal identity cannot be meant to achieve a definitive and comprehensive knowledge of ourselves but only a consistent and coherent one. This we achieve by selection and the creation of priorities, not primarily by integration. We do not normally try to integrate as many identifications of us as possible but select some to which we assign a special relevance for our identity. That is, we give priority to how certain others (individuals or groups) identify us by accepting their reflection of our identity (perhaps only temporarily) as normative for our own understanding of it.

The obvious danger with this is that we create wrong priorities and develop an inadequate self-identity through the appropriation of misleading identifications by others into our own self-knowledge. To become conscious of this process of appropriation is to be faced with three problems, i.e. (1) the *contingency*, (2) the *truth* and *certainty*; and (3) the *coherence* and *consistency* of our self-knowledge:

1 Why do (or did) I accept how this individual or group reflects my identity as normative for my own self-understanding? Would I not be a different sort of person if my self-knowledge were derived from some other person's view of me?
2 Do they really know me as I truly am? How can I be sure that their knowledge of me is really adequate and true so that I am not misled by assigning priority to their views in the working out of my own self-understanding?
3 Is their view and understanding of me supported by my own experiences of myself? Is what they reflect as my identity consistent with how I myself and others know and understand me?
   Our way from public self to private I will become increasingly self-critical the more we ask these sorts of questions.

None of these questions can be answered in a way that would not allow and require us to reiterate it. All we can do is to note that our self-knowledge depends on the contingent fact that and how these rather than other persons know us; that it may well miss what we truly are or could be; and that we cannot be sure that new experiences will not require us to revise our picture of ourselves in perhaps fundamental ways. Hence our identifying self-knowledge is always precarious: it may be based on wrong, misleading, inadequate or inappropriate views of us. For are we really as those with whom we communicate convey to us? Do they really reflect our identity? What is our true identity? Who are we, truly and essentially? When questions like these become pressing, they manifest the loss of certainty about our identity in our identifying self-knowledge. And to this we react typically in two kinds of ways.

The *non-religious reaction* is to reject the whole problem as misleading and confused. The distinction between actual and true identity, or between actual and true knowledge of myself, is illusory. No doubt, I could be different in many respects, but I could not be different in all respects without ceasing to be the person I am. In particular, it is part of my identity to be the one whom I know myself to be in the light of how others claim to know me. This may and does change. But it does not follow that I have a 'true identity' only approximately realized by my actual identity at a given time. I am who I am and whom I know myself to be at whatever time, and normally there are enough contingent continuities in my life to enable myself and others to ascribe it to one and the same person. Thus the adequate solution to the problem of my true identity is to accept my contingent actual identity as my true one and to content myself with identifying and locating myself relative to the relativities of this finite existence.

While coping with contingency in this way is possible and fairly common in our secular society, it does not silence the question as to my true identity. For whereas crocodiles have no difficulties in being crocodiles, this is not so in the case of human beings: we have actively and creatively to realize what and who we are; we can miss or achieve this end to a greater or lesser degree; and we are permanently faced with the difference between what in fact we achieve and what might and could have been achieved, who in fact we are and who we might and should (like to) be. The quest for our true identity, both individually and corporately, is thus part of our common human quest for standards of orientation in the precarious attempt at leading a human life to the best of our abilities, and the quest for adequate self-knowledge is an intrinsic part of our individual participation in this common quest.

However, we can opt for different standards of orientation, entertain different views about what is human life at its best, and follow different ideals in our individual life. Thus again we are caught within the circle of relative alternatives, unable ultimately to convince ourselves of the soundness of our self-knowledge and its actual ideals and standards. This is why the *religious reaction* tries a different way out. If certainty in these matters is to be achieved at all, we have to locate ourselves not merely concretely, i.e. relative to the actual and contingent knowledge of ourselves by some given others, nor merely abstractly, i.e. relative to the ideal and logically constructed knowledge of ourselves by all others, but absolutely, i.e. relative to a knowledge of ourselves

which is co-present with each of us at all times and in every situation; which not only knows who and what I am but also who and what all the

other persons are relative to whose knowledge of myself I (can)
constitute my own self-knowledge;
which for this reason knows everyone from all possible perspectives;
which constitutes its own identifying knowledge not relative to the
contingent knowledge of finite beings but absolutely, i.e. relative
to itself (which requires it somehow to be internally differentiated
by communicative processes) - although it does not follow that
this must also be true of its characterizing self-knowledge, so that
we must distinguish absolute (necessary) and relative (contingent)
aspects of this self-knowledge; and
which cannot be confused with some finite and contingent knowledge
of ourselves and everything else because it is a knowledge than
which no greater (more comprehensive, inclusive, detailed and
adequate) can be conceived.

This *absolute knowledge of ourselves and everything else* is the
divine knowledge which most theological concepts of God include as
an essential feature of God. Whatever else may have to be said about
him, he is the point of reference for our absolute location in the world
and, as such, must be conceived as absolute knowledge in the sense
outlined. The idea of such a knowledge is not generated by *generalization*: seeking to overcome the contingent particularity of our
actual communicative relationships by generalizing our partial interaction with *some* others to total interaction with *all* others can only
lead to the idea of the world as the totality of interactions, not to the
idea of God as the ultimate principle and absolute knowledge of all
actual and possible interactions. This latter idea is generated by *uni-
versalization*: we seek to ground the communicative relationships we
all have with *some* others in the constitutive relationship all of us
have with the *same* Other by universalizing the singular relationship
which we find to constitute our existence (and as such to be utterly
different from all our relations to others and ourselves in the realm of
worldly interactions) from being constitutive of us to being constitutive of everything actual and possible. Now, obviously, unless we
have reasons to assume this singular relationship to exist, we have no
reason to universalize it; and unless the idea of a universal singular
resulting from that operation is coherent, absolute location is impossible. For only self-knowledge perceiving my identity as reflected by
this absolute divine knowledge of myself and everything else is absolutely and not merely relatively localizing self-knowledge. I then
know myself as I am known by God, and I know God as the one who
truly and fully knows me and everything else in ways unsurpassable
by anything but himself. For he knows me and everything else not only

partially and selectively but totally, i.e. from the totality of all actual (and compossibly actual) external and internal perspectives. That is to say, the divine knowledge of me and everything else is non-perspectival, and to derive my identifying self-knowledge from there is to locate myself absolutely even though my knowledge will always be perspectival, partial and improvable.

However, to *believe* oneself to be absolutely located is not to *be* absolutely located. For the latter to be true God's absolute knowledge must exist and we must truly know it as it is and truly know ourselves as we are known by it. Neither of these necessary conditions is self-evidently true. Theology asserts the truth of all of them, but its arguments from revelation and faith carry little conviction outside the perspective of Faith. On the basis of God's revelation in Jesus Christ Christians hold that faith provides that access to the divine knowledge which alone enables us to locate ourselves absolutely. But they cannot establish the truth of this claim or show that in fact we are absolutely located, for it is an intrinsic part of their claim that only God himself can assure us of the truth of it. They can only testify to it, make it cognitively accessible by propagating the Gospel, and outline how it may become intelligible and credible to others; but finding out whether it really is will always be a personal matter. Its intelligibility comes from participation in the life of faith, not theoretical argument, and its credibility from faith's ability to provide opportunities for gaining and regaining certainty of absolute location in worship and religious ritual, not from adherence to independently formulated criteria. For identifying self-knowledge is individualizing self-knowledge and as such differs from person to person. Unless I myself know God and his knowledge of me by communicating with him (and not merely by communicating with others about him and his purported knowledge of me) I cannot have the identifying self-knowledge required, and unless he makes himself known to me I cannot know him. But as he has chosen to identify himself to us in and through his revelation in Christ, so that I cannot know him apart from the Gospel message, I cannot even begin to communicate with him in worship and prayer unless others have already communicated with me about him. Acquiring absolutely localizing self-knowledge, therefore, necessarily involves changing from communicating with others *about* God to communicating (together with others) *with* God. Both sides of this process are equally decisive: Absolutely localizing self-knowledge is no viable option unless there is a community communicating God's revelation in Christ to us; yet unless this second-hand knowledge is transformed into first-hand knowledge in communicating with God himself, we shall not be able in fact to localize ourselves absolutely. In short, absolutely localizing self-knowledge is possible only within the perspective of Faith and necessarily involves the transition from the external to the internal perspective.

Absolutely localizing self-knowledge thus depends on two basic conditions: we must be able to identify and know the divine knowledge because we must know how we are known by it; and we must be able to identify and know ourselves in the light of this divine knowledge because we must know ourselves as we are known by it. The two kinds of identifying knowledge are intrinsically related. They form the central core of theological knowledge as Reformation theology has seen when it summarized it as *cognitio dei et hominis* (Ebeling, 1966) or, more precisely, knowledge of the *homo reus et perditus et deus iustificans vel salvator*. Even these formulations, however, are not basic but already the first steps of a conceptual explication of the meaning and content of God's revelation in Jesus Christ. Here, not in those explications, we must look for the answer to the twofold problem of identification, i.e. the identification of the divine knowledge of us and the identification of ourselves in the light of this divine knowledge. We only have identifying knowledge of God because he has revealed his knowledge of us in Jesus Christ as summarized in the Gospel; and we can only have identifying knowledge of ourselves in the light of that knowledge by receiving and accepting the Gospel in faith. Without revelation and faith, therefore, we have no identifying knowledge of God and ourselves that would enable us to locate ourselves absolutely. And as faith is not merely the receiving of the Gospel message but its accepting as true, absolutely identifying self-knowledge can occur only *within* the perspective of Faith. We must change from what we know from others *about* God to knowing *God himself*, and from talking *about* God to talking *to* God: second-person address to God in prayer, not third-person statements about God in creed and proclamation are the primary form of the discourse of faith.

This change is not a matter of course nor of necessity. But neither is it a matter of decision or will. Of course I may voluntarily undertake to be conditioned into changing from talking about God to talking to God. I may try to acquire Christian beliefs by living a Christian life. But I cannot switch beliefs on and off at will, simply decide to accept as true now what I did not accept as true yesterday, or voluntarily change from knowing about God to knowing God. Unless God makes himself present and known to me, I cannot come to know him; and God communicates himself to us only in Jesus Christ and through the Spirit who assures us of the truth of the Gospel message. The only thing Christians can and must do, therefore, is to provide opportunities for the divine self-communication to take place by presenting the Gospel message in worship and ritual and by teaching the language of faith through catechesis and socialization.

Ordered worship and ritual in particular serve to present and re-present the decisive revelatory events of Jesus life and death in and through which God identifies himself to us. In stereotyped (biblical) word and (liturgical) action they symbolically reiterate the Christian rupture experience and its reception in faith. They thus transmit and safeguard the identity of the divine self-communication revealed in Christ, and this provides the context for the transition from the external perspective of third-person talk about God in proclamation and confession to the internal perspective of second-person talk to God in prayer and worship. Without this continuously renewed transition we cannot locate ourselves absolutely, either individually or communally. Because they symbolically repeat the decisive revelation and rupture-experience of the Christian faith, worship and ritual provide the opportunity for us to achieve and regularly renew certainty of our absolute location through participation in common worship. This is particularly true of Christian *baptism*, which is the *localizing ritual* of the Christian faith *par excellence*. By performing a symbolic action which manifests the total incorporation of the believer into the body of Christ the Christian community publicly witnesses to the exclusively divine constitution of the identity of every Christian; and this in turn enables Christians to develop their absolutely identifying self-knowledge by reference to this public manifestation of their true identity, i.e. the divine view of who they are: justified sinners. Ritual practice, therefore, not theoretical argument, is the primary way in which Christians achieve certainty of absolute location. And theoretical arguments like proofs for the existence of God are nothing but secondary attempts to conceptualize the absolutely localizing function of worship and ritual: they are conceptual constructions of primary religious convictions and usually fail as a means to induce such convictions.

To sum up; absolute location and identifying self-knowledge is possible only by reference to the divine knowledge of us and everything else by which we are known in ways unsurpassable for us. It can become actual because God has revealed his view of himself as creative love, and of everything else in the light of this love, in his self-revelation in Jesus Christ through the Spirit (Dalferth, 1984, pp. 212-25). And it becomes actual when this self-revelation is accepted in faith. But it cannot be accepted without being received; and it cannot be received without being propagated and made known. Thus propagating the Gospel is necessary for enabling us to acquire absolutely identifying self-knowledge. But it is not sufficient. Only

God the Spirit can make us accept this message as true and thus change from the external to the internal perspective of faith - a transition which we manifest as having been made by requiring baptism into the Christian community.

II

The organizing function of love

So far I have argued that God's revelation in Christ provides the focal point of reference for our absolute location and absolutely identifying self-knowledge. But to know one's place in the world is only one component of orientational knowledge; the other is that we must know the world somehow to be ordered so that we can find our way about it. And to this I turn now.

We are organisms and as such open systems in unceasing and intimate interrelation with our environments. Yet we not only register the effects of our environment and react to them; as conscious organisms we are aware of our interdependence with our environment, we differentiate ourselves from it as centres of spontaneous activity, and we actively relate to it by choosing one of different possible courses of action. This presupposes that we cognitively interpret our world, acquire (true) beliefs about what is the case (actual world), and deliberate possible courses of actions in the face of what might and should be the case (possible worlds). Thus without interpreting our environment and cognitively structuring it as a field of possible action we cannot act but only react to it.

This is something we do in many different ways. Our perceptual field, for example, has orientational structure derived from our bodily dimensions such as left-right, up-down, before-behind. More exactly, as Charles Taylor has argued, it 'marks our field as essentially that of an embodied agent'. Its up-down directionality is not simply related to my body. 'Rather, up and down are related to how one would move and act in the field' (C. Taylor, 1978, p. 154). Thus we structure our environment in directional perception as a field of action according to our bodily dimensions. We locate and identify individuals in this field by ostension or deixis and, because of the reciprocity of these processes, ourselves relative to the things and persons identified in this way. We communicate with others co-present with us by using indexicals like 'here' and 'there', 'you' and 'me', 'now' and 'then' to structure our common field of action. And we engender and organize our perception of and participation in the world as our common field of action by social intercourse with others in terms of non-verbal and verbal signs of a common system of communication. This is only possible at the price of conventionalizing this perception and participation and of establishing culturally fixed patterns or structures of experience into which we are born and which we internalize in the normal processes of socialization. On the other hand the use of such conventional systems and, in particular, of verbal signs enables us to transcend our actual situation and field of action by communicating about non-present, possible and counterfactual states of affairs and free ourselves from the limitations of the perceptually present. Thus language above all other things is what we use to organize our world and its patterns of conceptual organization structure reality for us. 'It is by language that order is summoned out of chaos, that tress stand out of forests, that blue is distinguished from green, that the child distinguishes Mother from other adults and Father from Mother' (Jennings, 1985, p. 48). Through language we create our world as an ordered cosmos and common field of action and interaction. Through language we communicate about the possible and most appropriate ways of acting in the world. But through language we also learn and internalize the legacy of our culture, its structures of experience, its patterns of cognitive, conceptual and social organization, its ways of organizing our common world in all its dimensions.

However, language does not create nor constitute these orders, and the structures of language are not beyond change, modification, disruption and evolution. Our language is part of our common cultural memory. It reflects, transmits and codifies the ways in which our culture structures reality and conceives the world as an ordered cosmos. And these include structures of reality which have been *decreed* as well as structures which have been *discovered*. In our acting and experiencing we depend on *orders of nature* or (statistical) *laws* which have been discovered, not created, by us; yet we also depend on *orders of culture* or (social and political normative) *rules* which others have created but which, in principle at least, can be changed by us. As *bodily* agents we have to conform in our actions to the laws which govern the interrelation between our bodies and their environments. But as bodily *agents* we transcend the natural orders by being able to follow normative systems which allow us consciously to choose one particular way of life or course of action rather than another. Although we cannot create the orders of nature we cannot act without them; and while we cannot act without the orders of culture we can create them. Thus we structure our reality on the one hand according to law-like or factual orders of nature which exist independently of our acting in the world and, on the other, according to rule-like or normative orders of culture which only exist because of our acting in the world. The two kinds of orders, and the corresponding duality of law-governed events and rule-governed actions, are irreducible to each other, and we necessarily participate in both of them in all our acting and experiencing. As bodily agents we are by nature cultural beings and thus depend permanently, though differently, on natural laws and on normative rules. We thus exist in permanent tension between the orders of nature (which we cannot explain in terms and as the result of our own actions) and the orders of culture (which we cannot deny or reduce to a kind of natural order without contradicting ourselves as free agents): we are dependent, yet free agents. Accordingly we find our world to be structured by an irreducible duality of (relatively stable) natural and (relatively variable) cultural orders; and we cannot overcome this duality and the corresponding duality between law-governed events and rule-governed actions but only reinforce it in all we do.

Our inability to overcome the duality between nature and culture and the underlying duality between events and actions and their organizing principles does not mean that they could not be interpreted in a homogeneous perspective and common frame of reference. There exist at least two such approaches. The one interprets acts as (kinds of) events, and cultural orders as open to the same sort of explanation as natural orders. The other interprets events as (aspects of) acts, and explains natural orders after the manner of cultural orders. Thus the first seeks to understand everything in terms of (e.g.) the model of causal efficacy as organized according to natural patterns; the second in terms of the model of personal agency as organized according to cultural patterns. The former does not necessarily require reference to God, whereas the latter does.

The first or *non-religious approach* tries to show that actions are certain kinds of events and that the orders of culture are not fundamentally distinct from the orders of nature. Both can be explained in terms of (e.g.) statistical principles which conceive both laws and rules as kinds of expectable regularities in events or actions. Laws hold for certain sets of events, not individual events; they allow for exceptions and thus approximate rules, which are normative precisely in that they allow obeying as well as violating their prescriptions. Similarly actions governed by rules lead to law-like results if only performed in large numbers and over a certain period of time. The orders of nature as well as of culture can thus be seen as self-stabilizing regularities of large numbers of events or actions over a period of time. However, it remains unexplained in this kind of approach why we find just this contingent structure or order in nature and culture and not one of the many possible other ones; why the chaos of possibilities results in just this and not some other kind of cosmos; why the interaction between individuals in nature and culture results in just these and not other regularities; which norms and rules we should accept and choose as guidance for our life, our interactions in the realm of culture and our actions in the realm of nature; what the measure is of human freedom and responsibility in a world which is characterized by an alarming expansion of what we can do without being able to assess its consequences. In short, while this kind of approach offers a homogeneous explanation of events and actions in terms of the actual orders of nature and culture, it does not explain these orders or offer the normative orientation necessary for choosing between different courses of action which are possible under these orders. It tells us what is the case; but it does not tell us what ought to be the case in the light of what is the case. It thus must be complemented by independently established systems of norms for the various fields of human life and action. The result is an unrelated dichotomy of 'is' and 'ought', of *Sein* and *Sollen*, which is precisely what this approach set out to overcome.

Here the second or *religious approach* takes another way. It claims both the orders of nature and the orders of culture to be norm-laden - not merely in the sense of having (e.g. technical or teleological) 'oughts' embedded in their descriptions but in the sense of incorporating a code of ethics or prescriptions for human conduct which can be fulfilled as well as violated by us. It supports this view by explaining both events and actions and the laws and rules governing them ultimately in terms of divine actions. Natural events and orders must be interpreted as acts of God which somehow embody the intention of their divine agent; and cultural actions and orders must be understood as acts of God at two removes in that he not only makes us make ourselves but, at the same time and in the long run, makes us realize his intentions by realizing our intentions. Moreover, the religious approach conceives the problem of natural and cultural orders not simply as a question of fact but as a question of meaning: it inquires into the ultimate significance of events, actions and the orders of nature and culture, and into the bearing they have on the way we should act and behave. Unless we know about their significance *for us* we cannot be sure whether we should place confidence in these orders as they actually are; and without knowing about their *ultimate* significance we cannot be sure whether they merit more than merely partial commitment and relative confidence, i.e. confidence relative to our actual knowledge about them and commitment proportioned to the evidence available.

Now for the religious approach nothing can possess ultimate significance for us and merit our absolute confidence and commitment unless it offers, or contributes towards, *salvation*: it must point out the most appropriate way to live; it must show how this kind of life can be achieved; and it must ground its account of the salvific life and of the way to achieve it in God. The religious approach not only privileges the model of (personal) agency in making sense of the world but combines the problems of order and of salvation by taking the orders of nature and culture to contribute, or to fail to contribute, towards salvation.

Religions have always linked order and salvation, the existence and reliability of structures and regularities in the realms of nature and culture and the divine foundation and preservation of these orders. At a fundamental level the divine is experienced as the manifestation of order in the chaos of events. Wherever this occurred the ancient Greeks responded to it by exclaiming *'theos'*, 'divine' (Kerényi, 1964, pp. 17ff). Accordingly, when they moved beyond this expletive and predicative use of *'theos'* (cf. Jennings, 1985, pp. 59ff) they conceived the divine as the multifarious ordering power which transforms chaos into cosmos in all areas of life and experience. We totally depend on this because we cannot live and act without relying on structures and regularities in our world which we can expect to obtain. All religions, therefore, offer means and (ritualized) practices of relating to these powers, pleasing them, asking for their help and receiving guidance for one's life from them. The Greek gods, for example, all embodied the ordering powers of particular realms of life which were experienced as chaotic, dangerous and beyond human control: Poseidon represented the ordering power of the sea, Aphrodite the elemental power of erotic love, Hera the numerous concerns of women, Zeus the powers of the sky with its clouds, rain and thunderstorms. Each deity represented a particular realm of life in which he or she guaranteed the transformation of chaos into cosmos, and together the Greek pantheon represented the ordered cosmos of the world as a whole. The gods themselves were unpredictable. But they guaranteed predictability in the particular areas of their power and responsibility. Because they were governed by a god these realms of life became reliable fields of human action. And because it was governed by the complex society of Olympian gods the whole world was taken to be in principle intelligible and reliably ordered. This did not silence the dangers of chaos or exclude conflict. Rather the unending quarrels between the gods reflected the continuous conflict between the various realms of life and their differing orders and underlined how precarious the existence of the order, reliability and intelligibility of the cosmos was in the face of the permanent threat of chaos. The world is a cosmos as the gods gave reason to believe; but this cosmos is permanently in danger of relapsing into chaos as the unending conflict between the gods never allowed humankind to forget.

Religions have developed different ways of coping with this problem. They have sought to banish the danger of relapsing into chaos by grounding all order in the power of a supreme god like Zeus, or in an non-personal principle of order which dominates even the gods like *tuche*, or in the immanent rational structure of the world-process which they identified with God, or in a singular personal deity who is responsible for both the existence and ultimate order of the world in all its conflicts. The biblical religions in particular have insisted that the existence, harmony and ultimate reliability of order in the cosmos is guaranteed by God, who creates, sustains and governs the world in all its infinite and conflicting details in nature, culture and history. They were thus required to regard all worldly events as divine actions, or means of divine actions, or embedded and participating in divine actions. If nature, culture and history are to be significant and meaningful for us they must somehow be manifestations of divine activity and embody the intentions of their agent. But then to understand this activity and the world in the light of it we have to know the divine intentions which govern it, and this is impossible without knowing the divine will. For if we can understand something as an action only if in the circumstances the agent could have done otherwise, we cannot understand the action without knowing why it has not been done otherwise, i.e. why the agent has chosen this rather than another possible course of action. Ultimately, therefore, it is *God's will* in terms of which the significance of events and the existence and reliability of order in the world must be understood. If there is an ultimate explanation of everything at all, it is the will of God who wills and does everything that he can, and can and does everything that he wills. In short, just as the localizing function of religion leads to conceptualizing God as *absolute knowledge*, so the ordering function of religion leads to conceptualizing him as *ultimate will*.

However, to conceive God with Austin Farrer as 'the Intelligent Will, or voluntary intelligence' (Farrer, 1963, p. 217) is not enough. What we want to know in order to make sense of the events and orders of the world is not merely that God is will but what his will is; for, as Farrer admits, 'the mere idea of his willing for us is valueless, we must have an idea what it is that he wills' (Farrer, 1972, p. 16). His will may ground the orders of nature and, indirectly, also the orders of cultu<u>r</u>e. But unless we can be sure that his will is a *saving* will because he wills only what is good for us, we cannot trust it absolutely and commit ourselves totally to it. Yet how do we know about God's will? And what do we know when we know it?

Christians answer both questions by reference to God's self-revelation as creative love in Jesus Christ. We know God's will because he discloses himself to us in Christ and through the Spirit; and we know it to be a saving will of love from what he thus reveals about the sort of person he is, the sort of persons we are, the reasons that guide all his actions, and therefore the ultimate *ratio essendi* of all there is. Of course, putting it this way is talking about God and the world in terms of the personal model of agency and will. But, from the way Christians respond to this rupture-experience and articulate their faith and understanding of God, world and human existence in worship, creed and reflection, this appears to be the most appropriate model for conceptualizing God in theological reflection. In faith I experience myself to be a sinner in need of salvation and God to be my saviour; I come to see how far I am from being the sort of person God wants me to be and how different I am from what I could and should be as God's creature; I realize that my actual life has estranged me from God in a, for me, irreparable way so that only God's grace can change my life into the kind expected of me; and I discover that, contrary to what I should have expected, God's love has actually brought about this change and set me on the path to life by making me conform to Christ in faith, thus reconciling me to him. In short, knowing God's will on the basis of revelation and faith is knowing it to be *saving* and *creative love*; and Christians confess this creative love 'which gives autonomy to that which it creates' (Jantzen, 1984, p. 152) to be the ultimate *raison d'être* of all there is.

The reason for this conviction is, as theological reflection tries to show, that faith's insight into its being passively constituted by God's saving love discloses the ultimate structure of all reality as being passively constituted by this love. Faith manifests the God-given certainty that the creative love disclosed in God's self-revelation in Christ is the true structure of reality and its ultimate principle of existence and order. Faith can thus be described, as Christoph Schwöbel has shown (1987), as a specific ordered relationship between certainty, truth and reality, all of which mark fundamental dimensions of our passive constitution disclosed in faith. In explicating it we must distinguish between three types of divine acts related in a specific way, i.e. creation, reconciliation and redemption or, as Schwöbel says, creation, revelation and inspiration.

1 The *certainty* of faith is constituted by divine inspiration through which God the Spirit opens our eyes to the truth of the Gospel message about his revelation in Jesus Christ, so that we respond to it in faith and are thus redeemed.

2 The *truth* of faith is constituted by God's self-revelation in Jesus Christ through which God the Son discloses the true character of God's attitude to his creation to be love - the saving love of reconciliation and the creative love of advance into novelty, freedom and loving response, with the urge to the final consummation of the adventure of creation in the free companionship of all creation with its creator.

3 The *reality* of faith, finally, is constituted by God's creative love through which God the Father creates *ex nihilo* not only the reality of faith but all reality; and as love hopes for reciprocity and free response which it cannot command, the process of creation out of love is the patient transformation of all there is into a free and loving response of created reality to the creative love of its creator. In short, inspiration opens our eyes to the truth of revelation, and revelation discloses God's creative love to be the ultimate ground and final goal of all there is.

Turning from theology's task of explicating faith to its task of elucidating our world in the light of faith, it is obvious that interpreting the world and our existence in the light of God's saving love disclosed in Christ is to open our eyes to what furthers or hinders our corresponding to this love in our own lives and actions. We cannot know that we are saved by faith in Christ and not, to the best of our abilities, try to conform to what we are by leading the kind of life which God has enabled us to lead. For apart from Christ we all exist *in via*, not *in patria*. Not that we are merely on the way to salvation. We *are* saved. But we are still on the way to the final consummation of our salvation. This dynamic tension between 'already' and 'not yet' provides the key to the Christian orientation in the world and attitude towards the orders of nature and culture. Through *faith* we already participate in the new eschatological life disclosed in Jesus Christ; in *hope* we expect the final consummation of what is already in the making for all humankind and, beyond it, for all creation; and *love* we know from faith to be the ultimate principle of the existence of the world as well as of the order and goal of the world-process. This is the principle which Christians explicitly accept as the basic norm of their individual and common actions and contributions to the creation of cultural orders in church and society in conformity with their faith. On the other hand, they also claim it to be the dynamic mystery of the world, i.e. the implicit, formative and creative principle of the existence, intelligibility and natural orders of the universe and its advance towards the final realization of love in a state in which the divine goodness and love is perfectly mirrored in creaturely goodness and love.

Faith, love and hope, then, summarize the three fundamental dimensions of the Christian orientation in the world. *Faith* locates us relative to God's revelation in Christ which ruptures or interrupts our given structures of experience in a way that renders everything radically questionable. It throws 'into question our habitual and conventional ways of perceiving, patterning, and participating in "reality" ' (Jennings, 1985, p. 55). It shatters the structures of our life, makes it impossible for us to continue as before, frees us from our past and liberates us for a new life full of promises which we can hardly imagine. But we cannot stop here. If we are to live this new life it must somehow answer to our basic human need for pattern, order and regularity. Thus we must restructure the patterns of our world and experience on the basis of these revelatory events by explicating their connectedness within the new pattern of meaning disclosed there: the pattern of *love*. The self-giving love of God is the ultimate ground and rationale of the events marked by the name Jesus Christ; conformity to Christ in faith is our mode of participating in, and being conformed to, this divine love; the rule of love is the normative principle by which we actively organize our Christian life in its personal, inter-personal, social and political dimensions according to the will of God; and as God's will has been revealed to be love, we believe this love also to be the ultimate ground and mystery of the world-process and its natural and cultural orders. For all these reasons, love has become the supreme Christian symbol for God, his relations to his creation, and the ideal of Christian existence in this life and beyond. But although Christian faith, life and theology have learned love to be the matrix for a new pattern of meaning and orientation in the world, whose cultural consequences and spiritual resources can hardly be overestimated, we cannot ignore that we can never control the divine creativity of love confronted in Christ. God's revelation cannot be domesticated by us. It eludes all attempts at domestication by our cultural apparatus of symbols, models, concepts and codes of conduct. When we talk of God, the term 'god' designates a gap in language which resists assimilation to the structures of our language and experience (Jennings, 1985, p. 56). Similarly when we talk of love we use the term to refer to the inexhaustible mystery and unfathomable source and goal of all created being and value, and its creative advance towards perfect realization. We see only darkly and in outline what this will involve by the pattern of Christ's life, death and resurrection. But - and this is the ground and content of Christian *hope* - we believe his story to be the paradigm of all our stories, and the manifestation of God's love in his life to be the promise and confirmation of what will be true of our own and every life as well. For, to quote Paul, 'as in Adam all die, even so in Christ shall all be made alive'. We do not know how this will be achieved and what it will involve. But we have confident hope that the creative love which has become manifest in Christ will continue its quiet work of transformation and achieve its end of turning creation into a free and perfect mirror of God's goodness and love.

Living a life of faith, love and hope in the sense outlined and conceiving the world to be ultimately ordered and organized by love is not normally the result of argument but of participation in the language and way of life of the Christian community. Of course, there are arguments for the Christian confidence and hope in love. But these are intratheological arguments based on revelation and faith which follow and do not precede participation. They presuppose the transition from the external to the internal perspective of Faith which, as we have seen, can be facilitated but not brought about by us through worship and the verbal and ritual presentation of the Gospel and the Christian response to it in faith. Yet again it is ritual practice rather than theoretical argument which helps us to achieve and renew confidence in the divine love as the fundamental principle of the existence and order of created reality as confessed by faith and explicated by theological reflection. For the ordering function of love disclosed by revelation and faith is rarely confirmed by the actual course of the world and has often to be maintained contrary to experience, especially in the light of evil, suffering and death. It thus has to be reaffirmed as a counterfactual truth in the face of everything that seems to contradict it. This is done by theological argument and reflection. But it is also, and more importantly, done by constantly returning in worship and ritual to the one place where it has unambiguously become manifest: the cross of Christ. Thus just as our certainty of absolute location is derived from baptism, so our certainty of the divine love as the ultimate principle of existence and order is derived from the *eucharist*. Just as baptism is the localizing ritual of the Christian faith, so the eucharist is its *ordering ritual*. In it we participate through the performance of a symbolic action in Christ's sharing of God's self-giving love with us by sharing it ourselves with our fellow Christians and thus preparing us individually and communally to share it with all our fellow-creatures. The dynamic structure and creative order of love is thus symbolically re-enacted and concretely accessible to our common experience. It originates solely with God; it becomes manifest in the life, death and resurrection of Christ; it conforms us to the will of God by conforming us to the cross of Christ in faith; it transforms us by thus incorporating us into the eschatological reality of the risen Christ; it works through us by making us instruments of love for our fellow-creatures; it induces us freely to worship God and to serve our neighbour; and it grounds our confidence and hope in the final advent of the kingdom of God in which the divine love will be perfectly mirrored in creaturely love.

To sum up; Christian faith and theology conceive created reality in all its dimensions to be constituted, sustained and organized by the saving love of God disclosed in Christ. This is not an obvious or self-evident fact. Theological reflection is thus faced with a twofold task in its attempt to work out a cognitive map of reality in the light of faith. It must explicate the character of the divine love by stating, amongst other things, who God is (doctrine of trinity); what God is (doctrine of Jesus Christ); what his actions are (doctrines of creation, revelation or reconciliation, and inspiration or redemption); and what his love is driving at (doctrine of the last things). One the other hand it must interpret the reality of our life and experience in the light of this understanding of the divine love. This involves, amongst other things, an exposition of how God's love is at work in his creation (pneumatology); how we react, or fail to react, to it (anthropology); and how the Christian faith manifests this love in its social and individual forms and institutions (ethics and ecclesiology). But it also involves the difficult task of critically diagnosing the obstacles to and the presence of God's love in our world in order to structure the world as a field of action according to the rule of love. Yet all this conceptual ordering of theology is secondary and dependent on the primary conviction of the Christian faith that God's love is indeed at work in all there is, a conviction permanently reinforced by worship and the symbolic re-enactment of the revelatory events of Jesus's life, death and resurrection in word and (liturgical) action.

Bibliography

(Literature published before the seventeenth century is quoted by reference to standard editions not listed below.)

Allen, D. 1985: *Philosophy for Understanding Theology*. Atlanta.

Apel, K.-O. 1980: *Toward a Transformation of Philosophy*, London.

(ed.) 1982: *Sprachpragmatik und Philosophie*. 3rd edn. Frankfurt.

Barbour, I. G. 1974: *Myths, Models and Paradigms. The Nature of Scientific and Religious Language*. London.

Barnes, J. 1982a: *The Presocratic Philosophers*. 2nd edn. London.

1982b: *Aristotle*. Oxford.

Barnes, W. H. F. 1950: *The Philosophical Predicament*. London.

Barth, K. 1919: *Der Römerbrief*. 1st edn. Zurich.

1922: *Der Römerbrief*. 2nd edn. Zurich.

1927: *Die Christliche Dogmatik im Entwurf. I: Die Lehre vom Worte Gottes. Prolegomena zur christlichen Dogmatik*. Ed. G. Sauter. Zurich.

1929: Schicksal und Idee in der Theologie. In K. Barth, *Theologische Fragen und Antworten*. Gesammelte Vorträge 3. Zollikon (Switzerland), 1957, 54-92.

1934: Nein! Antwort an Emil Brunner. In W. Fürst (ed.), *'Dialektische Theologie' in Scheidung und Bewährung (1933-1936). Aufsätze, Gutachten und Erklärungen*. Munich, 1966, 208-258.

1936: *Church Dogmatics*. Vol. I/1. Edinburgh.

1956: *Church Dogmatics*. Vol. I/2. Edinburgh.

1957: *Church Dogmatics*. Vol. II/1. Edinburgh.

1968: Nachwort. In H. Bolli (ed.), *Schleiermacher-Auswahl*. Munich, 290-312.

1973: *K. Barth-E. Thurneysen Briefwechsel*. Vol. 1: 1913-1921. Ed. E. Thurneysen. Zurich.

1979: *Das christliche Leben. Die Kirchliche Dogmatik IV/4. Fragmente aus dem Nachlaß. Vorlesungen 1959-1961*. Ed. H. A. Drewes and E. Jüngel. 2nd edn. Zurich.

Betzendörfer, W. 1924: *Die Lehre von der doppelten Wahrheit im Abendlande*. Tübingen.

Bieri, P., Horstmann, R. P. and Krüger, L. 1979: *Transcendental Arguments and Science*, Dordrecht.

Blumenberg, H. 1983: *Die Lesbarkeit der Welt*. 2nd edn. Frankfurt.

Bohm, D. 1972: Indication of a new order in physics. In T. Shanin (ed.), *The Rules of the Game. Cross-disciplinary Essays on Models in Scholarly Thought*. London, 249-75.

Brümmer, V. 1984: *What Are We Doing When We Pray? A Philosophical Inquiry*. London.

Budd, M. 1987: Wittgenstein on seeing aspects. *Mind*, 96, 1-17.

Buren, P. van 1972: *The Edges of Language. An Essay in the Logic of Religion*. London.

Burns, R. M. 1987: Bernard Lonergan's proof of the existence and nature of God. *Modern Theology*, 3, 137-56.

Burrell, D. B. 1967: How complete can intelligibility be? A commentary on *Insight*: chapter XIX. *Proceedings of the American Catholic Philosophical Association*, 41, 250-3.

— 1979: *Aquinas. God and Action*. London.

Busch, E. 1976: *Karl Barth. His Life from Letters and Autobiographical Texts*. London.

Caird, E. 1904: *The Evolution of Theology in the Greek Philosophers*. 2 vols. Glasgow.

Charlesworth, M. J. 1972: *Philosophy of Religion. The Historic Approaches*. London.

Chladenius, J. M. 1742: *Einleitung zur richtigen Auslegung vernünftiger Reden und Schriften*. Leipzig. Ed. L. Geldsetzer. Düsseldorf 1969.

Christian, C. W. 1979: *Friedrich Schleiermacher*. Waco (USA).

Clark, M. 1971: *Logic and System: A Study of the Transition from Vorstellung to Thought in the Philosophy of Hegel*. The Hague.

Craig, W. L. 1979: *The Kalam Cosmological Argument*. London.

— 1980: *The Cosmological Argument from Plato to Leibniz*. London.

Creel, R. C. 1986: *Divine Impassibility. An Essay in Philosophical Theology*. Cambridge.

Cupitt, D. 1979: *The Debate about Christ*. London.

Dalferth, I. U. 1981: *Religiöse Rede von Gott*. Munich.

— 1982: The visible and the invisible: Luther's legacy of a theological theology. In S. W. Sykes (ed.), *England and Germany. Studies in Theological Diplomacy*. Frankfurt, 15-44.

— 1984: *Existenz Gottes und christlicher Glaube. Skizzen zu einer eschatologischen Ontologie*. Munich.

— 1986: The one who is worshipped. Erwägungen zu Charles Hartshornes Versuch, Gott zu denken. *Zeitschrift für Theologie und Kirche*, 83, 484-506.

Davidson, D. 1983: A coherence theory of truth and knowledge. In D. Henrich (ed.), *Kant oder Hegel?*, Stuttgart, 423-38.

— 1984: *Inquiries into Truth and Interpretation*. Oxford.

Davis, S. T. 1983: *Logic and the Nature of God*. London.

Descartes, R. 1637: *Discours de la méthode*. Oeuvres de Descartes. Vol. VI. Ed. C. Adam and P. Tannery. Paris 1897-1913, 1-78.

Denzinger, H. and Schönmetzer, A. 1967: *Enchiridion Symbolorum*

Definitionum et Declarationum de Rebus Fidei et Morum. 34th edn. Freiburg.

Ebeling, G. 1966: Cognitio Dei et hominis. In G. Ebeling, *Lutherstudien*. Vol. 1. Tübingen, 1971, 221-72.

Edgley, R. 1969: *Reason in Theory and Practice*. London.

Evans, G. 1982: *The Varieties of Reference*. Ed. J. McDowell. Oxford.

Evans-Pritchard, E. E. 1965: *Theories of Primitive Religion*. Oxford.

Farrer, A. 1963: Causes. In A. Farrer, *Reflective Faith. Essays in Philosophical Theology*. Ed. C. C. Conti. London, 1972, 200-17.

1967: *Faith and Speculation*. London.

1972: The rational grounds for belief in God. In A. Farrer, *Reflective Faith. Essays in Philosophical Theology*. Ed. C. C. Conti. London, 7-23.

Fischer, J. 1983: *Handeln als Grundbegriff christlicher Ethik. Zur Differenz von Ethik und Moral*. Zurich.

Ford, D. 1979a: Barth's interpretation of the Bible. In S. W. Sykes (ed.), *Karl Barth. Studies of his Theological Method*. Oxford, 55-87.

1979b: Conclusion: Assessing Barth. In S. W. Sykes (ed.), *Karl Barth. Studies of his Theological Method*. Oxford, 194-201.

1981: *Barth and God's Story*. Frankfurt.

Galilei, G. 1623: *Il Saggiatore*. Opere VI. Rome, 1923, 197-372.

Geach, P. 1976: *Reason and Argument*. Oxford.

Gerrish, B. A. 1984: *A Prince of the Church. Schleiermacher and the Beginning of Modern Theology*. London.

Green, R. M. 1978: *Religious Reason. The Rational and Moral Basis of Religious Belief*. New York.

Gutting, G. 1982: *Religious Belief and Religious Skepticism*. Indianapolis.

Harnack, A. 1905: Der Vorwurf des Atheismus in den ersten drei Jahrhunderten. In O. von Gebhard and A. Harnack (eds), *Texte und Untersuchungen zur Geschichte der altchristlichen Literatur*. NS 13, Leipzig, 1-16.

Hartshorne, C. 1955: Some empty but important truths. In C. Hartshorne, *The Logic of Perfection*. La Salle, Ill, 1962, 280-97.

1964: *Man's Vision of God and the Logic of Theism*. Hamden, Conn.

1967: *A Natural Theology for Our Time*. La Salle, Ill.

Hegel, G. W. F. 1807: *Phänomenologie des Geistes. Works* (20 vols), vol. 3. Frankfurt, 1970.

1822: Foreword to H. Fr. Hinrich's *Die Religion im inneren Verhältnis zur Wissenschaft*. Trans. A. V. Miller. In F. G. Weiss (ed.), *Beyond Epistemology*. The Hague, 1974, 221-44.

1831: *Wissenschaft der Logik. I. Works* (20 vols), vol. 5. Frankfurt, 1969.

Helm, P. 1973: *The Variety of Belief*. London.

1982: *The Divine Revelation*. London.

Hepburn, R. W. 1958: *Christianity and Paradox. Critical Studies in Twentieth-Century Theology*. London.

Herms, E. 1978: *Theologie - eine Erfahrungswissenschaft*. Munich.

1982: Die Einführung des allgemeinen Zeichenbegriffs. Theologische Aspekte der Begründung einer reinen Semiotik durch Ch. W. Morris. In

E. Herms, *Theorie für die Praxis - Beiträge zur Theologie*. Munich, 164-88.

Hick, J. 1969: Religious faith as experiencing-as. In G. N. A. Vesey (ed.), *Talk of God*. London, 20-35.

1974: *Faith and Knowledge*. London.

1979: *Arguments for the Existence of God*. London.

1984: Seeing-as and Religious Experience. In J. Hick, *Problems of Religious Pluralism*. London, 1985, 16-27.

Hintikka, J. 1986: Kant on existence, predication, and the ontological argument. In S. Knuuttila and J. Hintikka (eds), *The Logic of Being. Historical Studies*. Dordrecht, 249-67.

Hume, D. 1779: *Dialogues concerning Natural Religion*. Ed. N. K. Smith. 2nd edn. Oxford, 1947.

Jaeger, W. 1947: *The Theology of Early Greek Philosophers*. Oxford.

Jantzen, G. 1984: *God's World, God's Body*. Philadelphia.

Jennings, T. W. 1985: *Beyond Theism. A Grammar of God-Language*. New York/Oxford.

Jones, H. O. 1985: *Die Logik theologischer Perspektiven. Eine sprachanalytische Untersuchung*. Göttingen.

Jüngel, E. 1982: *Barth-Studien*. Zurich/Cologne.

1983: *God as the Mystery of the World: On the Foundation of the Theology of the Crucified One in the Dispute between Theism and Atheism*. Edinburgh.

Kant, I. 1787: *Critique of Pure Reason*. Trans. N. Kemp Smith. London, 1933.

1936: *Opus postumum*. Kant's handschriftlicher Nachlaß. Vol. 8. Berlin/Leipzig.

Kaufman, G. D. 1960: *Relativism, Knowledge, and Faith*. Chicago, 1960.

1968: *Systematic Theology: A Historicist Perspective*. New York.

1972: *God the Problem*. Cambridge, Mass.

1981: *The Theological Imagination. Constructing the Concept of God*. Philadelphia.

Kellenberger, J. 1985: *The Cognitivity of Religion. Three Perspectives*, Berkeley/Los Angeles.

Kerényi, K. 1964: *Griechische Grundbegriffe. Fragen und Antworten aus der heutigen Situation*. Zurich.

King, R. H. 1974: *The Meaning of God*. London.

Kierkegaard, S. 1965: *The Last Years: Journals 1853-55*. Ed. and Trans. R. Gregor Smith, London.

Körner, S. 1984: *Metaphysics: Its Structure and Function*. Cambridge.

Kuhlmann, W. and Böhler, D. (eds) 1982: *Kommunikation und Reflexion. Zur Diskussion der Transzendentalpragmatik. Antworten auf Karl-Otto Apel*. Frankfurt.

Lakatos, I. 1976: *Proofs and Refutations*. Cambridge.

Lash, N. 1975: Method and Cultural Discontinuity. In P. Corcoran (ed.), *Looking at Lonergan's Method*. Dublin, 127-43.

Lindbeck, G. A. 1985: *The Nature of Doctrine. Religion and Theology in a Postliberal Age*. Philadelphia.

Locke, J. 1690: *An Essay concerning Human Understanding*. Ed. A. C. Fraser. 2 vols. New York, 1959.

Lohse, B. 1958: *Ratio und Fides. Eine Untersuchung über die ratio in der Theologie Luthers*. Göttingen.

Lonergan, B. J. F. 1958: *Insight. A Study of Human Understanding*. London.

1967a: *Verbum: Word and Idea in Aquinas*. Notre Dame.

1967b: Response. *Proceedings of the American Catholic Philosophical Association*, 41, 254-59.

1971: *Method in Theology*. London.

Louth, A. 1981: *The Origins of the Christian Mystical Tradition. From Plato to Denys*. Oxford.

Lüthi, K. 1963: Theologie als Gespräch. Das doppelte Dilemma der Theologie Karl Barths angesichts der Wandlungen der Theologie und der modernen Welt. In W. Dantine and K. Lüthi (eds), *Theologie zwischen Gestern und Morgen. Interpretationen und Anfragen zum Werk Karl Barths*. Munich, 302-32.

Mackie, J. L. 1982: *The Miracle of Theism. Arguments for and against the Existence of God*. Oxford.

MacKinnon, E. 1964: Understanding according to Bernard Lonergan. *The Thomist*, 28, 97-132, 338-372, 475-522.

McLelland, J. C. 1976: *God Anonymous. A Study in Alexandrian Philosophical Theology*. Philadelphia.

Macmurray, J. 1956: *The Self as Agent*. London.

Macquarrie, J. 1984: *In Search of Deity: An Essay in Dialectical Theism*. London.

Mavrodes, G. 1970a: *Belief in God. A Study in the Epistemology of Religion*. New York.

1970b: Introduction. In G. Mavrodes (ed.), *The Rationality of Religious Belief*, Englewood Cliffs, NJ, 1-25.

1979: Rationality and religious belief - a perverse question. In C. F. Delany (ed.), *Rationality and Religious Belief*. Notre Dame/London, 40.

Maywald, M. 1871: *Die Lehre von der zweifachen Wahrheit*. Berlin and Munich.

Mellor, D. H. 1980: Consciousness and degrees of belief. In D. H. Mellor (ed.), *Prospects for Pragmatism. Essays in Memory of F. P. Ramsey*. Cambridge, 139-73.

Meynell, H. 1982: *The Intelligible Universe*. London.

Miles, T. R. 1959: *Religion and the Scientific Outlook*. London.

Millar, B. 1975: In Defence of the predicate 'exists'. *Mind*, 84, 338-54.

Mitchell, B. 1973: *The Justification of Religious Belief*. London.

Moore, P. 1921: *The Religion of Plato*. Princeton.

Neuenschwandner, U. 1977: *Gott im neuzeitlichen Denken*. Vol. 1. Gütersloh (Germany).

Nielsen, K. 1967: Wittgensteinian Fideism. *Philosophy*, 42, 191-209.

Nygren, A. 1972: *Meaning and Method. Prolegomena to a Scientific Philosophy of Religion and a Scientific Theology*. London.

Osborne, E. 1981: *The Beginning of Christian Philosophy*. Cambridge.

Overbeck, F. 1963: *Christentum und Kultur. Gedanken und Anmerkungen zur modernen Theologie.* Ed. C. A. Bernoulli. Basel.

Penelhum, T. 1971: *Problems of Religious Knowledge.* London.

Phillips, D. Z. (ed.) 1967: *Religion and Understanding.* Oxford.

1970: *Faith and Philosophical Enquiry.* London.

1976: *Religion Without Explanation.* Oxford.

1983: *Primitive Reactions and the Reactions of Primitives.* The 1983 Marett Lecture. Oxford.

1985: The Friends of Cleanthes. *Modern Theology,* 1, 91-104.

Pieper, J. 1953: *Philosophia negativa.* Munich.

Plantinga, A. 1965: The free will defence. In M. Black (ed.), *Philosophy in America.* London, 204-20.

1967: *God and Other Minds. A Study of the Rational Justification of Belief in God.* Ithaca, NY.

1974: *The Nature of Necessity.* Oxford.

1975: *God, Freedom and Evil.* London.

1979: Is Belief in God Rational? In C. F. Delany (ed.), *Rationality and Religious Belief,* Notre Dame/London, 7-27.

1981: Is Belief in God Properly Basic? *Nous,* 15, 41-51.

Pöhlmann, H. G. 1965: *Analogia Entis oder Analogia Fidei? Die Frage der Analogie bei Karl Barth.* Göttingen.

Polanyi, M. 1962: *Personal Knowledge. Towards a Post-Critical Philosophy.* 2nd edn. London.

Popper, K. R. 1972: *Objective Knowledge. An Evolutionary Approach.* Oxford.

Putnam, H. 1983: *Realism and Reason. Philosophical Papers.* Vol. 3. Cambridge.

Raeder, S. 1977: *Grammatica Theologica. Studien zu Luthers Operationes in Psalmos.* Tübingen.

Ramsey, I. T. 1957: *Religious Language. An Empirical Placing of Theological Phrases.* London.

1973: *Models for Divine Activity.* London.

Reichenbach, B. R. 1972: *The Cosmological Argument. A Reassessment.* Springfield, Ill.

Rescher, N. 1973: *The Coherence Theory of Truth.* Oxford.

Ritschl, D. 1984: *Zur Logik der Theologie. Kurze Darstellung der Zusammenhänge theologischer Grundgedanken.* Munich.

Ritschl, D. and Jones, H. O. 1976: *'Story' als Rohmaterial der Theologie,* Munich.

Roberts, R. H. 1979: Karl Barth's doctrine of time: its nature and implications. In S. W. Sykes (ed.), *Karl Barth. Studies of his Theological Method.* Oxford, 88-146.

1980: The ideal and the real in the theology of Karl Barth. *New Studies in Theology,* 1, 163-80.

Root, H. E. 1962: Beginning all over again. In A. R. Vidler (ed.), *Soundings. Essays Concerning Christian Understanding.* Cambridge, 1-19.

Rorty, R. 1979: *Philosophy and the Mirror of Nature.* Princeton.

1986: Pragmatism, Davidson and truth. In E. LePort (ed.), *The Philosophy of Donald Davidson: A Perspective on 'Inquires into Truth and Inter-pretation'*. Oxford.

1987: Non-Reductive Physicalism. In K. Cramer, H. F. Fulda, R. P. Horstmann and U. Pothast (eds), *Theorie der Subjektivität.* Frankfurt, 278-96.

Rosen, M. 1982: *Hegel's Dialectic and its Criticism.* Cambridge.

Rowe, W. 1975: *The Cosmological Argument.* Princeton/London.

Russell, B. 1914: *Our Knowledge of the External World.* 7th edn. London, 1972.

1921: *The Analysis of Mind.* 10th edn. London 1971.

Schleiermacher, F. D. E. 1830a: *The Christian Faith.* Trans. H. R. Mackintosh and J. S. Stewart. Edinburgh, 1928.

1830b: *Brief Outline of the Study of Theology.* Trans. T. N. Tice. Richmond.

1942: *Dialektik.* Ed. R. Odebrecht. Leipzig.

Schlesinger, G. 1977: *Religion and Scientific Method.* Dordrecht/Boston.

Schwöbel, C. 1987: Die Rede vom Handeln Gottes im christlichen Glauben. Beiträge zu einem systematisch-theologischen Rekonstruktionsversuch. *Marburger Jahrbuch Theologie,* 1, 56-81.

Shepherd, J. J. 1975: *Experience, Inference and God.* London.

Smart, N. 1971: *The Religious Experience of Mankind.* London.

Solmsen, F. 1942: *Plato's Theology.* Ithaca, NY.

Spiekermann, I. 1985: *Gotteserkenntnis. Ein Beitrag zur Grundfrage der neuen Theologie Karl Barths.* Munich.

Stead, C. 1977: *Divine Substance.* Oxford.

Strawson, P. F. 1971: Identifying reference and truth-values. In P. F. Strawson, *Logico-Linguistic Papers.* London, 75-95.

Surin, K. 1986: The Trinity and philosophical reflection: a study of David Brown's *The Divine Trinity. Modern Theology,* 2, 235-56.

Swinburne, R. 1977: *The Coherence of Theism.* Oxford.

1979: *The Existence of God.* Oxford.

1981: *Faith and Reason.* Oxford.

Taylor, A. E. 1971: *Plato. The Man and His Works.* 7th edn. London.

Taylor, C. 1978: The Validity of Transcendental Arguments. *Proceedings of the Aristotelian Society,* 79, 151-65.

Thiemann, R. F. 1985: *Revelation and Theology. The Gospel as Narrated Promise.* Indianapolis.

Toulmin, S. E. 1969: *The Uses of Argument.* Cambridge.

Työrinoja, R. 1987: *Nova Vocabula et Nova Lingua.* Luther's conception of doctrinal formulas. In T. Mannermaa, A. Ghiselli and S. Peura (eds), *Thesaurus Lutheri. Auf der Suche nach neuen Paradigmen der Luther-Forschung.* Helsinki, 221-36.

Tyrell, B. 1974: *Bernard Lonergan's Philosophy of God.* Dublin.

Vlastos, G. 1952: Theology and philosophy in early Greek thought. *Philosophical Quarterly,* 2, 97-123.

Wagner, F. 1986: *Was ist Religion? Studien zu ihrem Begriff und Thema in Geschichte und Gegenwart.* Gütersloh (Germany).

Walsh, W. H. 1970: *Metaphysics.* 3rd edn. London.

Ward, K. 1982: *Rational Theology and the Creativity of God*. Oxford.

Whitehead, A. N. 1926: *Religion in the Making*. New York.

— 1929: *Process and Reality. An Essay in Cosmology*. New York.

Williams, R. R. 1978: *Schleiermacher the Theologian. The Construction of the Doctrine of God*. Philadelphia.

Winch, P. 1958: *The Idea of a Social Science and its Relation to Philosophy*. London.

— 1967: Understanding a primitive society. In D. Z. Phillips (ed.), *Religion and Understanding*, Oxford, 9-42.

Wisdom, J. 1944: Gods. *Proceedings of the Aristotelian Society*, 45, 185-206.

— 1953: *Philosophy and Psychoanalysis*. Oxford.

— 1965: *Paradox and Discovery*. Oxford.

Wittgenstein, L. 1964: *Philosophical Remarks*. Oxford.

— 1967: *Zettel*. Oxford.

— 1968: *Philosophical Investigations*. 3rd edn. Oxford.

— 1969: *Philosophical Grammar*. Oxford.

— 1970: *Lectures and Conversations on Aesthetics, Psychology and Religious Belief*, ed. C. Barrett. Oxford.

— 1980: *Remarks on the Philosophy of Pyschology*. Vol. 1. Oxford.

Zaehner, R. C. 1962: *The Comparison of Religions*. Boston.

Index

actions/events duality, 214-15; non-religious approach to, 215-16; religious approach to, 216-17
analogy: of faith, 122; rule of, 201-2
Anselm, St, 200-1
apologists, 65-6
Aquinas, St Thomas, 71, 82, 156
Aristotelianism, 169, 170
Aristotle, 25-30, 71, 77, 78; concept of primary divinity, 28-9; models of causality, mind, substance, 28, 29; sciences categorized by, 26; theory of causality, 27-8, 77; theory of inductive knowledge, 25-6; theory of substances, 26-8; 'unmoved mover' argument, 27-8
Augustine, St, 31, 67-8
authorization, divine, 42

baptism, 212, 213
Barnes, W.H.F., 185
Barth, K., 11, 39; christological bias in theology of, 117, 123-4; conception of reality, 118-21; eschatological theology of, 113-18, 125-6; levels in dogmatics of, 122-4; theological integration of perspectives by, 121-2; view of religion, 125-6
beliefs: and articles/preambles of faith, 156; information embodied in, 48-9; justified v. reasonable, 5; rationality of, 4-10; religious v. scientific, 6; second-order, 7-8

causality: Aristotelian theory of, 27-8, 77
Christian theology: in ancient world, 35-6; belief related to faith in, 44-6; dualist position in, 64; exclusivist position in, 64; and faith, 39-40, 43, 44-6, 49-50, 57, 63-6; inclusivist position in, 65; influence of Ancient Greek theology on,

31-2; and interpretation, 54-5; and perspectives, 54-5, 56-8, 63-6; pluralist position in, 65; relation to other disciplines, 57-8; and revelation, 39-46, see also revelation; standards for, 58-9; v. philosophical theology, 46-7
christology, 37-8, 103
Cobb, J., 94
cognition: and Common Reality Argument, 134
Collingwood, R.G., 183, 184-5
Common Reality Argument, 127-8; based on god, 129-30; based on ontological categories, 133; based on science and history, 130-3; and cognition, 134
communication: and structuring of reality, 213-14
conditioning: of expressions of faith, 198-9
consciousness: Schleiermacher on, 105-11
contingent/necessary reality; and existence of God, 137-41
coram deo v. coram mundo perspectives, 77-8, 85-8
creed, 202
culture/nature duality, 214-15; non-religious approach to, 215-16; religious approach to, 216-17; and semiotic activity, 146-8

Davis, S.T., 13
Democritus, 18
dependence, feeling of: Schleiermacher on, 107-11
Descartes, René, 69, 90, 92; method of doubt, 171-2
description and interpretation, 130-3
difference-in-unity model, 99-111
dogma, 200
doubt: Descartes' method of, 171-2

empiricism, 92-3
Enlightenment, the: philosophy in, 89-91;
theism in, *see* theism, Enlightenment;
theology in, 91-8
epistemology, 90
eucharist, 222-3
Eusebius of Caesarea, 31
Evans-Pritchard, E.E., 156
evil, problems of, 95-6
experience: evidential, 90 and God as
interpretive concept, 185-7
experiences: mystical, 186-7 religious,
186-7
experiential theologies, 15
explication, theological, 151, 152

fact and interpretation, 130-3
faith, 39-40, 43, 44-6, 49-50; and absolutely localizing self-knowledge,
210-13; analogy of, 122; articles v.
preambles of, 156; certainty of, 219-20;
and Christian theology, 39-40, 43, 44-6,
49-50, 57, 63-6; conditioning of expressions of, 198-9; discourse of, models in,
200-2; external/internal perspectives,
63-6; reality of, 219-20; and theological
reflection, 152, 153-4, 157; truth of,
219-20; v. reason, 57, 63-6
Farrer, A., 170, 218
Feuerbach, Ludwig, 109
foundationalism, 155-6, 183

Galilei, Galileo, 69
God: as absolute knowledge, 209-13;
biblical models of, 198, 199, 200;
consequent/primordial nature of,
138-9; as contingent necessity, 166;
creativity/order polarity in concepts of,
196; dependency argument for
existence of, 107-11; existence of, and
contingent/necessary reality, 137-41;
existence of, and intelligibility of
reality, 210-13; features of Christian
concept of, 196-7; identification of, 188,
193-4; revelation-based, 191-2; inferred
cosmologically, 170; as interpretive
concept, and experience, 185-7; knowledge of, 80, 114, 159-63; as love, 159,
219-20, 221-2; Luther on, *see* Luther;
models of, in Christian faith, 199-201;
necessity of, 95, 166-7; and orientation,
195-6, 203; orientational function of
concept of, 202; possibility of, 95; as
practical necessity, 167; rationalist
argument for existence of, 172-3;

rationality of belief in, 166; self-
identification of, *see under* self-identification of God; singularity of, 95; as
theoretical construct, 165-6; as
transcendental necessity, 166-7;
transcendental subjectivity and existence of, 135; will of, 218-19
Gospel, 189, 190, 193, 194, 202, 210, 211,
212; *see also* Law-Gospel model
grace: in Lutheran theology, 84; *see also*
Nature-Grace model
Greek gods, 217-18
Greek philosophers: *see* Aristotle; Plato;
Presocratic philosophers; Stoicism

Hartshorne, C., 129, 138, 167, 172
Hegel, G.W.F., 113, 167; absolutist metaphysics of, 177-82; difficulty of criticizing philosophy of, 181; on knowledge
and self-knowledge, 178-9; philosophy
of, and Christian faith, 181-2; on
rationality of reality, 177-8, 179-81
Heidegger, M., 183, 184
Herbert of Cherbury, Edward Herbert,
1st Baron, 92
Herms, E., 144
Hesiod, 19
Hick, J., 53-4, 93, 166
history: and common reality, 130-3
Homer, 19
hope: in Christian faith, 220, 222
Hume, D., 96, 172
hypostatic union, 119, 126

identification, 204-5, 210-11; of God, 188,
191-4; *see also* self-knowledge
identity: actual/true, 207-8; development
of, *see* self-knowledge
inspiration, divine, 219-20
intelligibility of reality, 176; existence of
God inferred from, 136, 176
interpretandum/interpretans, 183-4, 185
interpretation, 54-5; and Christian
theology, 54-5; and description, 130-3;
fact and, 130-3; hierarchy of, 53; metaphysical, 183-7; and perspectives, 52-6;
religious, 54-5

James, W., 187
Jennings, T.W., 186
Jesus Christ: God's revelation in, 38-9,
42-3, 76, 79, 80-2; God's self-
identification in, 189-90, 191, 193, 197;
interpretations of, 53, 54; models used

to explain, 199; terms used in referring to, 199
Judaism, Hellenistic, 36

Kant, I., 96, 166-7, 172; transcendental metaphysics of, 174-5, 178
Kellenberger, J., 7
Kierkegaard, S., 3, 182
knowledge: absolutely localizing, and communication, 210-11; descriptive, demonstrative and reflective, 161-2; divine, 209-13; Enlightenment concept of, 89-90; of God, 80, 114, 159-63; and location of self, 190-1; orientational, 185, 190, 193, 197, 203, 204; practical, 190-1; reflective, about God, 164-8; and revelation, 159-63; theoretical, 190; *see also* self-knowledge

language, and structuring of reality, 214
language-games, 143
Leibniz, G., 92, 96, 172
Lindbeck, G. A., 143-4
location of self: and knowledge, 190-1; *see also* self-knowledge
Locke, J., 92, 172
logos, 21, 30, 66
Lonergan, B., 175-6; on intelligible universe, 136; reality defined by, 136-7; on transcendental subjectivity, 134-6
love: God's creative, 219-20, 221-2; organizing function of, 213-23; rule of, 202
Luther, M.: on concepts of God, 80-1; *coram deo/coram mundo* perspectives distinguished by, 77-8, 85-8; eschatology of, 78-9; on God's activity in Law and Gospel, 84-5, 87; on God's revelation in Christ, 80-2; *grammatica theologica* of, 82-3; on hiddeness of God, 81; on identification of God, 79-80; on modes of divine activity, 84; on natural/spiritual presence of God, 83-4; on philosophical theory of creation, 79-80; philosophy distinguished from theology by, 76-8, 82-3, 86, 87-8; on theological discourse, 82-3

Mackie, J. L., 140
Macquarrie, J., 185
Marx, K., 180
mentalist approach: to knowledge about God, 170-3
meta-rules: and discourse of faith, 200-1
metaphysical theology: and knowledge of

God, 162; and reflection, 169-73; and self-reflection, 174-87
metaphysics: *a posteriori* v. *a priori*, 170; absolutist, 177-82; cosmological, 169-70; ideological, 170-2; immanent v. transcendent, 169-70; interpretative, 183-7; descriptive/revisionary, 184; rational, 172-3; scientific, 169; transcendental, 174-6
models: biblical, of God, 198, 199, 200; Christian, of God, 199-201; in discourse of faith, 200-2; theological, 25
monotheism: development in Ancient Greece, 18-20
morality: and necessary existence of God, 167
Morris, C. W., 144
mystical experiences, 186-7
mythical theology: and knowledge of God, 162
mythology, 18-20, 38, 217-18

natural theology, 92-3, 96-7
nature: as book, 67-70; Nature-Grace model, 71-5
nature/culture duality: *see* culture/nature duality
necessary/contingent reality: and existence of God, 137-41
Nicholas of Cusa, 174
Nielsen, K., 7
nominalism, 74-5
nous, 28, 30

onto-theological tradition, 172
ontologies: and Common Reality Argument, 133
order: Greek gods and, 217-18; and salvation, 217
orders of culture/nature: *see* culture/nature duality
Otto, R., 187
Overbeck, F., 112-13, 121

Panaitios of Rhodes, 31
perception, 213
person: world conceived on model of, 140
perspectives, 7-8, 50-2, 54-5, 56-8; and Christian theology, 54-5, 56-8, 63-6; common linguistic medium of, 141-7; common reality and, *see* Common Reality Argument; *coram deo/coram mundo*, 77-8, 85-8; external/internal, on faith, 63-6; and interpretation, 52-6;

and transcendental subjectivity, 134-6; translation between, 148
phenomena, religious, 186-7
Phillips, D.Z., 6-7, 143
philosophical theology, 15-17, 79, 86; v. Christian theology, 46-7
philosophy: apologetic use in theological reflection, 154-5; constructive use in theological reflection, 153-4; critical use in theological reflection, 154; formal use in theological reflection, 153; foundational use in theological reflection, 155-7; hermeneutical use in theological reflection, 153; instrumental use in theological reflection, 153-5
Piaget, J., 172
Plantinga, A., 96, 166, 172
Plato, 21-5, 170; concept of the Good, 22-3; doctrine of soul, 22-3; on intelligibility of god, 23-4; philosophical theology developed by, 21-2
Platonism, 169, 170
Polanyi, M., 51, 55
polytheism, *see* mythology
Popper, K., 181
Presocratic philosophers, 18-19
presuppositions: absolute and ultimate, 184-5
Process philosophy, 169
Protagoras, 18

Ramsey, I.T., 196
rational theology, 92-3, 97
rationality: of beliefs, 4-10; external v. internal, 5-6; of reality, 177-8, 179-81; scientific, 4; self-conscious, in theology, 12-13
reality: common, *see* Common Reality Argument; contingent/necessary, 137-41; contingent/necessary, and existence of God, 137-41; intelligibility of, 136, 210-13; Lonergan on, 134-5, 136-7; rationality of, 177-8, 179-81; structuring of, 213-14
reason: empiricist v. rationalist conceptions of, 92, 92-3; v. faith, 57, 63-6
reason-revelation model, 91-8; theological reactions to, 99-100
reductionist arguments: and theological problems, 13-14
reflection, 47-9; theological, *see* theological reflection
religion v. theology, 33-4
religious experiences, 186-7
Rescher, N., 64

resurrection, 112, 114
revelation, 39-46, 80-2; and absolutely localizing self-knowledge, 211-12; and Christian theology, 39-46; concepts of God based on, 197, 202; content of, 158-9; Enlightenment conception of, 91; epistemologically, 43-4; knowledge disclosed in, 160; and knowledge of God, 159-63; localizing function of, 204-13; pragmatically, 41; processes of identification in, 193-4; semantically, 41-2; structurally, 40-1; theological explication of, 195, 197; theologically, 43; v. proclamation, 41; *see also* God, self-identification of; reason-revelation model
revelational theology, 15-17; and knowledge of God, 162-3
revelatory experiences, 187
ritual: and absolutely localizing self-knowledge, 212; and certainty of divine love, 222-3
Roman Catholicism, 74
Russell, B., 50

salvation, 160, 220; and divine will, 219; order and, 217
Schleiermacher, F.D.E., 99-100, 112, 115-16, 121, 129; doctrinal exposition, 101, 102-3; on God-consciousness, 106-11; on self-consciousness, 105-6; on sin/grace antithesis, 103; theory of piety, 101, 103-11; theory of religion, 101, 102; on world-consciousness, 105
Schlesinger, G., 170
Schwöbel, C., 219
science, 69; and common reality, 130-3
scientific beliefs, 6
scientific rationality, 4
self-knowledge, 205-13; absolutely localizing, 209-13; and communication with God, 210-11: and faith, 210-13; and problem of identification, 210-11; and ritual, 212; and communication, 205-6; non-religious approach to, 208; religious approach to, *see* knowledge, divine; and views of others, 207
self-reflection: metaphysical theology and, 174-87
self-identification of God, 188; in Christ, 189-90, 191, 193, 197; and eschatological rupture, 195 and orientation, 195-6; *see also* revelation through phenomena, 192-3; through the Spirit, 189-90, 191,

194; v. descriptive identification of, 189-91
semiotic activity: and common linguistic medium of perspectives, 144-8; and culture/nature duality, 146-8; and 'dependence on transcendence' argument, 144-5; selection in, 145; and translation between perspectives, 148
signs, 41-2, 192; *see also* semiotic activity
Smart, N., 187
Spinoza, B., 92, 93
Spirit: God's self-identification through the, 189-90, 191, 194; Hegel's concept of the, 177, 178-82
Stoicism, 30-1
subjectivity: transcendental, 134-6
suprarationalist theology, 100
Swinburne, R., 13, 93, 94, 139-40, 155, 166, 170

Taylor, C., 213
Tertullian, 31
Thales, 18
theism, 186
theism, Enlightenment, 93-4; arguments for existence of God, 94-5, 96-8; cosmological and religious motifs, 94; and problem of evil, 95-6
theological problems, 10-17

theological reflection, 46, 49-50; concepts of God in, 194-5; foundational use of philosophy in, 155-7; instrumental use of philosophy in, 153-5; levels of problems in, 152
theological standards, 10-12
theology: as autonomous discipline, 13-14; first- and second-order disputes in, 12; interpretive tasks of, 151
theology, metaphysical, *see* metaphysical theology; metaphysics
two-books mode, 66-7

unity-in-difference model, 112-26

Varro, Marcus Terentius, 31
via moderna, 74-5

Wagner, F., 155
Ward, K., 13, 129, 138, 139, 167, 170
Ward, Keith, 93
Whitehead, A.N., 138, 170
will, divine, 218-19; as creative love, 219
Williams, R.R., 109
Wittgenstein, L., 6, 51, 53, 143
worship: and absolutely localizing self-knowledge, 212; God as object of, 16

Xenophanes, 18, 19

Index by Justyn Balinski